# First World War
## and Army of Occupation
# War Diary
## France, Belgium and Germany



19 DIVISION
56 Infantry Brigade,
Brigade Machine Gun Company
7 November 1915 - 28 February 1918

WO95/2082/2

The Naval & Military Press Ltd
www.nmarchive.com
**Published in association with The National Archives**

Published by

The Naval & Military Press Ltd

Unit 10 Ridgewood Industrial Park,

Uckfield, East Sussex,

TN22 5QE England

Tel: +44 (0) 1825 749494

www.naval-military-press.com

www.nmarchive.com

# Contents

| Document type | Place/Title | Date From | Date To |
|---|---|---|---|
| Heading | WO95/2082-2 | | |
| Heading | 56th Machine Gun Coy. Oct 1915-Feb 1918 | | |
| Heading | 56th Infantry Brigade Machine Gun Company October 1915 Feb 18 | | |
| Miscellaneous | Machine Gun Company 56th Infantry Brigade | 02/11/1915 | 02/11/1915 |
| Miscellaneous | Operation Orders For The 25th September 1915 by Capt. H.O. Collyer Comdg. 56th Brig M.G. Coy. | | |
| Heading | 56th Infantry Brigade Machine Gun Company November 1915 | | |
| War Diary | | 07/11/1915 | 30/11/1915 |
| Miscellaneous | Machine Gun Company 56th Infy Brigade. | 07/11/1915 | 07/11/1915 |
| Heading | 56th Infantry Brigade Machine Gun Company December 1915 | | |
| Heading | War Diary Of Machine Gun Co. 56th Infy Brigade from Dec. 1st Dec 31st 1915 | | |
| War Diary | In The Field | 01/12/1915 | 31/12/1915 |
| Miscellaneous | Appendices 1, 2 & 3. | | |
| Miscellaneous | Appendix 1 | | |
| Miscellaneous | Certificate to be Signed before Fire is Opened. app 2 | 14/12/1915 | 14/12/1915 |
| Map | Appendix 3 | | |
| Heading | War Diary Of 56 Machine Gun Company From 9th February To 29th Feb 1916 Volume I | | |
| War Diary | Havre | 09/02/1916 | 13/02/1916 |
| War Diary | Merville | 14/02/1916 | 14/02/1916 |
| War Diary | St Venant | 14/02/1916 | 16/02/1916 |
| War Diary | La Huit Maisons | 17/02/1916 | 29/02/1916 |
| War Diary | Havre | 09/02/1916 | 13/02/1916 |
| War Diary | Merville | 14/02/1916 | 14/02/1916 |
| War Diary | St Venant | 14/02/1916 | 16/02/1916 |
| War Diary | La Huit Maisons | 17/02/1916 | 29/02/1916 |
| Heading | 56 M G Coy Vol 6 | | |
| Heading | War Diary of 56 Machine Gun Coy. from March 1st 1916 To March 31st 1916 Volume II | | |
| War Diary | La Huit Maisons | 01/03/1916 | 02/03/1916 |
| War Diary | Euston Coy H.Q | 03/03/1916 | 13/03/1916 |
| War Diary | Paridis | 14/03/1916 | 23/03/1916 |
| War Diary | Euston Corner | 24/03/1916 | 31/03/1916 |
| Heading | War Diary Of 56th Coy. Machine Gun Corps. From 1st April To 30th April 1916 Vol 3 | | |
| War Diary | Euston Corner | 01/04/1916 | 16/04/1916 |
| War Diary | Lestrem | 17/04/1916 | 17/04/1916 |
| War Diary | St Venant | 18/04/1916 | 19/04/1916 |
| War Diary | Linghem | 20/04/1916 | 30/04/1916 |
| War Diary | La Chaussee | 13/05/1916 | 07/06/1916 |
| War Diary | Bellevue | 08/06/1916 | 14/06/1916 |
| War Diary | Villers-Bocage | 15/06/1916 | 15/06/1916 |
| War Diary | Rainneville | 16/06/1916 | 26/06/1916 |
| War Diary | Baizieux | 27/06/1916 | 30/06/1916 |
| Heading | 56th Machine Gun Company. July 1916 | | |
| Heading | War Diary Of 56th Coy M.G. Corps. 1-7-16-31.7.16 | | |

| | | | |
|---|---|---|---|
| War Diary | Albert | 01/07/1916 | 08/07/1916 |
| War Diary | Henencourt | 09/07/1916 | 18/07/1916 |
| War Diary | Albert | 19/07/1916 | 19/07/1916 |
| War Diary | Mametz Wood | 20/07/1916 | 21/07/1916 |
| War Diary | Bazentin | 22/07/1916 | 27/07/1916 |
| War Diary | Mametz Wood | 28/07/1916 | 31/07/1916 |
| Heading | Memorandum 010616 From 300616 | | |
| Heading | 56th Brigade Machine Gun Company August 1916 | | |
| Heading | 56th Inf. Bde. | 05/09/1916 | 05/09/1916 |
| War Diary | Franvillers | 01/08/1916 | 03/08/1916 |
| War Diary | Gorenflos | 04/08/1916 | 06/08/1916 |
| War Diary | Locre | 07/08/1916 | 09/08/1916 |
| War Diary | Kemmel | 10/08/1916 | 31/08/1916 |
| Operation(al) Order(s) | 56 Coy. Machine Gun Corps. Operation Order No. V.95 | 24/08/1916 | 24/08/1916 |
| Heading | War Diary Of 56th M.G, Coy From 1.9.16 To 30.9.16 | | |
| War Diary | Kemmel | 01/09/1916 | 03/09/1916 |
| War Diary | Ploegsteert | 04/09/1916 | 12/09/1916 |
| War Diary | Ploegsteert Wood | 13/09/1916 | 20/09/1916 |
| War Diary | Papot | 21/09/1916 | 21/09/1916 |
| War Diary | Oultersteen | 22/09/1916 | 28/09/1916 |
| War Diary | Outtersteen | 29/09/1916 | 04/10/1916 |
| War Diary | Coigneux | 05/10/1916 | 06/10/1916 |
| War Diary | Sailly-Au-Bois | 07/10/1916 | 15/10/1916 |
| War Diary | Coigneux | 16/10/1916 | 16/10/1916 |
| War Diary | Vadencourt | 17/10/1916 | 19/10/1916 |
| War Diary | Aveluy (Beighty Wood) | 20/10/1916 | 24/10/1916 |
| War Diary | Aveluy | 25/10/1916 | 12/11/1916 |
| War Diary | Stuff Trench | 13/11/1916 | 13/11/1916 |
| War Diary | St Pierre Divion | 14/11/1916 | 20/11/1916 |
| War Diary | Aveluy | 21/11/1916 | 21/11/1916 |
| War Diary | Warloy | 22/11/1916 | 22/11/1916 |
| War Diary | Vadencourt | 23/11/1916 | 23/11/1916 |
| War Diary | Beauval | 24/11/1916 | 24/11/1916 |
| War Diary | La Vacquerie | 25/11/1916 | 25/11/1916 |
| War Diary | Dommesmont | 26/11/1916 | 26/11/1916 |
| Miscellaneous | 56 Coy. M.G. Corps. Operation Order No. 115A. App 3 | 01/11/1916 | 01/11/1916 |
| Operation(al) Order(s) | 7th Lan. R. Order No. 119 App 4 | 29/10/1916 | 29/10/1916 |
| Operation(al) Order(s) | 56th Infantry Brigade Order No. 123 App 5 | 07/11/1916 | 07/11/1916 |
| Miscellaneous | Table Of Reliefs Appendix To 56 Infy Bde. Order No. 123 | | |
| Operation(al) Order(s) | 56th Infantry Brigade Order No. 124 App 6 | 11/11/1916 | 11/11/1916 |
| Miscellaneous | Addendum to 56th Infantry Brigade Order No. 124 | 12/11/1916 | 12/11/1916 |
| Operation(al) Order(s) | 56th Infantry Brigade Order No. 125 App 7 | 11/11/1916 | 11/11/1916 |
| Miscellaneous | Table Of Moves Appendix To 56th Bde Order No. 125 | | |
| Operation(al) Order(s) | 7th East Lancashire Regiment Operation Order No. 5 App 8 | 12/11/1916 | 12/11/1916 |
| Miscellaneous | A Form Messages And Signals. | 18/11/1916 | 18/11/1916 |
| Operation(al) Order(s) | 56th Infantry Brigade Order No. 132 | 17/11/1916 | 17/11/1916 |
| War Diary | Domesmont | 01/12/1916 | 18/12/1916 |
| War Diary | Nr. Berneuil | 19/12/1916 | 19/12/1916 |
| War Diary | Domesmont | 20/12/1916 | 09/01/1917 |
| War Diary | Beauquesne Coigneux | 10/01/1917 | 21/01/1917 |
| War Diary | Hebuterne And Bavencourt | 22/01/1917 | 31/01/1917 |

| | | | |
|---|---|---|---|
| Operation(al) Order(s) | 56 Coy. M.G. Corps. Operation Order No. 1A Appendix A | 21/01/1917 | 21/01/1917 |
| | | | |
| War Diary | Hebuterne & Bayencourt | 01/02/1917 | 28/02/1917 |
| Operation(al) Order(s) | Operation Order No. 3A. | | |
| Miscellaneous | Amendment I To Operation Order 3 A | 21/02/1917 | 21/02/1917 |
| Miscellaneous | Amendment II Operation Order 3 A | 21/02/1917 | 21/02/1917 |
| War Diary | Bus | 01/03/1917 | 04/03/1917 |
| War Diary | Vauchelles | 05/03/1917 | 09/03/1917 |
| War Diary | Longuevillette | 10/03/1917 | 10/03/1917 |
| War Diary | Ligny-S-Canche | 11/03/1917 | 12/03/1917 |
| War Diary | Pethonval | 13/03/1917 | 13/03/1917 |
| War Diary | Sachin | 14/03/1917 | 15/03/1917 |
| War Diary | Laires | 16/03/1917 | 18/03/1917 |
| War Diary | Cohem | 19/03/1917 | 19/03/1917 |
| War Diary | Sercus | 20/03/1917 | 20/03/1917 |
| War Diary | Larecousse | 21/03/1917 | 02/04/1917 |
| War Diary | Wizernes | 03/04/1917 | 03/04/1917 |
| War Diary | Scherpenberg | 04/04/1917 | 17/04/1917 |
| War Diary | Trenches & La Clytte | 18/04/1917 | 30/04/1917 |
| Operation(al) Order(s) | 56 Coy. M.G. Corps. Operation Order No. 6 A Appendix A | | |
| | | | |
| War Diary | In The Line | 01/05/1917 | 01/05/1917 |
| War Diary | Scherpenberg | 02/05/1917 | 02/05/1917 |
| War Diary | In The Line | 03/05/1917 | 08/05/1917 |
| War Diary | Laclyte | 09/05/1917 | 10/05/1917 |
| War Diary | In The Line | 11/05/1917 | 21/05/1917 |
| War Diary | Scherpenberg | 22/03/1917 | 24/03/1917 |
| War Diary | Westoutre | 25/03/1917 | 29/03/1917 |
| War Diary | In The Line | 30/03/1917 | 31/03/1917 |
| War Diary | La Clytte | 01/06/1917 | 14/06/1917 |
| War Diary | Vierstraat | 15/06/1917 | 15/06/1917 |
| War Diary | Klondyke Farm Kemmel | 16/06/1917 | 20/06/1917 |
| War Diary | Locre | 21/06/1917 | 30/06/1917 |
| Miscellaneous | Relief Orders No. 2 Appen I | 03/06/1917 | 03/06/1917 |
| Miscellaneous | 2nd St Dummett 56 Mg Coy App II | 05/06/1917 | 05/06/1917 |
| Miscellaneous | Barrage Sections Preliminary Operation Orders App III. | | |
| Miscellaneous | 56 Coy. M.G. Corps. App IV | 02/06/1917 | 02/06/1917 |
| War Diary | Locre | 01/07/1917 | 04/07/1917 |
| War Diary | Siege Fm | 05/07/1917 | 20/07/1917 |
| War Diary | Kemmel | 21/07/1917 | 29/07/1917 |
| War Diary | Siege Fm | 30/07/1917 | 31/07/1917 |
| Operation(al) Order(s) | Company Operation Order No.1 Bg. Capt R.L. Hartley App I | 09/07/1917 | 09/07/1917 |
| Operation(al) Order(s) | Coy Operation Orders No. 2 By Captain R L. Hartley App II | 11/07/1917 | 11/07/1917 |
| | | | |
| Miscellaneous | 56 Coy M.G. Corps. Company Orders By Capt R L. Hartley. App II | 12/07/1917 | 12/07/1917 |
| Miscellaneous | A Form Messages And Signals. | 13/07/1917 | 13/07/1917 |
| Miscellaneous | Relief Orders By Capt R.L. Hartley App IVA | 22/07/1917 | 22/07/1917 |
| Miscellaneous | 56 Coy. M.G. Corps. Operation Orders By Captn R.L. Hartley. App V | 28/07/1917 | 28/07/1917 |
| Miscellaneous | 56 Coy M.G. Corps. Operation Orders No. 9.B. App VI | 28/07/1917 | 28/07/1917 |
| War Diary | Siege Fm | 01/08/1917 | 08/08/1917 |
| War Diary | Berthen | 09/08/1917 | 10/08/1917 |
| War Diary | Watterdal | 11/08/1917 | 11/08/1917 |
| War Diary | Colembert | 12/08/1917 | 22/08/1917 |

| | | | |
|---|---|---|---|
| War Diary | Watterdal | 23/08/1917 | 29/08/1917 |
| War Diary | Westoutre | 30/08/1917 | 31/08/1917 |
| Miscellaneous | Company Operation Orders By Lt. E.W.C. Flavell | 09/08/1917 | 09/08/1917 |
| War Diary | Westoutre | 01/09/1917 | 06/09/1917 |
| War Diary | Locre | 07/09/1917 | 19/09/1917 |
| War Diary | Kleine Vierstraat | 19/09/1917 | 30/09/1917 |
| Map | | | |
| Miscellaneous | Make Use Of Paragraphs As Required Give Map reference or mark of map at back. | | |
| Miscellaneous | Operation Orders By Captn F. H. Champion Commanding 56th Coy Machine Gun Corps | 18/09/1917 | 18/09/1917 |
| Miscellaneous | 56th Inf Bde | | |
| War Diary | Klein Vierstraat | 01/10/1917 | 31/10/1917 |
| Operation(al) Order(s) | App I Company Operation Order No. 1 By L. E. W. C. Flavell Commanding 56th Machine Gun Company | 31/10/1917 | 31/10/1917 |
| Operation(al) Order(s) | App II Copy No03a Operation Order No. 1 By Capt A S Warren | 25/10/1917 | 25/10/1917 |
| Miscellaneous | 56th Inf Bde | | |
| War Diary | Klein Vierstraat | 01/11/1917 | 01/11/1917 |
| War Diary | Zillebeke Sector In The Line Klein Verst | 02/11/1917 | 09/11/1917 |
| War Diary | Frontier Camp Westoutre | 10/11/1917 | 10/11/1917 |
| War Diary | Le Labourer | 11/11/1917 | 27/11/1917 |
| War Diary | Wallon Cappell | 28/11/1917 | 30/11/1917 |
| Miscellaneous | Relief Orders By Capt F.H. Champion. M.R. 1/10,000 Hollebeke. | 07/01/1917 | 07/01/1917 |
| Miscellaneous | 56 Coy M G Comm Orders By Captn F. H. Champion | 08/11/1917 | 08/11/1917 |
| Miscellaneous | Appex III 56 Infy Bde M G. Coy | | |
| Miscellaneous | 56th Inf Bde. | 01/01/1918 | 01/01/1918 |
| War Diary | Wallon Cappel | 01/12/1917 | 07/12/1917 |
| War Diary | Bellacourt | 08/12/1917 | 08/12/1917 |
| War Diary | Courcelles-Le-Comte | 09/12/1917 | 09/12/1917 |
| War Diary | Etricourt | 10/12/1917 | 13/12/1917 |
| War Diary | Fins | 14/12/1917 | 21/12/1917 |
| War Diary | Havrincourt Wood | 22/12/1917 | 31/12/1917 |
| War Diary | Havrincourt Wood | 01/01/1918 | 10/02/1918 |
| War Diary | Havrincourt Wood P.18.c. Central 57 C1/40000 | 11/02/1918 | 28/02/1918 |

19TH DIVISION

56TH INFY BDE

56TH MACHINE GUN COY.

OCT 1915-FEB 1918

19th Div.

WAR
DIARY

56th INFANTRY BRIGADE MACHINE GUN COMPANY.

O C T O B E R

1 9 1 5

Feb '18

Machine Gun Company

56th Infantry Brigade

War Diary  Ref. Trench Map 36 S W

~~Date~~ No. of guns in front line remains 6, numbered 5. 6. 7. 9. 10. 11

| Gun | Position |
|---|---|
| No. 5 | S 27 b 5.4 |
| No 6 | S 21 d 7.5 |
| No 7 | S 21 d 6.6 |
| No 9 | S 21 d 7.9 |
| No. 10 | S 21 b 7 4 |
| No 11 | S 21 b 7 9 |

| Date | Target | Gun | No. of rounds fired |
|---|---|---|---|
| 10.10.15 | (a) Rue d'Ouvert (Indirect) | No. 5 | 1000 |
| | (b) Rue du Marais do | Nos 6 & 7 | 500 |
| | Working parties | do | 700 |
| | (b) Rue du Marais (Indirect) | Nos 9 & 10 | 600 |
| 11.10.15 | (a) | No 5. | 1200 |
| | (b) | Nos 6. 7. 9 & 10. | 550 |
| | Working party | No 6 | 300 |
| | do | No 9 | 300 |
| | (c) Ferme Cour d'Avoué | No 10 | 200 |
| 12.10.15 | (a) | No. 5 | 600 |
| | (b) | Nos 6. 7. 9. 10. | 1600 |
| | (c) | No 11 | 400 |

2/Machine Gun Coy. 56th Inf Bde War Diary Contd.

| Date | Gun | Target | No. of rounds. |
|---|---|---|---|
| 13.10.15 | Nos 6.7.9.10 | b | 3000 |
| | No. 11 | c. | 500 |
| | No. 6 | Enemy parapet | 420 |
| | No 9 | Working party | 200 |
| 14.10.15 | No. 5 | a. | 700 |
| | do | Parapet | 200 |
| | Nos 6 & 7 | Working parties | 1320 |
| | Nos 9 & 10 | b | 400 |
| | do | Working parties | 200 |
| 15.10.15 | No 5 | a | 500 |
| | do | Parapet | 200 |
| | Nos 6 & 7 | b | 550 |
| | do. | Working parties & parapet | 2100 |
| | No 9 & 10 | b | 800 |
| | No. 11 | c | 250 |
| 16.10.15 | No. 5. | a & working party | 800 |
| | Nos 6. & 7 | Working party & parapet | 670 |
| | Nos 9. & 10 | do. | 500 |
| 17.10.15 | No 5 | Working party | 400 |
| | Nos 6 & 7 | Parapet | 200 |
| | Nos 9.10 & 11. | Working party etc & parapet | 400 |
| 18.10.15 | No 5. | Working parties | 400 |
| | Nos 6 & 7 | do | 400 |
| | Nos 9 10 & 11 | do | 750 |
| 19.10.15 | No. 5 | do. | 300 |
| | Nos 6 & 7 | do | 150 |
| | Nos 9.10 & 11 | do | 300 |

O/M. G. Co. 56th Inf. Bde. Nr Bois Carré

| Date | Gun | Target | No. of rounds. |
|---|---|---|---|
| 20·10·15 | No 5. | Working party S27d38 | 300 |
| | Nos 6 & 7 | Working parties | 400 |
| | Nos 9 & 10 | Parapet | 300 |
| | No 11 | Working party S22a07 | 200 |
| 21·10·15 | No 5 | " | 500 |
| | No. 9 | Snipers post | 200 |
| | No 11 | M. G. emplacement | 200 |
| 22·10·15 | No. 5 | Working parties | 200 |
| | No 6 | Cupola | 200 |
| | No 9 | S22c28 to S22d94. Trenches | 100 |
| 23·10·15 | No 5 | — | |
| | Nos 6 & 7 | Working parties & cupola | 300 |
| | Nos 9 & 10 | Parapet & cupola | 800. |

23·10·15 Company relieved by 58th Inf Bde M. G. Co I
6 pm.

F. W. Taylor Lt
for O.C. M. G. Co
56th Inf. Bde.

2·11·15

Secret

R

Operation Orders for the 25th September 1915
by Capt. H.O. Collyer. Comdg.
56th Brig M-G- Coy.

General Idea. The 2nd Division on our right are going to attack the Enemy at Zero.
The 58th Brigade on our immediate right will also go forward. Their Northern limit is about A.3.a.75.
They will time their attack from the right & will probably advance about 0.30. Their signal to advance is a sheap of many coloured rockets.

Special Idea. The 56th Brigade Machine Guns will endeavour to assist the advance by bringing Enfilade fire to bear on the Enemy's Trenches.
The following are the times & targets of the guns to be employed.

1 Gun S.W.B. Regt. at S. 26. d. 2. 8. will fire on Support Trench A. 9. b. 1. 8. to A. 9. b. 6. 1. from 0. 5. to 0. 8.

This gun must stop sharp at 0. 8. From 0. 8. to 0. 30 it will fire on Communication Trench A. 4. C. 0. 7. to A. 4. C. 9. 6. 2 guns S.W.B. Regt will fire on Communication Trench A. 3. B. 6. 5 to A. 4. C. 9. 6 from 0. 5 to 0. 30.

They will then cease fire & search the Rue du Marais.

Nos. 1 & 2 guns will Enfilade German front line Trench. Target A. from 0. 5 to 0. 10.

The extreme range of 1000 yards must on <u>NO</u> account be passed. Then No. 1. gun from 0. 10. onwards must fire at target B.

& No. 2. at target A.

No. 3 gun will fire from 0. 5 to 0. 15 at Rue D'Ouvert Target C. then it will fire on targets A & B.

No. 4. gun will fire its targets from 0. 10. continuously.

No. 6. will fire on target C continuously.

No. 7. will fire on target C for ½ an hour after Zero.

No. 1. will fire on target B continuously from 0. 10.

No.11. will fire on La. Towelle from 0.5. continuously.

Zero. The time Zero has not been definitely decided on but will be probably 4.50. a.m. The exact time will be communicated later.

Targets. When a target is referred to as target A. B or C it refers to the targets mentioned in the former list issued on 22nd Inst.

Time Watches must be checked with signal time.

Visibility. As we shall be using smoke bombs observation of fire will be improbable therefore great accuracy must be expended in laying the guns.

Night Firing. So as to reduce the chances of breakages as little fire as possible should be used to-night. (24th)

Damaged Guns. If any gun is out of action or likely to become so it must be replaced by another if necessary from the South Lancs Detachment.

H.O. Colley. Capt.
B.G. in-G. Coy.
[illegible] . 55th

19th Div.

WAR
DIARY

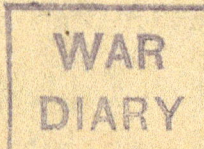

56th INFANTRY BRIGADE MACHINE GUN COMPANY.

N O V E M B E R

1 9 1 5

Machine Gun Co. 56th Inf Brigade

# War Diary November 1915.

Nov 1st - 7th In reserve to XIX Division at LOCON.

Scheme for attack by 56th Brigade on enemy line S of CANADIAN ORCHARD arranged. Fac simile trenches made under R.E. supervision near LOCON. Scheme practised in conjunction with Brigade Grenadier Co.

Scheme abandoned owing to state of trenches, parapet and ground between the lines through continual rain

Nov. 8th Left LOCON at noon and proceeded to GORRE Co. Hd. Qrs. at F 4 a 10.3 (BETHUNE combined Sheet). 13 teams of 1 N.C.O. + 3 men each went up to trenches.

| | | |
|---|---|---|
| No 1 Team | INDIA | Bay 19 |
| 2 | do | do 26 |
| 3 | do | do 43 |
| 4 | LEE'S KEEP. | |
| 5 | INDIA | Bay 81 |
| 6 | do 1B | do 9 |
| 7 | do | do 22 |
| 8 | FESTUBERT E | Post. |
| 9 | IND 1B | 25 |
| 10 | IND 1C | Bay 72 |
| 11 | do | 85 |
| 12 | COLONET KEEP | |
| 13 | B REDOUBT. | |

Reliefs complete at 10.5 p.m.

Relief reported to 54th Inf Brigade.

Reliefs made very difficult owing to state of communication trenches which were in many places impassable, teams having to move across the open.

Machine Gun Coy 56th Inf Brigade

War Diary contd

Nov. 9th

Teams 1-4 Nothing to report. No firing

5-8 No. 6 gun dispersed working party barn.

9-12 Nothing to report.

Nov. 10th Nothing to report. Work practically impossible owing to difficulty ~~to~~ of taking up material.

Nov. 11th Working parties fired on by Nos. 4. 6. & 7

No. 5 fired 200 rounds at enemy M.G. emplacement.

All teams relieved.

Nov. 12th Drying shed built for clothing of men coming out of trenches.

No 9 fired 200 rounds at working party.

Nos 3 & 6 fired 500 rounds at M.G. emplacements.

Working party of 20 sent to begin conversion scheme. Bays 31 & 32 heightened by 2 sandbags.

Nov. 13th No 2 Detachment 7 E. Lan R. relieved by No 4 7 N. Lan R. Other teams relieved.

Nos 1-4 2 magazines fired at enemy parapet.

5-12 Breach in enemy parapet fired on at intervals during the day.

Parapet traversed, M.G. emplacements, snipers posts & patrols fired on.

Enemy replied with M.G fire & 2 H.E. shells on BARNTON RD.

Wire received from XIX Divn. – "7th Div will be blowing up a mine about 4.30 p.m. to-day. Look out for possible targets". No targets were visible.

Nov. 14th Teams 1-4 No target. 50 rounds fired at parapet.

Teams 5-8 Working party dispersed from wire in front of No. 5 emplacement. attempts to repair wire frustrated. Trench ammunition stores built.

Teams 9-12 No firing. Water pumped out of trenches.

Working party of 20 raised bays 31-32 by 4 sandbags.

# Machine Gun Coy 56th Inf Brigade.

## War Diary Contd

Nov. 15th 19 men reported sick.

O.C. Coy proceeded to M.G. School G.H.Q for a course of instruction for B.M.G.O's and Brigade Staff Officers.

Teams 1-4. Nothing to report.

5-8. Fire at breaches made in enemy parapet by artillery. Enemy replied with rifle + M.G. fire. Water depth reduced by 1' near No. 5 emplacement.

9-12. 100 rounds fired at working parties.

By instruction of the Brigadier General, a gun was placed in the post known as FESTUBERT C.

Reliefs were made at each gun.

Working party of 24 raised the breastwork in Bays 31 + 32 by 3 sandbags.

Nov. 16th Working party dispersed by No. 2 gun.

Nos 5-8 fired at parapet, working parties and snipers posts. Casualties were observed.

Enemy snipers active. Two men killed by bullets through breaches in parapet.

A carrying party of 20 took dug out frames from R.E. depôt in reserve trenches to front line. Two of party killed by one bullet.

Nov. 17th 1200 rounds fired at working parties, parapets and posts.

No. 2 (7 E. Lancs R) Detachment relieved No 1 (7 R. Lanc R.) and other teams relieved.

Nov. 18th No. 2 gun moved to new emplacement in Bays 31 + 32. Dug outs + traverses made.

Nos. 5-8 fired 1300 rounds. Enemy artillery swept front apparently searching for M.G.S.

Nos 9-12 fired 450 rounds at breach in parapet.

Nov. 19th Nos 5-8 fired 950 rounds at usual targets

Nos 9-12 " 350 " " parapet

Nov. 19th Contd

Report received from XIX Div. "Unconfirmed report that Germans are using gas on left of VII Div. Be prepared and report" At once repeated to Detacht. officers. Reports received that preparations had been made but no traces of gas were felt.

Teams relieved.

Nov. 20th Teams 9-12 250 rounds fired at enemy working party in mouth of sap.

Nov. 21st Officer sent to Corps reserve area to arrange for billets K 26 a 5.7 Sheet 36A.

Teams 1-4 200 rounds fired at working party 9.0pm.

Teams 5-8 600 rounds at working parties.

No 3 Detacht. relieved by 7 S. Lan R No 1.

Other teams relieved.

A M.G. officer of the 20th Brigade met the OMGO at the 56th Brigade office to discuss arrangements for taking over.

Nov 22nd Teams 5-8 100 rounds fired at working party near old German communication trench.

Motor lorry & seven limbers left for new billets with Coy stores.

Teams from posts in FESTUBERT C & E relieved by 6th Gordon Highlanders

Nov. 23rd. M.G. officer from 4th Camerons T.F. came to make arrangements for taking over three guns on the right.

Reports Teams 1-4 200 rounds fired at working parties.

5-8 600 " " " "

9-12 1200 " " " "

No observation possible owing to mist. Parties could be heard working.

All ranks of Coy not in trenches moved off from GORRE and marched to LOCON occupying the billets vacated 8.11.15.

20th Brigade relieved the Coy's teams, who arrived

War Diary Contd.

Nov. 23rd Contd.

at LOCON 12.30 am. 24.11.15.

Nov. 24th. Coy moved off at 11.20 am to new billets. A cyclist orderly met the Coy near MERVILLE with a message to say that the billets to which the Coy was moving were occupied by the Div. Squadn of the Guards Div. who had no instructions to move. The O.C. Coy went forward to 56th Brigade new headquarters and was given a new area. (K29 - K4 Sheet 36A) Coy arrived in new billets at 4.45 pm.

Nov. 25th. Day given up to billeting, cleaning of equipment and clothing.

Nov. 26th. Parades for inspection of clothing and equipment.

Field General Court Martial held at Coy Hd. Qrs.

~~for~~ President. Major RCW Goodwyn 7 E. Lan R.

Members. Capt BAD Leverson 7 N. Lan R.

Capt E.O. Sewell 7 S. Lan R

for the purpose of trying 13080 Pte. Jackson 7 E. Lan. R M.G. Detachment.

The 7 S. Lan R. and 7 E. Lan R Detachts. went to their battalions for inspection by the Brigadier Genl.

Nov. 27th. Extract from Routine Orders by Brig. Genl B.G. Lewis G.O.C. 56th Inf. Brigade dated 26.11.15.

"Complimentary. The Brigadier congratulates the officers and men of the Lancashire Brigade on their behaviour during the last very trying time in the trenches.

Their cheerful pluck and fortitude were admirable and worthy of the best traditions of the army."

Nov. 28th. Instruction classes were arranged for officers and men of the 7 E. Lan R, 7 S. Lan R and 7 N. Lan R by officers and men of the M.G. Coy. to be held in the morning of each day during the week.

The N.C.O's + men of the above detachments who

Machine Gun Coy 56th Inf. Brigade.
War Diary Contd

Nov. 28th Contd.
were not required as instructors reported to their battalions and were instructed to carry out the same programme daily.

Nov. 29th Instruction classes held as yesterday.
The O.C., a subaltern and a sergeant of the 5th Batt. Motor Machine Guns gave instruction to 3 classes of officers, N.C.O's & men of the Coy in the Vickers Gun.

Nov. 30th Promulgation of Field General Court Martial 13080 Pte. Jackson 7. E. Lan. R. fined 10/- and awarded 3 months F. P. No 1 for
i Being drunk
ii Threatening an N.C.O.
Classes of instruction held as yesterday.

5. 12. 15

T. W. Taylor 2/Lt
for O.C.
Machine Gun Coy
56th Inf. Brigade

Operation R

# Machine Gun Company.
## 56 Infantry Brigade.

Routine Orders by Lt. J.W. Cox. Tempy Commanding.

The Company will relieve the Machine Gun Company, 57th Inf. Brigade tomorrow.

<u>Special Orders</u>

The Company will form up in the order previously arranged, with head of column at road junction W.6 D.4, ready to move off at 12.0 noon.

Dinners will be clear by 11.15 am. Each man will carry his own tea ration. Men going into trenches will carry firewood. Extra biscuit & meat will be issued for teams remaining in trenches.

All braziers, heavy tripods, & tools, (except 1 pick & 1 shovel per team, to be carried by No. 1) to be at guard room at 9. am.

All men not told off to teams, or as officers' servants or observers, report to Sgt. Major at guard room at 8.30 am.

Section Sgts, gun [illegible] & officers' observers will attend at guard room at 9. a.m.

Amm. limbers, stores limber to be at guard room at 8.30 am; ration limbers remain loaded.

| SECT. | TEAM. | EMPLACEMENT. | S.A.A. CARRIED. | S.A.A. LOOSE. | S.A.A. TAKEN OVER. IN BOXES. | GUIDES. |
|---|---|---|---|---|---|---|
| | No. 1. | No. 1. | 20 mags full 36 – empty. | 1692 | 12.000 | [illegible] |
| K.D. | No. 2. | No. 2. | " | " | 12.000 | |
| | No. 3. | No. 3 | " | " | 9.000 | |
| | No. 4. | LEE'S KEEP. | " | " | 16000. | |
| | No. 5. | No. 7. | 18 mags full 36 empty. | 1692 | | [illegible] |
| E.L. | No. 6. | No. 8. | " | " | 38.000 | |
| | No. 7. | No. 9. | " | " | | |
| | No. 8. | [illegible] | " | " | 24.000 | |
| | No. 9. | No. 4. | 18 mags full. 36 – empty. | 1692 | 8.000 | [illegible] |
| S.L. | No. 10. | No. 5. | " | " | 8.000. | |
| | No. 11. | No. 6. | " | " | 8.000 | |
| | No. 12. | [illegible] KEEP. | " | " | 16.000 | |
| N.L. | No. 13. | REDOUBT. B. | 18 mags full 36 – empty. | 1692 | 7000. | [illegible] |
| | No's 14 15 & 16 | IN RESERVE. | 54 mags full. | | | |

[illegible]

7. 11. 15

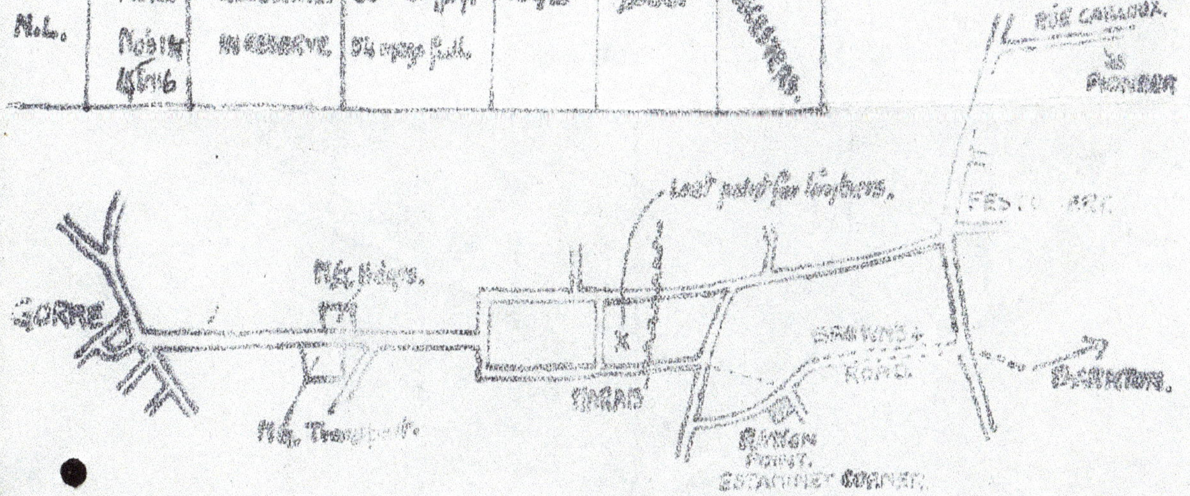

19th Div.

WAR DIARY

56th INFANTRY BRIGADE MACHINE GUN COMPANY.

D E C E M B E R

1 9 1 5

Attached:

Appendices 1, 2 & 3.

Confidential

War Diary

of

Machine Gun Coy

56th Infy Brigade

from Decr 1st – Decr 31st 1915.

J. W. Coe. Lieut

Commanding M. G. Coy

56th Infy Bde.

Army Form C. 2118

Instructions regarding War Diaries and Intelligence Summaries are contained in F. S. Regs., Part II. and the Staff Manual respectively. Title Pages will be prepared in manuscript.

# WAR DIARY
*or*
# INTELLIGENCE SUMMARY
*(Erase heading not required.)*

| Place | Date | Hour | Summary of Events and Information | Remarks and references to Appendices |
|---|---|---|---|---|
| In the Field | 1.12.15 | . | In Corps Reserve at MERVILLE. Instructional classes held in VICKERS GUN by M.M.G Battery and instruction given by officers N.C.O's & men of the M G Coy to officers N.C.O.s & men of Batt^ns of 56th Brigade | |
| | 2.12.15 | – | Classes as yesterday. O.C. Coy lectured to officers of 4 R Lanc R. at the Batt H.Q. on M.G tactics. | |
| | 3.12.15 | 3a.m | Orders received to prepare to move off at 11.0 am as the XIX Div^n was to take over to-morrow the line held by the 46th Div^n. | |
| | | | All arrangements for classes & baths cancelled. | |
| | | 10.0 – | Further orders to move at 12 noon to PARADIS and to send billeting officer in advance. | Nos 1.2.3.5.7. 10.11. & Reserve |
| | | 2.30p | Coy billeted at PARADIS. B.M.G.O went to 139th Brigade to arrange for taking over. | |
| | 4.12.15 | 9.45a | Coy moved off from PARADIS. * Eleven teams went directly into the trenches. The remainder found billets along road running through M256 (BETHUNE combined). Relief complete at 6.0pm | * App. 1 Pos^n of guns |
| | 5.12.15 | | No 2 gun fired 200 rounds at enemy parapet. Nos 8–11 fired 400 rounds at working parties. No. 9 gun fired 100 rounds in direction indicated by patrol officer. a few minutes later patrol returned reporting that fire had caused great confusion. | |
| | 6.12.15 | | Two teams of No. 3. Detach^t went with their guns to the front line * 400 rounds fired at enemy front line. | Nos 6 & 8 |
| | 7.12.15 | | Two other guns were sent up to front line * 400 rounds fired at enemy front line & working parties. B.M.G.O. & 2nd in command went to select pos^ns for indirect fire. | Nos 9–12 |
| | 8.12.15 | | Operation Orders. There will be a combined artillery & M.G. action against enemy salient S5d 2.3. to-morrow morning. | |
| | | | 1. Zero. All troops along line will cheer. | |
| | | | 2. 0.5 Bouquet of shrapnel; upon which M.G's & Trench Mortars will fire as scheduled below | |

1875 Wt. W593/826 1,000,000 4/15 J.B.C. & A. A.D.S.S./Forms/C. 2118.

Instructions regarding War Diaries and Intelligence Summaries are contained in F. S. Regs., Part II. and the Staff Manual respectively. Title Pages will be prepared in manuscript.

# WAR DIARY
*or*
# INTELLIGENCE SUMMARY
*(Erase heading not required.)*

Army Form C. 2118

| Place | Date | Hour | Summary of Events and Information | Remarks and references to Appendices |
|---|---|---|---|---|
| In the Field | 8.12.15 | Contd | 0.30 - till dusk slow & steady bombardment by artillery | |
| | | | dusk till 8.0 pm pause | |
| | | | 8.0 pm whiff of shrapnel upon which signal artillery & M.Gs will fire at irregular intervals through the night | |
| | | | 2. Guns in front line will not fire during daylight except one magazine each after signal of shrapnel at 0.5. They will fire at irregular intervals during the night. The following guns appear to cover the position Nos 3. 4. 5 (to go to to emplace) 7 and 9 | |
| | | | 3. The following guns will move at 5pm today to positions notified and will be under the command of Lt. Cox. | |
| | | | (a) CHATEAU gun to PONT LOGY via ~~LA BASSÉE ROAD~~ CHATEAU RD. CHIMNEY CRESCENT & RUE TILLELOY | |
| | | | (b) HILL'S KEEP " " " " LA BASSÉE ROAD | |
| | | | (c) PORT ARTHUR " " WINDY CORNER via " + FORESTER'S LANE | |
| | | | (d) RUE DU BOIS Cellar " " " " " Tramline F " " | |
| | | | 4. Teams of these four guns will take all kit. gun. heavy tripod. spare parts. 9 magazines with case. Rations and ammunition will be brought to their new positions | |
| | | | 5. Instructions will be sent to the teams on arrival at their new positions. | |
| | | | 1000 rounds fired at working parties on enemy wire | |
| | 9.12.15 | | 200 " " " enemy parapet. | |
| | | | Guns 1 & 3 fired 600 rounds according to instructions | |
| | | | " 5-4 & 6 " ~~2000~~ 400 " " " " | |
| | | | " ~~8 & 9~~ 7-9 " 2000 " " " " | |

1875 Wt. W593/826 1,000,000 4/15 J.B.C. & A. A.D.S.S./Forms/C. 2118.

Instructions regarding War Diaries and Intelligence Summaries are contained in F. S. Regs., Part II. and the Staff Manual respectively. Title Pages will be prepared in manuscript.

Army Form C. 2118

# WAR DIARY
*or*
# INTELLIGENCE SUMMARY
*(Erase heading not required.)*

| Place | Date | Hour | Summary of Events and Information | Remarks and references to Appendices |
|---|---|---|---|---|
| In the Field | 9.12.15 | Cont^d | Guns 10-12 fired 1200 rounds. | |
| | | | Indirect Fire – 7500 rounds fired on LA TOURELLE, DISTILLERIE, FERME du BIEZ, roads leading through BOIS du BIEZ, railhead & communication trenches, from houses at PONT LOGY and in FORESTER'S LANE. | * App^x Indirect Fire Orders |
| | 10.12.15 | | Guns 1-3 fired 1200 rounds at enemy's front line & supports. | |
| | | | " 4-6 " 2500 " at breach in parapet and working parties | |
| | | | " 7-9 dispersed working party at S5d 2.1. French map 36 SW Sheet 3 | |
| | | | " 10-12 fired 1400 rounds at patrols & parapet. | |
| | | | Indirect Fire 1000 rounds fired on LA TOURELLE, DISTILLERIE, FERME du BIEZ. | |
| | | | 1500 " " at BOIS du BIEZ, roads leading through, railhead & comm^n trenches | |
| | 11.12.15 | | Guns 1-3 fired 900 rounds at enemy salient, & parapet. | |
| | | 6.0am | No 4 " 100 " " working party | |
| | | 11.0am | " 5 " 50 " " | |
| | | | " 6 " 550 " enemy salient LES BRULOT | |
| | | | Nos 7-9 " 400 " " houses S5d 5.1½ | |
| | | | " 10-12 " at German M.G. emplacement | |
| | | | Indirect fire 2 guns fired 1500 rds. from FORESTER'S LANE at LES BRULOTS and country behind. | |
| | 12.12.15 | | Guns 1-3 fired 550 rounds at enemy parapet and breach | |
| | | | " 7-9 " 930 rounds at " " , LES BRULOT, S5d 4.5, searching parapet | |
| | | | Sentry at No 1 gun THE NEB killed by M.G. fire | |
| | 13.12.15 | | 2200 rounds fired at enemy wire, parapet and at three working parties. | |
| | 14.12.15 | | 3200 " " " " " breaches in parapet & green mound FERME du BIEZ | |

Instructions regarding War Diaries and Intelligence Summaries are contained in F. S. Regs., Part II. and the Staff Manual respectively. Title Pages will be prepared in manuscript.

# WAR DIARY
*or*
# INTELLIGENCE SUMMARY
*(Erase heading not required.)*

Army Form C. 2118

| Place | Date | Hour | Summary of Events and Information | Remarks and references to Appendices |
|---|---|---|---|---|
| In the Field | 15.12.15 | - | 300 rounds fired at enemy working party. | |
| | | | 400 " " in conjunction with artillery | |
| | | | N.C.O. & 2 men of No. 11 gun wounded by shrapnel | |
| | 16.12.15 | " | 1500 rounds fired at enemy parapet, working parties, green mound & gaps in wire | |
| | | | N.C.O. of No 7 gun killed by bullet | |
| | | | Man of team relieving No. 5 gun killed in OXFORD ST by bullet | |
| | 17.12.15 | " | 1-3 fired 750 rounds at enemy parapet. | |
| | | | 4-6 " 800 " " " " | |
| | | | 7-9 " 1200 " " mound & breaches in parapet. | |
| | | | 10-12 " 800 " " gaps in wire opposite No 11 gun | |
| | | | Sentry at No. 2 gun killed by bullet. | |
| | 18.12.15 | | 1-3 fired 1000 rounds at parapet & reported working parties. | |
| | | | 4-6 " 900 " traversing parapet & single shots at breaches. | |
| | | | 7-9 " 2650 " according to special instructions from B.M.G.O. at special targets and breaches in parapet, also at 2 Germans reported in ditch S5 b 2.0 | |
| | | | 10-12 fired 2700 rounds at enemy's front line & wire. | |
| | 19.12.15 | | The Coy was relieved by the 58th Infy Bde. M.G. Coy. The officers & other ranks not in the trenches moved off from VIEILLE CHAPELLE and arrived at new billets at LES LOBES at 3 pm. | |
| | | | The relief was complete and all men had arrived in the new billets by 9.30 pm. | |
| | 20.12.15 | | Guns were cleaned and inspected and new gun equipment issued. Rest of day given up to cleaning. Special order of the day issued by Brig Gen Lewis D.S.O. on relinquishing command of the 56th Infy Bde | |

1875 Wt. W593/826 1,000,000 4/15 J.B.C. & A. A.D.S.S./Forms/C. 2118.

Instructions regarding War Diaries and Intelligence Summaries are contained in F. S. Regs., Part II. and the Staff Manual respectively. Title Pages will be prepared in manuscript.

# WAR DIARY
*or*
# INTELLIGENCE SUMMARY
*(Erase heading not required.)*

Army Form C. 2118

| Place | Date | Hour | Summary of Events and Information | Remarks and references to Appendices |
|---|---|---|---|---|
| In the field | 21.12.15 | - | Gun Cleaning. Clothing & equipment issued. Men's clothing & equipment cleaned. Capt H.O. Collyer having been transferred to the Machine Gun Corps, left for England this day, being succeeded by Lieut J.W. Cox 7 E. Lan R. as actg. in command of the Coy. | |
| | 22.12.15 | - | Kit Inspection. Short march | |
| | 23.12.15 | - | Short march. Inspection by O.C. Coy Gun cleaning & issue of equipment. 2 off. 150 men attended an entertainment given by XIX Divn Follies at LESTREM | |
| | 24.12.15 | - | Gun cleaning. Changing clothes. Short march. Lectures by officers | |
| | 25.12.15 | - | R.C.s. Church Parade. Short March. Gun cleaning & inspection. | |
| | 26.12.15 | - | Coy relieved the M.G. Coy 57th Infy Bde. in the trenches from ROPE to COPSE ST. The Coy Headquarters being established at R35d 2,9 [BETHUNE combined] | app x 3 Map of posn |
| | 27.12.15 | | 650 rounds fired at parapet. working parties. and M.G. emplacements | |
| | 28.12.15 | | 1050 " " " " " gaps in enemy wire. 2/Lt W.E.A. Milward 7E. Lan R joined the Coy to replace Lt J.W. Cox appointed a/B.M.G.O. | |
| | 29.12.15 | | 800 rounds fired at enemy parapet & breaches in parapet, M.G. emplacements & working parties | |
| | 30.12.15 | | 950 rounds " " " " " " " working parties. | |
| | 31.12.15 | | 1105 rounds " at enemy wire. M.G. emplacements and at FERME COUR D'AVOUÉ. | |

A P P E N D I C E S 1, 2 & 3.

Appendix 1.

Position of guns in trenches from COPSE ST & SIGN POST LANE

Ref. 36 S.W. Sheet 3.

| | | | |
|---|---|---|---|
| No. 1. | S 10 c 9.7 | No. 2 | S 10 b 5.½. |
| No. 3 | S 10 c 7.7 | No. 4 | S 11 a 1.8. |
| No. 5 | S 5 c 2½. 2½ | No. 6 | S 5 c 4.5 |
| No. 7 | S 5 c 1.9 | No. 8 | S 5 b ½.2. |
| No. 9 | S 5 b 5.0 | No. 10 | S 5 b 6.1. |
| No. 11 | M 35 d 2.0. | No. 12 | M 35 d 3.4. |

CHATEAU REDOUBT.
HILL'S do
PORT ARTHUR do.
Cellar on RUE du BOIS S 10 a 4 2½.

-2199 50,000 7/15 H W V (M127)

App 2

## Certificate to be Signed before Fire is Opened.

have checked all calculations and line of fire of gun.

he Brigadier-General commanding the line of trenches, *i.e.*, Nos. ________, has sanctioned fire from 14/12/15 to ________ date.

The troops occupying trenches No. ________ have been notified.

(Signed) Ho. Collyer Capt. B. M. G. O.

fficer in charge of Gun Capt. Collyer Sheet ______ Square ___

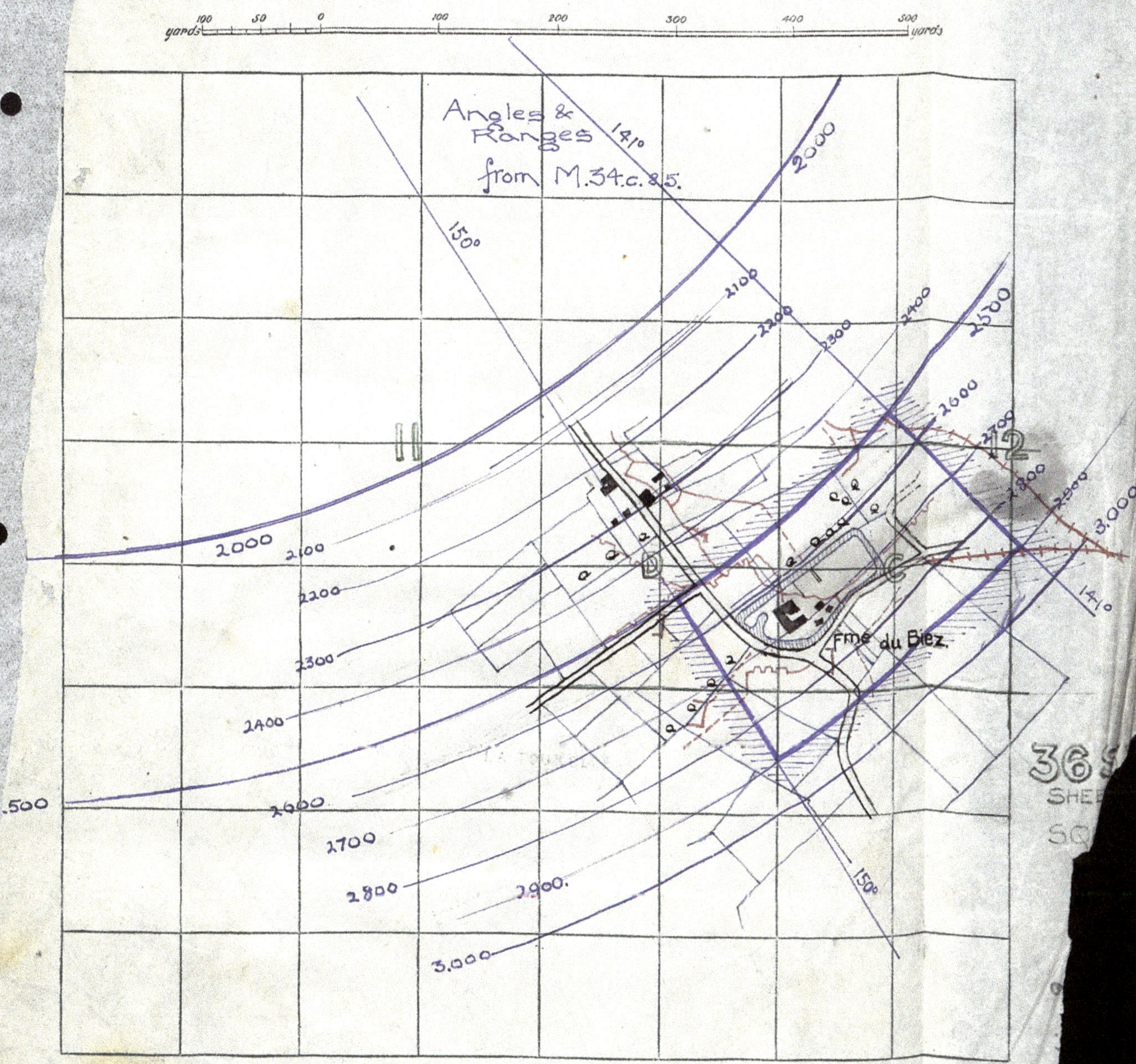

Appendix 3.

9
10
GUARDS
TEETOTAL CORNER
FACTORY POST.
BOND
VINE
HUN LINE
CONNAUGHT.
OLD BRITISH LINE
CHOCOLATE CORNER.
15
16
FERME DU BOIS.
Farm Corner
CADBURY.
DEAD COW.
PIPE.
PRINCES ROAD.
TUBE STATION.
FERME COUR D'AVOUE.
Marsden Keep.
HUN LINE
21
22
RUE DE CAILLOUX
ROPE.
Rope Keep.
LA QUINQUE RUE
SQUARE S.
Machine Gun Company.
56th Infantry Brigade

CONFIDENTIAL

3/3

# War Diary

of.

56. MACHINE, GUN COMPANY.
MACHINE GUN CORPS.

From 9th February To 29th Feb 1916

VOLUME I

Instructions regarding War Diaries and Intelligence Summaries are contained in F. S. Regs., Part II. and the Staff Manual respectively. Title pages will be prepared in manuscript.

# WAR DIARY
*or*
~~INTELLIGENCE SUMMARY.~~
*(Erase heading not required.)*

No 56 COY. MACHINE GUN CORPS.

Army Form C. 2118.

| Place | Date | Hour | Summary of Events and Information | Remarks and references to Appendices |
|---|---|---|---|---|
| HAVRE | 9/2/16 | 1 A.M. | Disembarked & arrived @ rest camp @ SANVIC. Telegram received from H.M. THE KING wishing success to the Company. | [illegible] |
| " " | 10/2/16 | 10. P.M. | Nothing of importance to report. | [illegible] |
| " " | 11/2/16 | 10 " | 2nd Lieut. KEMP. F. admitted to hospital | [illegible] |
| " " | 12/2/16 | 11. A.M. | Word received that the Coy had to move @ 1.A.M. on 13.2.16. Coy paraded @ 10.45 pm. moved off 11pm | [illegible] |
| " " | 13/2/16 | 3.40 A.M. | Entrained @ GARE MARITIME HAVRE. Destination unknown. Stopped @ ABBEVILLE. 2.30 A.M. Watered & fed mules & horses. Left @ 3.30 pm & Stopped @ BETHUNE about 10 pm | [illegible] |
| ~~MERVILLE~~ | | | | |
| MERVILLE | 14.2.16 | 12.5 A.M. | Arrived @ MERVILLE & started detraining & started to march to billets @ ST VENANT. | [illegible] |
| ST VENANT. | 14.2.16 | 5.50 A.M. | Arrived @ Billets @ ST VENANT. In the afternoon No 4391. was admitted to Divisional hospital | [illegible] |
| ST VENANT. | 15.2.16. | | In billets. Received orders to move up to the trenches, Stopping to billet @ LA. HUIT MAISONS. | [illegible] |
| ST. VENANT. | 16.2.16 | 6.40 A.M. | Coy paraded, & marched to LA. HUIT. MAISONS. via CALONNE-SUR-LA-LYS. PARADIS, ZELOBES. and VIELLE-CHAPELLE. Put men in billets & @ 5 pm one gun was placed in each of the following posts:- ST VAAST. LANSDOWNE. EUSTON, and LORRETTO under the command of 2nd Lieuts LOMAX & SOPER. Men supplied from No 1 Section | [illegible] |
| LA. HUIT. MAISONS | 17/2/16 | 6 pm. | ~~(A Gun placed in)~~ 14 men sent to front line trenches for instruction & @ 4 pm rations were sent up to the KEEPS | [illegible] |

T.2134. Wt. W708—776. 500000. 4/15. Sir J. C. & S.

Instructions regarding War Diaries and Intelligence Summaries are contained in F. S. Regs., Part II. and the Staff Manual respectively. Title pages will be prepared in manuscript.

# WAR DIARY
or
~~INTELLIGENCE SUMMARY.~~
*(Erase heading not required.)*

No 56 COY. MACHINE GUN CORPS.

Army Form C. 2118.

| Place | Date | Hour | Summary of Events and Information | Remarks and references to Appendices |
|---|---|---|---|---|
| LA-HUIT-MAISONS | 18/2/16 | 6 P.M. | A gun placed in CURZON POST. manned by 1 N.C.O + 3 men. No 4322 admitted into Hospital. F.A 131. | [illegible] |
| " " | 19/2/16 | | Nos 4393. 4316. + 7971. admitted to F.A. 131. Serjt Smith + 5 men went to 1st line trenches | [illegible] |
| " " | 20-2-16 | | Captn LANE + 2 Lieut GROVE made a tour of the M.G. Emplacements. | [illegible] |
| " " | 21-2-16 | 4. P.M. | Relief of Keeps. In the evening 2 guns opened over head fire, in conjunction with Artillery from LA. BASSEE ROAD. to a DISTILLERIE behind the GERMAN lines, Range about 2,900x Casualties nil, Gun placed in CHATEAU REDOUBT. with 3,000 rounds. S.A.A. No 4355 admitted to F.A. 131. | [illegible] |
| " " | 22/2/16 | | No 4381 admitted to F.A. 131. Muster Parade. Heavy fall of Snow. | [illegible] |
| " " | 23-2-16 | | Emplacements strengthened @ all posts held. Nothing of Tactical progress to report. | [illegible] |
| " " | 24-2-16 | 4. P.M. | Relieved Lewis guns in front line with 8. M.G.s 2nd Lieuts PRICE, LOMAX, + SOPER in Command. 2nd Lieut DUFFIELD took command of guns in all posts held. No 4322 discharged from F.A. 131. | [illegible] |
| " " | 25-2-16 | | Brigade order No 48 received, 33.000 rounds S.A.A. sent to front line guns. In the afternoon, Brigade order No 48. was cancelled. | [illegible] |
| " " | 26-2-16 | | Guns tested in Keeps Operation order No 49. received, | [illegible] |
| " " | 27-2-16 | | 2nd Lieuts LOMAX, PRICE, + SOPER, relieved by 2nd Lieut GROVE + WILGARS | [illegible] |
| " " | 28-2-16 | 6. A.M. | Gun under, 2nd Lieut GROVE fired 1,000 rounds @ target on enemys parapet, Gun @ LANSDOWNE post fired 2,000 rds overhead fire on enemys reserve line, Gun @ CURZON POST, fired 3.000 rds overhead fire on enemys reserve line. 2nd Lieut PRICE + Serjt No 4284, proceeded to Divl School of Instruction @ MERVILLE | [illegible] |

T2134. Wt. W708—776. 500000. 4/15. Sir J. C. & S.

Instructions regarding War Diaries and Intelligence Summaries are contained in F. S. Regs., Part II. and the Staff Manual respectively. Title pages will be prepared in manuscript.

# WAR DIARY
*or*
~~INTELLIGENCE SUMMARY~~.
*(Erase heading not required.)*



Army Form C. 2118.

| Place | Date | Hour | Summary of Events and Information | Remarks and references to Appendices |
|---|---|---|---|---|
| LA HUIT. MAISON. | 29-2-16. | | Reorganised relief of guns, Abolishing Section arrangement & supplying reliefs by teams. Nothing of tactical importance to report. | [illegible initials] |

Instructions regarding War Diaries and Intelligence Summaries are contained in F. S. Regs., Part II. and the Staff Manual respectively. Title pages will be prepared in manuscript.

# WAR DIARY
*or*
# ~~INTELLIGENCE SUMMARY.~~
*(Erase heading not required.)*

No 56 COY. MACHINE GUN CORPS.

Army Form C. 2118.

| Place | Date | Hour | Summary of Events and Information | Remarks and references to Appendices |
|---|---|---|---|---|
| HAVRE | 9/2/16 | 1 A.M. | Disembarked & arrived @ rest camp @ SANVIC. Telegram received from H.M. THE KING wishing success to the company. | J.D.W. |
| " " | 10/2/16 | 10 P.M. | Nothing of importance to report. | J.D.W. |
| " " | 11/2/16 | 10 " | 2nd Lieut. KEMP. F. admitted to hospital | J.D.W. |
| " " | 12/2/16 | 11 A.M. | Word received that the Coy had to move @ 1 A.M. on 13.2.16. Coy paraded @ 10.45 pm. moved off 11pm | J.D.W. |
| " " | 13/2/16 | 3.20 AM | Entrained @ GARE MARITIME HAVRE. Destination unknown. Stopped @ ABBEVILLE 2.30 A.M. Watered & fed mules & horses. Left @ 3.30 pm. Stopped @ BETHUNE about 10 pm. | J.D.W. |
| ~~MERVILLE~~ | | | | |
| MERVILLE | 14.2.16 | 12.5 AM | Arrived @ MERVILLE & started detraining & started to march to billets @ ST VENANT. | J.D.W. |
| ST VENANT. | 14.2.16 | 5.50 AM | Arrived @ Billets @ ST VENANT. In the afternoon No 4391. was admitted to Divisional hospital | J.D.W. |
| ST VENANT. | 15.2.16. | | In billets; Received orders to move up to the trenches, stopping to billet @ LA HUIT MAISONS. | J.D.W. |
| ST. VENANT. | 16.2.16 | 6.40 A.M. | Coy paraded & marched to LA HUIT MAISONS via CALONNE-SUR-LA-LYS. PARADIS. ZELOBES. and VIELLE CHAPELLE. Put men in billets & @ 5 pm. one gun was placed in each of the following posts:- ST VAAST-LANSDOWNE. EUSTON, and LORRETTA under the command of 2nd Lieuts LOMAX & SOPER. Men supplied from No 1 Section | J.D.W. |
| LA-HUIT-MAISONS | 17/2/16 | 6 pm. | ~~(A Gun placed in)~~ 14 men sent to front line trenches for instruction & @ 4 pm rations were sent up to the KEEPS | J.D.W. |

T2134. Wt. W708-776. 500000. 4/15. Sir J. C. & S.

Instructions regarding War Diaries and Intelligence Summaries are contained in F. S. Regs., Part II. and the Staff Manual respectively. Title pages will be prepared in manuscript.

# WAR DIARY
*or*
# ~~INTELLIGENCE SUMMARY.~~
*(Erase heading not required.)*



Army Form C. 2118.

| Place | Date | Hour | Summary of Events and Information | Remarks and references to Appendices |
|---|---|---|---|---|
| LA HUIT MAISONS | 18/2/16 | 6 P.M. | A gun placed in CURZON POST manned by 1 NCO + 3 men. No 4322 admitted into Hospital F.A 131. | [illegible] |
| " " | 19/2/16 | | Nos 4393. 4316 + 7971 admitted to F.A 131 Sergt Smith + 5 men went to 1st line trenches. | [illegible] |
| " " | 20-2-16 | | Capt. Frame + 2 Lieut GROVE made a tour of the M.G. Emplacements. | [illegible] |
| " " | 21-2-16 | 4 Pm | Relief of Keeps. In the evening 2 guns opened overhead fire in conjunction with Artillery from LA BASSEE ROAD to a DISTILLERIE behind the GERMAN lines, Range about 2900x Casualties nil. Gun placed in CHATEAU REDOUBT with 3000 rounds S.A.A. No 4305 admitted to F.A. 131. | [illegible] |
| " " | 22/2/16 | | No 4381 admitted to F.A 131. Muster Parade. Heavy fall of Snow. | [illegible] |
| " " | 23-2-16 | | Emplacements strengthened @ all posts held. Nothing of Tactical progress to report. | [illegible] |
| " " | 24-2-16 | 4 pm | Relieved Lewis Guns in front line with 8 M.G. 2nd Lieuts PRICE, LOMAX + SOPER in Command. 2nd Lieut DUFFIELD took command of guns in all posts held. No 4322 discharged from F.A 131. | [illegible] |
| " " | 25-2-16 | | Brigade order No 48 received. 33.000 rounds S.A.A sent to front line guns. In the afternoon, Brigade order No 48. was cancelled. | [illegible] |
| " " | 26-2-16 | | Guns tested in Keeps @ position order No 49. received. | [illegible] |
| " " | 27-2-16 | | 2nd Lieuts LOMAX, PRICE + SOPER relieved by 2nd Lieuts GROVE + WILGARS | [illegible] |
| " " | 28-2-16 | 6 a.m. | Guns under 2nd Lieut GROVE fired 1.000 rounds @ targets in enemy parapet. Gun @ LANSDOWNE post fired 2000 rds overhead fire on enemy reserve line. Gun @ CURZON POST, fired 3.000 rds overhead fire on enemy reserve line. 2nd Lieut PRICE + Sergt No 4284. proceeded to Div's School of Instruction @ MERVILLE | [illegible] |

T2134. Wt. W708—776. 500000. 4/15. Sir J. C. & S.

Instructions regarding War Diaries and Intelligence Summaries are contained in F. S. Regs., Part II. and the Staff Manual respectively. Title pages will be prepared in manuscript.

# WAR DIARY
*or*
~~INTELLIGENCE SUMMARY.~~
*(Erase heading not required.)*



Army Form C. 2118.

| Place | Date | Hour | Summary of Events and Information | Remarks and references to Appendices |
|---|---|---|---|---|
| LA HUTT. MAISON. | 29-2-16. | | Reorganised relief of guns, abolishing section arrangement & supplying relief by teams. Nothing of tactical importance to report. | [illegible] |

Confidential

War - Diary

of

56. Machine Gun Coy.

From March 1st 1916 To March 31st 1916

Volume II

Instructions regarding War Diaries and Intelligence Summaries are contained in F. S. Regs., Part II. and the Staff Manual respectively. Title pages will be prepared in manuscript.

# WAR DIARY
or
~~INTELLIGENCE SUMMARY.~~
(*Erase heading not required.*)



Army Form C. 2118.

| Place | Date | Hour | Summary of Events and Information | Remarks and references to Appendices |
|---|---|---|---|---|
| LA HUIT MAISONS | 1/3/16 | 10 p.m | Company reorganised, Sections arranged into gun teams which enable reliefs to be carried out easier. M.G. emplacement at CHURCH REDOUBT destroyed by shell fire, no casualties | FK. |
| " " | 2/3/16 | 10 p.m. | The men were employed strengthening all gun positions during day. Capt FANE made a tour of all positions & Keeps held by Coy. | FK. |
| EUSTON. COY. H.Q. | 3/3/16 | 10 p.m | Coy. Hd. Qrs. moved up nearer the firing line & occupied building on the LA BASSEE ROAD. Fatigue party were busy all day strengthening building with sand bags etc. | FK. |
| " " | 4/3/16. | 10 p.m. | A fatigue party busy all day strengthening Coy Hd Qrs. Capt FANE made tours of emplacements & Keeps held by the company. | |
| " " | 5/3/16. | 10 p.m | Successful reliefs of front line & Keeps were made. 2ND LT. KEMP from Hospital @ rest camp HAVRE Nothing of tactical importance to report. | FK. |
| " " | 6/3/16 | 10 p.m. | Capt FANE made a tour of front line trenches to note suggested improvements. New emplacement made. Enemy working party dispersed by our M.G. fire @ 6.30 p.m. | FK. |
| " " | 7/3/16. | 10 p.m | Proceeded with work on new dug out in front line. Iron girders procured from R.E. dump sent to front line. Some snow fell during the day interfering with improvements | FK. |
| " " | 8/3/16. | 10. p.m | Work proceeded with on gun emplacements. Enemy shelled Coy H.Q. Scoring one direct hit. no casualties. Nothing of tactical importance to report. | [illegible] |

Instructions regarding War Diaries and Intelligence Summaries are contained in F. S. Regs., Part II. and the Staff Manual respectively. Title pages will be prepared in manuscript.

# WAR DIARY
*or*
~~INTELLIGENCE SUMMARY.~~
*(Erase heading not required.)*



Army Form C. 2118.

| Place | Date | Hour | Summary of Events and Information | Remarks and references to Appendices |
|---|---|---|---|---|
| EUSTON. Coy. H.Q. | 9/3/16. | 10 pm | Relief of front line + Keeps. Parapet repaired @ CURZON, and emplacement at CHATEAU given a wider field of fire. Fired 500 rds over head fire @ left edge of BOIS DU BIEZ | J.B.W. |
| " " | 10/3/16 | 10 pm. | Men employed filling sand bags, + strengthening Coy. H.Q. During the night 1600 rds were fired @ enemys working party, + enemys parapet. Weather dull, some snow. | J.B.W. |
| " " | 11/3/16. | 10 pm. | Men @ H.Q. employed filling sand bags. 3,750 rds were fired @ enemys parapet, + also dispersed enemys working party. Progress was made in the repairing of the dug outs in the front line. | J.B.W. |
| " " | 12/3/16 | 10 pm | Received orders to the effect that 58 M.G. Coy would relieve us on the 13th + that the Coy would move into rest billets @ PARIDIS. Nothing of Tactical importance to report. | J.B.W. |
| " " | 13/3/16 | " | At 9.30 Am guides were sent off to meet 58 Coy. Owing to being unable to bring the limbers up the road in day light, the relief of Keeps + front line was not completed until 5 pm. @ 6.15 pm the Coy paraded, + was marched off to billets @ PARIDIS. | J.B.W. |
| PARIDIS. | 14/3/16 | 10 pm | Coy in rest billets. In the forenoon limbers were unpacked + guns cleaned. In the afternoon O.C. Sections made an inventory of stores etc. in each section. | J.B.W. |
| " " | 15/3/16. | 10 pm | Capt: orderly room @ 10 Am. + Money drawn from Field Cashier @ HINGE. Arrangements made with Lewis Gun Coy whereby men from 56 M.G. Coy can be instructed in Lewis Gun. | J.B.W. |
| " " | 16/3/16 | " | At 8 Am. 4 Sgts + 28 men proceeded to Lewis Gun Coy H.Q for instruction, + 30. Lewis gunners arrived @ Coy. H.Q for instruction in Vickers Gun. Instruction proceeded until 3 pm when the classes were dismissed | |

Instructions regarding War Diaries and Intelligence Summaries are contained in F. S. Regs., Part II. and the Staff Manual respectively. Title pages will be prepared in manuscript.

# WAR DIARY
*or*
~~INTELLIGENCE SUMMARY.~~
*(Erase heading not required.)*

NO. 56 COY. MACHINE GUN CORPS.

Army Form C. 2118.

| Place | Date | Hour | Summary of Events and Information | Remarks and references to Appendices |
|---|---|---|---|---|
| PARIDIS | 17/3/16 | 10 pm | Men from Lewis Gun Coy for instruction on Vickers gun. Coy paraded & marched to Baths @ MERVILLE where they received baths, & clean underclothing. Limber got ready for inspection by Brigadier on the 18th | JRmw |
| " " | 18/3/16 | 10 pm | Coy paraded @ 9-30 Am. & were inspected by the Brigadier General. In the afternoon the men were exercised in Gas Helmet drill. | JRmw. |
| " " | 19/3/16 | 10 pm. | Coy paraded, for church parade, @ H. Qrs of 7th N. LANC R. when word was received that this was to be cancelled. In the afternoon men proceeded to LA GORGUE, where a concert was provided for them by 2nd Lt A D GROVE. In the evening word was received from Bde HQ. that the Company was to be divided into two sections & ~~(the sec)~~ which were to be attached to 7/E. LAN. R. & 7/ R. LAN. R. for Drill discipline, this only to apply as long as Coy was in rest billets. To take effect from the 21/3/16. | JRmw |
| " " | 20/3/16 | 10 pm | Men from Lewis Gun Coy for instruction on Vickers Gun & party from 56 M.G.Coy reported to Lewis Gun Coy for instruction on Lewis Gun. | JRmw. |
| " " | 21/3/16. | 10 pm | Coy were divided into two Sections & attached to 7th E LAN R. & 7th R. LAN R. for drill discipline. | JRmw |
| | 22/3/16 | 10 pm. | Word received that Coy was to relieve 58. M.G.Coy in front line, & supporting points. After men came off parade, the limbers were packed, & 1 & 2 Sections left rest billets @ 5-30 pm for billets nearer firing line, so as to be able to relieve front & second line in the morning. | JRmw |
| " " | 23/3/16 | 10 pm | Coy paraded @ 9.30 Am. & marched to Coy HQ @ EUSTON CORNER & remainder of Stores & transport | |

T2134. Wt. W708—776. 500000. 4/15. Sir J. C. & S.

Instructions regarding War Diaries and Intelligence Summaries are contained in F. S. Regs., Part II. and the Staff Manual respectively. Title Pages will be prepared in manuscript.

# WAR DIARY
or
~~INTELLIGENCE SUMMARY~~
(Erase heading not required.)

Army Form C. 2118

No 53 COY. MACHINE

| Place | Date | Hour | Summary of Events and Information | Remarks and references to Appendices |
|---|---|---|---|---|
| PARIDIS. | 23/3/16 | 10pm | arrived @ Coy H.Q about 6 p.m. Relief of front line + Supporting points was completed by 12.45 pm | JDMW |
| EUSTON CORNER | 24/3/16 | 10pm | Captn Gane made tour of front line, inspected gun emplacements. During the night our guns in front line traversed the enemys parapet, + @ target indicated by the Infantry, firing 3,250 rds. Report received that No 4344 was wounded @ 11.30pm 23/3/16. During the night enemys working party was fired on, + enemys parapet traversed. | JDMW. |
| " " | 25/3/16 | 10pm. | Enemy shelled Coy H.Q. from 8.45AM till 9.45AM 54 Shells falling within a radius of 50 yds of building, doing slight damage to walls, the gases from the shells caused slight smarting of the eyes. Nothing of tactical importance to report. | JDMW |
| " " | 26/3/16 | 10pm | 2Lt Gane went to 2nd LONDON C.C.S. Hospital. The enemy bombarded our front line, + our guns traversed the enemys parapet. | JDMW. |
| " " | 27/3/16 | 10pm. | Front line, supporting points relieved. During the night an enemy working party was observed from No 1 emplacement fire was directed on it + dispersed the party. Enemys communication trenches, + roads behind his front line, were searched with overhead fire during the night @ intervals. Two new gun emplacements were occupied. | JDMW |
| " " | 28/3/16 | 10pm | During the night 1700 rds were fired. An enemy patrol was observed close to our wire, + was dispersed by our fire, breach in enemys parapet was also traversed during the night @ intervals | JDMW |
| " " | 29/3/16 | 10pm. | Work proceeded with on new emplacements. Working partys of the enemy were dispersed during the night by our guns in front line. Nothing of tactical importance to report. | JDMW |
| " " | 30/3/16 | 10pm | The work was proceeded with on the new emplacements, + Coy H.Q was further strengthened, by the addition of Sand bags etc | |
| " " | 31/3/16 | | During the night over head fire was directed on the enemys communication trenches, + main roads behind his front line. | JDMW. |

1875 Wt. W593/826 1,000,000 4/15 J.B.C. & A. A.D.S.S./Forms/C. 2118.

# Confidential

War — Diary

of

56th Cay. Machine Gun Corps.

From. 1st April — to 30th April. 1916.

XIX

Vol. 7

56 M G Coy
vol 7

Instructions regarding War Diaries and Intelligence Summaries are contained in F. S. Regs., Part II. and the Staff Manual respectively. Title Pages will be prepared in manuscript.

# WAR DIARY
*or*
~~INTELLIGENCE SUMMARY~~
*(Erase heading not required.)*

Army Form C. 2118

56 COY. MACHINE GUN CORPS.

| Place | Date | Hour | Summary of Events and Information | Remarks and references to Appendices |
|---|---|---|---|---|
| EUSTON CORNER | 1/4/16 | 10 p. | Work proceeded with on new emplacements. Nothing of Tactical Importance to report. | J.D.M.W. |
| " " | 2/4/16. | 10 p. | During the night over head fire was directed on enemys communication trenches, & main roads behind his lines | J.D.M.W. |
| " " | 3/4/16 | 10. | Transport H.Q were moved to R.23·B·5·1· to make room for Battery of Artillery. Overhead fire was directed on enemys communication trenches by day & night. Emplacements improved & strengthened. | J.D.M.W. |
| " " | 4/4/16 | 10. " | Relief of Front line & Supporting points carried out. Nothing of Tactical Importance to report. | J.D.M.W. |
| " " | 5/4/16 | 10 p. | During the night fire was directed on enemys parapet @ intervals & Captn made a tour of front line emplacements. Work proceeded with on new emplacements @ PONT LOGY. | J.D.M.W. |
| " " | 6/4/16 | 10 p.m. | Nothing of Tactical importance to report. improvements made to dugouts in front line. No 7970 wounded | J.D.M.W. |
| " " | 7/4/16 | 10 p. | During the night enemys parapet was traversed. At 3·55 p.m. the enemy shelled bay. H.Q. 8 shells were fired. slight damage to walls etc. | J.D.M.W. |
| " " | 8/4/16 | 10. p. | Repairs to emplacements & parapets carried out. & preparation made for relief of front line supporting points & 2 line Reps. | J.D.M.W. |
| " " | 9/4/16 | 10 p. | Relief carried out & completed by 4 p.m. Nothing of Tactical importance to report. | J.D.M.W. |
| " " | 10/4/16 | 10 p. | Work proceeded with on new emplacements & dug out @ Prom, ST. A hostile M.G. was located @ S·6·C·1·7½ in a ruined house, @ edge of wood. | J.D.M.W. |
| " " | 11/4/16 | 10 p. | Work proceeded with on new emplacement; existing emplacements altered & improved | J.D.M.W. |
| " " | 12. | 10 p. | Nothing of tactical importance to report. Heavy rain all day which hindered progress of work. | J.D.M.W. |

1875 Wt. W593/826 1,000,000 4/15 J.B.C. & A. A.D.S.S./Forms/C. 2118.

Instructions regarding War Diaries and Intelligence Summaries are contained in F. S. Regs., Part II. and the Staff Manual respectively. Title Pages will be prepared in manuscript.

# WAR DIARY
*or*
~~INTELLIGENCE SUMMARY~~
*(Erase heading not required.)*

Army Form C. 2118

| Place | Date | Hour | Summary of Events and Information | Remarks and references to Appendices |
|---|---|---|---|---|
| EUSTON CORNER | 13/4/16 | 10 p.m. | Relief of Front line, Front line Keeps & supporting points completed by 4 pm. Nothing of tactical importance to report. | J.D.M.W. |
| " " | 14/4/16 | 10 p. | Bde order. No 55 received. Informing us that the Bde moves into Divn'l Reserve on 16th & 17th. | J.D.M.W. |
| " " | 15/4/16. | 10 pm | During the night fire was directed on Enemys communication trenches, & on tracks & roads behind his front line as it was believed he had a relief in progress. Enemy replied with considerable M.G. fire. | J.D.M.W. |
| " " | 16-4-16 | 10 p | The Coy was relieved by the 106th Bde. Machine Gun Coy. @ 1 pm At 3 pm the Coy marched off to Billets @ LESTREM. | J.D.M.W. |
| LESTREM. | 17-4-16. | 10 pm. | Orders received to move to Billets @ St. VENANT. The Coy marched off @ 12.30 pm preceded by transport | J.D.M.W. |
| ~~St VENANT~~ | ~~18-4-16~~ | ~~10 p~~ | Coy arrived @ 3-30 pm. Billets arranged. | |
| St VENANT. | 18-4-16 | 10 p | During the day the men were employed in cleaning the guns & overhauling the spare parts checking & noting deficiencies. In the forenoon orders were received to move to Divisional training area, on the 19th | J.D.M.W. |
| St VENANT. | 19-4-16 | 10 AM | Coy paraded @ 8-45 AM. & @ 9 AM. proceeded to join main body of Division. Orders were to billet @ LINGHEM which was reached @ 2.45 pm. | J.D.M.W. |
| LINGHEM. | 20-4-16 | 10 pm. | During the forenoon Coy rested. The Brig'd General visited Coy H.Q. & arranged for men from LEWIS GUN Coy to join M.G. Coy. In the afternoon, the men were exercised in rifle exercises under Section officers | J.D.M.W. |
| " " | 21. | 10 pm | During the forenoon & afternoon, the numbers 1 & 2 of the Sections & gun numbers were [illegible] on the range. Programme of work arranged by Capt. C. G. Yane. | J.D.M.W. |
| " " | 22 | 10 pm | Work carried on indoors, as weather would not permit of outside operation, very wet. | J.D.M.W. |

1875 Wt. W593/826 1,000,000 4/15 J.B.C. & A. A.D.S.S./Forms/C. 2118.

Instructions regarding War Diaries and Intelligence Summaries are contained in F. S. Regs., Part II. and the Staff Manual respectively. Title Pages will be prepared in manuscript.

# WAR DIARY
*or*
# INTELLIGENCE SUMMARY
*(Erase heading not required.)*

Army Form C. 2118

| Place | Date | Hour | Summary of Events and Information | Remarks and references to Appendices |
|---|---|---|---|---|
| LINGHEM. | 23-4-16 | 10.p.m | Brigade Church parade was held @ RELY @ 11 A.M. The remainder of the day was observed as a holiday. | JSMW |
| " " | 24-4-16 | 10 p.m | Coy programme of training carried out. Rifle exercises, Gun drill etc. | JSMW |
| " " | 25-4-16 | 10 p.m. | " " " " " " " " .. Sanction was given for the transfer of 29 men from the Lewis Gun Coy to the 56 M.G. Coy per letter A.G., G.H.Q No A/6864 of 8/4/16 + First Army Nos: 2224/414/A. of 9th + 22nd April 1916 | JSMW |
| " " | 26-4-16 | 10 p.m. | In the forenoon, the Defence of a village, + rear guard action, was carried out. + in the afternoon the men were exercised in Rifle drill | JSMW |
| " " | 27/4/16 | 10 p.m | In the forenoon the men were trained in mechanism etc, + in the afternoon the Coy was on the manoeuvre area, | JSMW |
| " " | 28-4-16 | 10 p.m | During the day the Coy was out with the Bde, on the manoeuvre area. | JSMW |
| " " | 29-4-16 | 10 p.m | The day was spent on the manoeuvre area, with the Bde, carrying out an attack, on a wood | JSMW |
| " " | 30-4-16 | 10 p.m | During the forenoon, Bde church parade, + the afternoon was observed as a holiday. | JSMW |

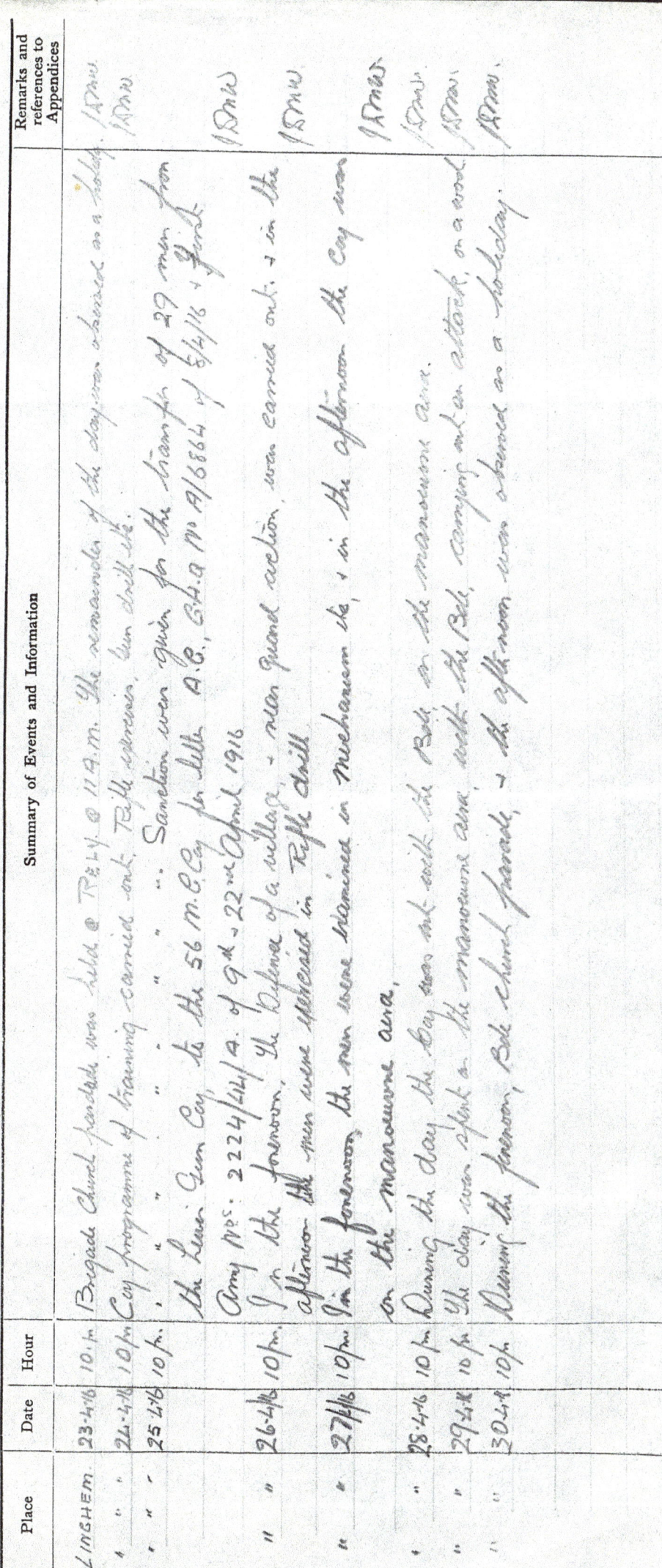

1875 Wt. W593/826 1,000,000 4/15 J.B.C. & A. A.D.S.S./Forms/C. 2118.

Instructions regarding War Diaries and Intelligence Summaries are contained in F. S. Regs., Part II. and the Staff Manual respectively. Title Pages will be prepared in manuscript.

# WAR DIARY
*or*
~~INTELLIGENCE SUMMARY~~ XIX
*(Erase heading not required.)*

Army Form C. 2118



Vol 8

| Place | Date | Hour | Summary of Events and Information | Remarks and references to Appendices |
|---|---|---|---|---|
| LA CHAUSSEE | 13.5.16 | 10 pm | In the forenoon, mechanism & immediate action was carried out. | |
| do | 14.5.16 | 10 pm | Church Parade. 2/Lt Grove proceeded on leave to U.K. | Fcwy |
| do | 15.5.16 | 10 pm | Gun Drill with limbers. Mechanism & Immediate Action. Four Sergeants & 4 Cpls went to Div^l M.G. School with two guns & limbers | Fcwy |
| do | 16.5.16 | 10 pm | Scheme. Advancing sections holding positions. Elementary Tests & Fire orders. F.G.C.M. held on 12237 Pte ROTHWELL for "When on Active Service Refusing to obey an order." | Fcwy |
| do | 17.5.16 | 10 pm | Gun Drill with limbers over broken ground. Mechanism & Immediate Action | Fcwy |
| do | 18.5.16 | 10 pm | Defence of Village Scheme. Mechanism & Immediate Action. Stripping | Fcwy |
| do | 19.5.16 | 10 pm | Gun Drill with limbers over broken ground. Mechanism. Immediate action | Fcwy |
| do | 20.5.16 | 10 pm | Promulgation of F.G.C.M. of 16.5.16. Sentence Three months F.P. No 1. Nos 1 & 2 Section a.m. and Nos 3 & 4 pm firing on Range | Fcwy |
| do | 21.5.16 | 10 pm | No parades. 4th Army No. A 263/130 d/18.5.16 authorised transfer of 2/Lt F.C.W. TAYLOR 7 N. Lan R. and 2/Lt S.G. CAMPION 7 S. Lan R. to this Coy. | |
| do | 22.5.16 | 10 pm | Parades for Coy Drill. Gun Drill. 2/Lt McWilliam proceeded to Base | |
| do | 23.5.16 | 10 pm | The Coy was inspected this day by the G.O.C. 56th Infy Brigade. He expressed his satisfaction with the appearance and work of the Coy. 9 Reinforcements. | |
| do | 24.5.16 | 10 pm | Physical Exercises. Coy Drill and Range Practice | |
| | 25.5.16 | 10 pm | As yesterday am. Drill with limbers pm. 1 Reinforcement | |

Instructions regarding War Diaries and Intelligence Summaries are contained in F. S. Regs., Part II. and the Staff Manual respectively. Title Pages will be prepared in manuscript.

# WAR DIARY
*or*
# INTELLIGENCE SUMMARY
*(Erase heading not required.)*

Army Form C. 2118



| Place | Date | Hour | Summary of Events and Information | Remarks and references to Appendices |
|---|---|---|---|---|
| LA CHAUSSÉE | 26/5/16 | 10pm | Scheme - Advancing over unknown country. | F.W.T. |
| do | 27.5.16 | 10pm | Divisional Sports at FLESSELLES. CoJ entered a team in the M.G. Competition. O.C. CoJ one other officer and 2 NCO.S left for a tour of the trenches. | F.W.T. |
| do | 28.5.16 | 10pm | No parades. 2/Lt CAMPION from 7 S. Lan R arrived. | F.W.T. |
| | 29.5.16 | 10pm | Route march of 23 miles. 7.0am - 12.15pm 4.30pm - 8.0pm. 8 N.C.O.s + men went to Div! M.G. School, in place of 8 others having finished their course. | F.W.T. |
| do | 30.5.16 | 10pm | Baths 8-10 am. Range Practice | F.W.T. |
| do | 31-5-16 | 10pm | Physical exercise - Company Drill - Gun drill with limbers - 2/Lt Taylor proceeded on leave to U.K. | [signature] |

XIX

June

Army Form C. 2118

Vol 9

No 56 COY. MACHINE GUN CORPS

Instructions regarding War Diaries and Intelligence Summaries are contained in F. S. Regs., Part II. and the Staff Manual respectively. Title Pages will be prepared in manuscript.

# WAR DIARY
or
# ~~INTELLIGENCE SUMMARY~~

*(Erase heading not required.)*

| Place | Date | Hour | Summary of Events and Information | Remarks and references to Appendices |
|---|---|---|---|---|
| LA CHAUSÉE | 1-6-16 | 10 p.m. | Physical exercises - Cleaning guns & ammunition - Coy. paraded at 5·30 p.m. & marched to BOIS du GARD to bivouac for the night | JK. |
| - Do - | 2-6-16 | 10 p.m. | Field operations in & near the BOIS du GARD immediately N of the "Y" in YZEUX. - all day. | JK. |
| — " — | 3-6-16 | 10 p.m. | Physical drill - Cleaning guns, equipment etc. - Range practices with guns & rifles. - Four re-inforcements - | JK. |
| — " — | 4-6-16 | 10 p.m. | No parades. | JK. |
| — " — | 5-6-16 | 10 p.m. | Gun drill with limbers - mechanism & immediate action. | JK. |
| — " — | 6-6-16 | 10 p.m. | Rain in morning. Afternoon, route-march: - BREILLY - AILLY - LA CHAUSSEE | AL. |
| — " — | 7-6-16 | 11 am. | Marched to new billets at BELLE VUE Farm near VILLERS-BOCAGE. Arrived 3 p.m. 2/Lt. Kemp, Sergt. Titcombe proceeded on leave to U.K. | AL. |
| BELLEVUE | 8-6-16 | 10 am. | Co-operated with rest of Brigade in an Attack Scheme on FREMONT from the Sports Ground at FLESSELLES. | AL. |
| — " — | 9-6-16 | 9 am to 4 pm. | Section training, overhauling stores, kit inspection. In the afternoon, practice in tactical handling of guns under concealment. | AL. |
| — " — | 10-6-16 | 9.30 am. | Scheme of 8.6.16 repeated. Coy. was paid out at 3·15 p.m. 2/Lt. ROSE joined the Coy. from BASE. | AL. |
| — " — | 11-6-16 | | R.C. Parade. Two men sent on a Sanitary Course. | AL. |
| — " — | 12-6-16 | | Physical Exc. Arms Drill. Mechanism. Immediate Action. Section Sergts. witnessed Stokes Trench Mortar Demonstration at FLESSELLES. | AL. |
| — " — | 13-6-16 | 10 p.m. | Scheme of 10.6.16 repeated. 2/Lt. Taylor returned from leave | [illegible] |

1875 Wt. W593/826 1,000,000 4/15 J.B.C. & A. A.D.S.S./Forms/C. 2118.

Instructions regarding War Diaries and Intelligence Summaries are contained in F. S. Regs., Part II. and the Staff Manual respectively. Title Pages will be prepared in manuscript.

# WAR DIARY
*or*
# ~~INTELLIGENCE SUMMARY~~
*(Erase heading not required.)*

Army Form C. 2118

| Place | Date | Hour | Summary of Events and Information | Remarks and references to Appendices |
|---|---|---|---|---|
| BELLEVUE | 14.6.16 | 10pm | Cpt. Fane proceeded to U.K. on leave. 2/Lt H.W. Duffield arrived from Base as reinforcement. Physical & Arms Drill. Mechanism & Immediate action. Summer Time adopted 11pm. | FCWT |
| VILLERS-BOCAGE | 15.6.16 | 10pm | Brigade Attack Scheme practised again. Rest of day devoted to preparation for move. O.C. Coy attended a lecture at D.H.Q. by G.S.O.1 on forthcoming operations. | FCWT |
| RAINNEVILLE | 16.6.16 | 10pm | Coy moved to new billets arriving at 9.45am. Inspection of kit and equipment by Section officers. Guns and tripods painted. | FCWT |
| | 17.6.16 | 10pm | Physical Coy, Arms & Gun Drill. Lecture on Anti Gas Measures by Sect. officers. 2/Lt. Kemp returned from leave. | FCWT |
| | 18.6.16 | 10pm | Church Parades. Lecture by N.C.O. from Div. Anti Gas School to officers & N.C.O.s with demonstration | FCWT |
| | 19.6.16 | 10pm | Baths parades. Immediate action & Gun Drill. 2/Lt Flood proceeded to HAVRE on transport course. 2/Lt Lomas proceeded to U.K. on leave. Conference at Bde H.Q. on forthcoming operations. | FCWT |
| | 20.6.16 | 10pm | Scheme of attack through woods. 3 men transferred from 56th Brigade to replace 3 sent to Base | FCWT |
| | 21.6.16 | 10pm | Scheme. Protection of village against attack. Immediate action. Belt and SAA cleaning. | FCWT |
| | 22.6.16 | 10pm | Physical Exc. Route march 12 mls. Immediate action. Smoke Helmet Drill. | FCWT |
| | 23.6.16 | 10pm | Physical Exc. Coy & Arms Drill. Bayonet Exc. Limber Packing. Gun Drill. Advance Party sent to prepare camping ground in BAIZIEUX WOOD | FCWT |
| | 24.6.16 | 10pm | Coy and Arms Drill. Inspection & cleaning of Belts & Boxes. Boy returned to Base under age. Capt. Fane returned from leave | FCWT |
| | 25.6.16 | 10pm | Church Parades. | |

1875 Wt. W593/826 1,000,000 4/15 J.B.C. & A. A.D.S.S./Forms/C. 2118.

Instructions regarding War Diaries and Intelligence Summaries are contained in F. S. Regs., Part II. and the Staff Manual respectively. Title Pages will be prepared in manuscript.

# WAR DIARY
*or*
~~INTELLIGENCE SUMMARY~~
*(Erase heading not required.)*

Army Form C. 2118

| Place | Date | Hour | Summary of Events and Information | Remarks and references to Appendices |
|---|---|---|---|---|
| RAINNEVILLE | 26.6.16 | 10 p.m. | Overhauling all kit and equipment. Cleaning Billets. Left RAINNEVILLE at 7.30 p.m. Arrived at BAIZIEUX WOOD at 11 p.m. Brigade bivouacked in WOOD. Heavy rain | FCWT |
| BAIZIEUX | 27.6.16 | 10 p.m. | Advance party sent to next area. Brigade moved off at 9.0 p.m. and marched to HENENCOURT WOOD. Huts and shelters provided. | FCWT |
| | 28.6.16 | 10 p.m. | Preparations to move to "Intermediate Line" - trenches N.W. of ALBERT. Order received for all troops to stand fast for 48 hours. Heavy rain. | FCWT |
| | 29.6.16 | 10 p.m. | Route March. All guns fired for testing purposes. | FCWT |
| | 30.6.16 | | Left HENENCOURT WOOD 10.12 p.m. Coy moved to "Intermediate Line," limbers unpacked. Transport returned to Brigade Transport Depôt 1 mile E.N.E. of MILLENCOURT. 50% of officers moved up, remainder at Transport Depôt.<br>List No 86 Appointments etc "2nd Lieut F.C.W. Taylor, Machine Gun Corps to be second in Command, 56th Brigade Coy and to be Temp'y Lieut. vice 2nd Lieut H.W. Duffield (sick) dated 18.5.16." | FCWT |

1875 Wt. W593/826 1,000,000 4/15 J.B.C. & A. A.D.S.S./Forms/C. 2118.

56th Inf.Bde.
19th Div.

WAR DIARY

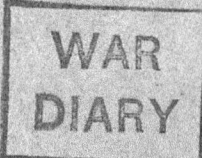

56th MACHINE GUN COMPANY.

J U L Y

1 9 1 6

MACHINE GUN CORP
1. 8. 16

CONFIDENTIAL.

War Diary of
56th Coy. M. G. Corps

1-7-16 – 31-7-16.

J. W. Taylor Lt.
for Adj.

Instructions regarding War Diaries and Intelligence Summaries are contained in F. S. Regs., Part II. and the Staff Manual respectively. Title Pages will be prepared in manuscript.

# WAR DIARY or ~~INTELLIGENCE SUMMARY~~

*(Erase heading not required.)*



Army Form C. 2118

Vol 10

| Place | Date | Hour | Summary of Events and Information | Remarks and references to Appendices |
|---|---|---|---|---|
| ALBERT | 1.7.16 | 10pm | Coy moved from "Intermediate Line" with the Brigade and proceeded to W23C 3.0. (Sheet 57D SE) where it remained all day. | FcwJ |
| do | 2.7.16 | 10pm | Coy moved back to a position in the SE outskirts of ALBERT | FcwJ |
| do | 3.7.16 | 10pm | Coy moved at 3.0 am. back to the position occupied 1.7.16. Nos 3 & 4 sections moved up into the front line at 6pm. | FcwJ |
| do | 4.7.16 | 10pm | (Capture of LA BOISSELLE by 56th Inf Brigade) 8 guns advanced to new line. Two men killed 10 wounded. | FcwJ |
| do | 5.7.16 | 10pm | 2/Lt. Grove became a casualty through shell shock. One man killed, 10 wounded, One reported missing. Nos 1 & 2 sections relieved Nos 3 & 4 | FcwJ |
| do | 6.7.16 | 10pm | Guns followed up infantry advance through LA BOISSELLE. | FcwJ |
| do | 7.7.16 | 10pm | Guns take up new position on LA BOISSELLE – CONTALMAISON road. 5 men wounded by shell fire. Relief of half company | FcwJ |
| do | 8.7.16 | 10pm | Village of LA BOISSELLE cleared of enemy. Two men wounded by shell fire. | FcwJ |
| do HENENCOURT | 9.7.16 | 10pm | Brigade relieved by 111th Brigade. One section relieved at 8.0pm. Other section not relieved till 3.0am 10.7.16. Three casualties to carrying party. Coy moved to HENENCOURT WOOD, No 4 Section arriving at 9.15am. | FcwJ |
| do | 10.7.16 | 10pm | Day given up to rest. changing clothing. kit inspection. Total Casualties killed 4 wounded 1 off 35 OR. Missing believed wounded 1 | FcwJ |
| do | 11.7.16 | 10pm | Overhauling Guns & Gun equipment. Cleaning personal equipment. | FcwJ |

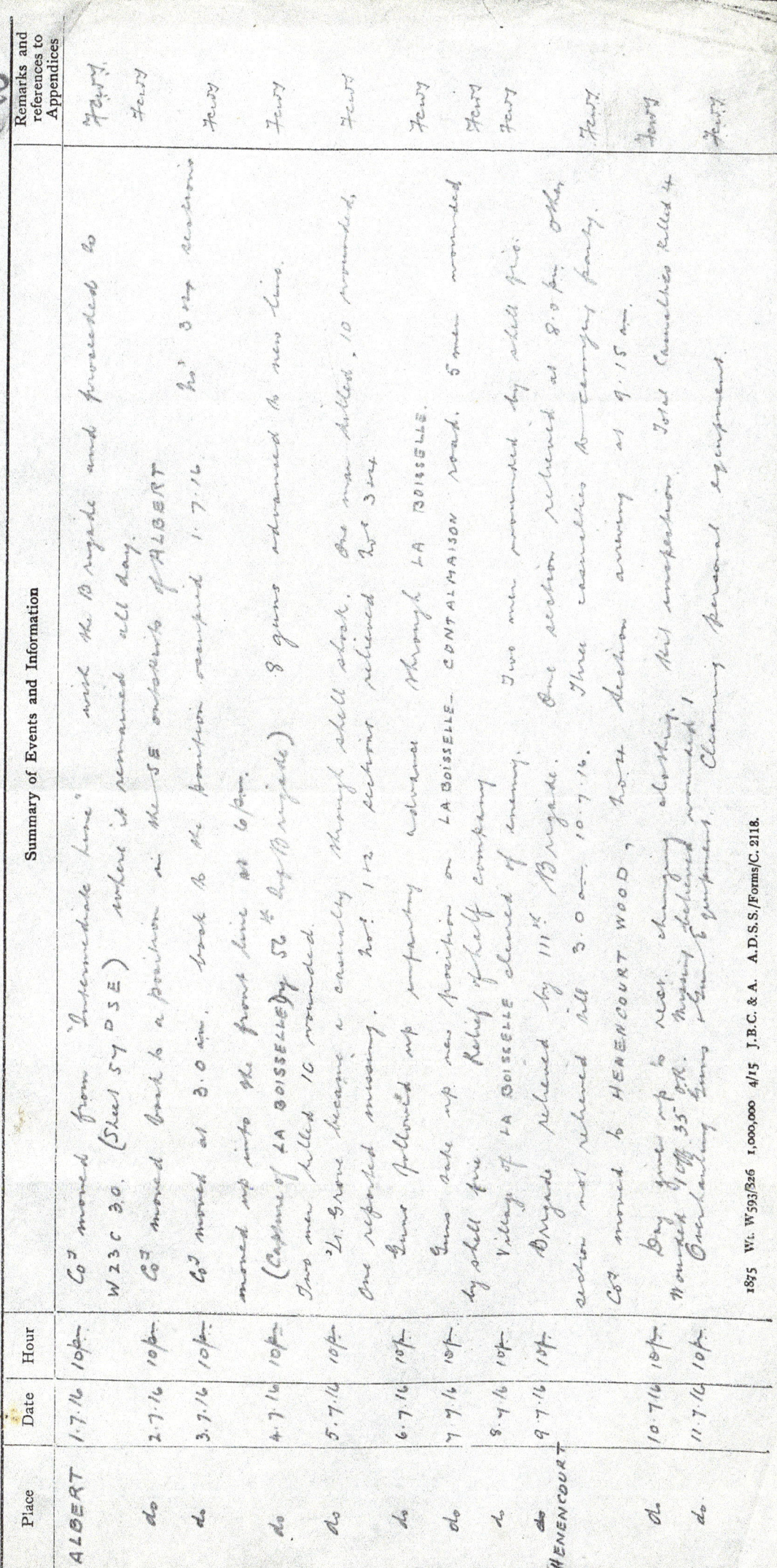

1875 Wt. W593/826 1,000,000 4/15 J.B.C. & A. A.D.S.S./Forms/C. 2118.

Instructions regarding War Diaries and Intelligence Summaries are contained in F. S. Regs., Part II. and the Staff Manual respectively. Title Pages will be prepared in manuscript.

# WAR DIARY
*or*
~~INTELLIGENCE SUMMARY~~
*(Erase heading not required.)*

Army Form C. 2118

No 56 COY. MACHINE GUN CORPS.

| Place | Date | Hour | Summary of Events and Information | Remarks and references to Appendices |
|---|---|---|---|---|
| HENENCOURT | 12/7/16 | 10pm | Route March. Special Orders of the Day from G.O.C.s XIX Div^n & 56^th Inf Brigade congratulating the Brigade on its successful work of last week. 2/Lt GROVE evacuated to U.K. 2/Lt FLOOD returned from Transport course at HAVRE | Fcw? |
| do | 13.7.16 | 10pm | Coy Arms & Physical Drill. Coy present p.m. at review of Brigade by the ~~Army~~ 3rd Corps Commander who congratulated the Brigade on its work of last week. 26 O.R. Reinforcements arrived | Fcw? |
| do | 14.7.16 | 10pm | Coy Arms Gun Drill. Smoke Helmet Inspection & Drill. 2/Lt H.a. Price rejoined as re-inforcement. | Fcw? |
| do | 15.7.16 | 10pm | Orders to be prepared to move at an hour's notice. Gun cleaning. Limber packing. "Stand by" Order annulled. | Fcw? |
| do | 16.7.16 | 10pm | No Parades. | |
| do. | 17.7.16 | 10pm | Coy and Arms Drill. Smoke Helmet Drill. Inspection & Cleaning of Guns. 17 men attached from Batt^ns in Brigade. | Fcw? |
| do. | 18.7.16 | 10pm | Inspection by G.O.C. XIX Div^n | |
| ALBERT | 19.7.16 | 10pm | Route March. Orders to prepare for move about 7 pm. Half Coy with gun limbers left at 8.0 and relieved the 98^th Coy at BAZENTIN LE PETIT. Remainder of Coy with transport proceeded to a position N. of the ALBERT-FRICOURT RD. 5 men wounded. | Fcw? |
| MAMETZ WOOD | 20.7.16 | 10pm | Half Coy moved from ALBERT to MAMETZ WOOD with guns. 2 men killed | Fcw? |

1875 Wt. W593/826 1,000,000 4/15 J.B.C. & A. A.D.S.S./Forms/C. 2118.

Instructions regarding War Diaries and Intelligence Summaries are contained in F. S. Regs., Part II. and the Staff Manual respectively. Title Pages will be prepared in manuscript.

# WAR DIARY
*or*
# INTELLIGENCE SUMMARY
*(Erase heading not required.)*

Army Form C. 2118



| Place | Date | Hour | Summary of Events and Information | Remarks and references to Appendices |
|---|---|---|---|---|
| MAMETZ WOOD | 21.7.16 | 10 pm | During shelling of BAZENTIN one officer wounded. 3 men killed + one wounded. | FCWT |
| BAZENTIN | 22.7.16 | 10 pm | Half Coy moved up from MAMETZ to BAZENTIN WOOD. Enemy shelled position S of MAMETZ WOOD four times. One officer (i/c Brigade Water Supply) + one man wounded. Position in BAZENTIN wood also shelled during night | FCWT |
| | 23.7.16 | | 56th + 57th Bdes attacked SWITCH LINE unsuccessfully. No targets for M.G.'s. One officer, 8 O.R. killed + one O.R. wounded by one shell 3.15 am. 3 other O.R. wounded. Team sent up to replace casualties. Two guns placed on left of drive running E-W near N end of WOOD, since line seemed lightly held. Coy relieved by 58th Coy. Coy moved to S edge of MAMETZ WOOD. Relief complete 9.15 pm. | FCWT |
| | 24.7.16 | 2.30 am | Enemy shelled position – two men buried by shell. | FCWT |
| | 25.7.16 | 6.0 pm | Enemy shelled position continuously for 4 hrs. Two O.R. (including C.Sgt Major) wounded | FCWT |
| | 26.7.16 | 10.0 pm | Position bombarded with gas shells – all ranks warned – helmets put on. gas cleared. Repeated 11.20 pm. | FCWT |
| | 27.7.16 | 3.0 am | Gas shells twice – no casualties. | |
| | | 4.0 pm | Two guns by orders of XIX Divn sent to HIGHWOOD about S4b4.2 (MARTINPUICH) to give flanking fire to attack by 58th Bde. attack postponed. | FCWT |
| | | 6.0 pm | Position shelled – 2 men buried but both rescued | |

1875 Wt. W593/826 1,000,000 4/15 J.B.C. & A. A.D.S.S./Forms/C. 2118.

Instructions regarding War Diaries and Intelligence Summaries are contained in F. S. Regs., Part II. and the Staff Manual respectively. Title Pages will be prepared in manuscript.

# WAR DIARY
or
~~INTELLIGENCE SUMMARY~~
(Erase heading not required.)

56th Coy M. G. Corps.

No 56 CO. MACHINE GUN CORPS.

Army Form C. 2118

| Place | Date | Hour | Summary of Events and Information | Remarks and references to Appendices |
|---|---|---|---|---|
| MAMETZ WOOD | 28.7.16 | 2.0pm | Orders for all movements to be suspended for 24 hrs. Report of observation of German Intermediate Line by Capt FANE sent to 56th Inf. Bde. | |
| | | | Ten Reinforcements arrived. | F.C.W.J. |
| | | 11.0pm | Instructions received to send guides to meet officers of 111th M. G. Coy which would eventually relieve this Coy. | |
| | 29.7.16 | 9.0am | Instructions re Guides cancelled. | |
| | | 2.0pm | Guns in HIGH WOOD relieved by two teams of No 3 Sectn. | |
| | | 2.30pm | Position shelled – no casualties. | F.C.W.J. |
| | | 6.0pm | Relief complete. | |
| | 30.7.16 | 11.0am | O.C. 111th M. G. Coy arrived to arrange for relief. | |
| | | 2.15pm | Position shelled till 5.15pm. Two men buried – released safely. One man wounded | F.C.W.J. |
| | | 5.30pm | Orders from 56th Infy Bde. refng relief by 111th M. G. Coy to-morrow. | |
| | | | One man wounded at gun in HIGH WOOD. | |
| | 31.7.16 | 2.0pm | 111th M. G. Co arrived at MAMETZ WOOD. Relief carried out without casualties. | |
| | | | 2 guns in HIGH WOOD to be relieved under arrangements by the 57th Brigade | |
| | | | One man killed 4 wounded in HIGH WOOD | F.C.W.J. |
| | | | Coy marched to billets at FRANVILLERS arriving at 8pm. | |

[827] W1332-1132 5000m 12/15R G & S 77 77 Forms C. 348 61

Army Form C. 348.

# MEMORANDUM.

| | |
|---|---|
| From 56th Coy M. G. Corps | From |
| To Officer i/c Adjutant General's Branch Base | To |
| | ANSWER. |
| 2. 7. 1916. | 191 . |
| Attached is War Diary of 56th Coy M. G. Corps. from 1. 6. 16 — 30. 6. 16. Please<br><br>F. W. Taylor Lt<br>Adjt | |

56th Brigade.

19th Division.

-----------

56th BRIGADE MACHINE GUN COMPANY

AUGUST 1 9 1 6

No 56 COY.
1.9.16
MACHINE GUN CORPS

To 56th Inf Bde

Passed to you please for transmission to D.A.G. 3rd Echelon.

A Thomas 2Lt
a/Adj. for O.C.

Instructions regarding War Diaries and Intelligence Summaries are contained in F. S. Regs., Part II. and the Staff Manual respectively. Title Pages will be prepared in manuscript.

# WAR DIARY
or
~~INTELLIGENCE SUMMARY~~
(Erase heading not required.)

Army Form C. 2118

Vol 11

| Place | Date | Hour | Summary of Events and Information | Remarks and references to Appendices |
|---|---|---|---|---|
| ~~[illegible]~~ FRANVILLERS | 1/8/16 | | Gun & Belt + S.A.A. inspection + cleaning. | Fcws |
| | | | 2 Gun Teams from HIGH WOOD arrived in new billets 7.30pm. | |
| | 2.8.16 | 9.0-12.30 | Physical, Coy + Arms Drill | |
| | | 3.30 | Brigade Parade. Lieut. Genl. Pulteney addressed the Brigade on its leaving the Corps | Fcws |
| | 3.8.16 | ~~[illegible]~~ 10.0am | Bathing Parade | |
| | | 4.0pm | Coy. marched to FRECHENCOURT. Entrained at 9.20pm. | Fcws |
| GORENFLOS | 4.8.16 | 1.30 | arrived at LONGPRE. Marched to billets at GORENFLOS arriving at 6.0 am. Rest of day spent in preparing billets + resting. | Fcws |
| | 5.8.16 | | Cleaning guns + limbers + personal equipment | Fcws |
| | 6.8.16 | 6.0am | Coy marched to PONT REMY entraining at 9.30, transport having been entrained 2 hours earlier; proceeded via BOULOGNE + CALAIS to BAILLEUL: detrained | Fcws |
| | | 8.0pm | at 7.20; Marched from BAILLEUL to position occupied by 151st M.G. Coy near LOCRE arriving at 9.40pm. | |
| LOCRE | 7.8.16 | | O.C. Coy + Section officers went round line to see positions occupied by 151st Coy. Guns and equipment overhauled | Fcws |
| | 8.8.16 | | Coy relieved 151st Coy. 4 guns in Left sub-section 4 guns in Right. 2 guns with Battn in Divl. Reserve | Fcws |

1875 Wt. W593/826 1,000,000 4/15 J.B.C. & A. A.D.S.S./Forms/C. 2118.

Instructions regarding War Diaries and Intelligence Summaries are contained in F. S. Regs., Part II. and the Staff Manual respectively. Title Pages will be prepared in manuscript.

# WAR DIARY
*or*
~~INTELLIGENCE SUMMARY~~
*(Erase heading not required.)*

Army Form C. 2118

| Place | Date | Hour | Summary of Events and Information | Remarks and references to Appendices |
|---|---|---|---|---|
| LOCRE | 9.8.16 | | No firing done. Gun moved for Indirect fire. Night emplacements repaired. Coy Hd Qrs at N 24 d 1.9. Refce Sheet 28 S.W. 1/20,000. | Fcwt |
| KEMMEL | 10.8.16 | | Coy Hd Qrs. moved to KEMMEL village. 3000 rounds fired indirect fire from N 29 a 5.9. on to road leading to WYTSCHAETE. Patrol reported hearing cries of wounded. Ranging fire obtained on trench from which T.M.'s were fired. | Fcwt |
| | 11.8.16 | | 5000 rounds along KEMMEL-WYTSCHAETE ROAD. Houses at O 19 c 8.8 fired at during day. Usual T.M. activity did not take place at usual time owing to fire from gun ranged with yesterday. 3000 rounds fired at C.T's round PECKHAM. BLACK REDOUBT + HOP POINT. 250 rounds at suspected O.P. O 19 C 60.75 | Fcwt |
| | 12.8.16 | | 4000 rounds fired along KEMMEL-WYTSHAETE RD. and C.T.s near PECKHAM and SPANBROECKMOLEN. O.C. Coy admitted to Fld Ambce. 2 Lts SHEFFIELD + SMART reinforcements reported. Lt. F.C.W. TAYLOR assumes command of Coy. 2/Lt LOMAX acting 2nd in Comd. | Fcwt |
| | 13.8.16 | | 4 Guns of No 1 Secn in Left Sub Section, ~~4~~ 4 of No. 2 Secn in Right + 2 of No. 3 with Battn in Divl Reserve relieved by 4 of No 3, 4 of No 4 and 2 of No. 1 respectively. | Fcwt |
| | 14.8.16 | | Brigadier visited gun positions. Indirect fire on usual targets 1000 rounds fired | Fcwt |

1875 Wt. W593/826 1,000,000 4/15 J.B.C. & A. A.D.S.S./Forms/C. 2118.

Instructions regarding War Diaries and Intelligence Summaries are contained in F. S. Regs., Part II. and the Staff Manual respectively. Title Pages will be prepared in manuscript.

# WAR DIARY
*or*
~~INTELLIGENCE SUMMARY~~
*(Erase heading not required.)*

Army Form C. 2118

| Place | Date | Hour | Summary of Events and Information | Remarks and references to Appendices |
|---|---|---|---|---|
| KEMMEL | 15.8.16 | | 800 rounds fired on usual targets. Sgt. and two men sent down from the line under arrest. Men in reserve improving billets. | FCWJ |
| | 16.8.16 | | 1250 rounds at usual targets. Notes on present positions occupied, proposed alterations, and proposed action in case of attack drawn up and submitted to Brigadier | FCWJ |
| | 17.8.16 | | Proposals approved. Emplacement + Dug. out Frames got from R.E. Men practised in assembling the parts. Working party sent up to gun in left sector to dig sap leading to new position. Re-inforcement arrived - 1 Sgt. No firing. | FCWJ |
| | 18.8.16 | | No firing. Work continued on emplacements dug outs and trenches | FCWJ |
| | 19.8.16 | 4.0pm | Message received from Bde. H.Q. that enemy would relieve in trenches opposite this sector to-night. Indirect fire on roads + C.T's leading to trenches. Section relief. Gun placed in FORT REGINA. | FCWJ |
| | 20.8.16 | | 1000 rounds fired on usual targets. Work on emplacements etc continued. | FCWJ |
| | 21.8.16 | | 2/Lt T. WALL late 3rd WEST YORKS REGT. reported as re-inforcement. Work continued. Gun at FERME D'HOINE began indirect fire. Other indirect fire gun fired 1250 rounds. | Map 2 FCWJ |
| | 22.8.16 ~~23.8.16~~ | | Teams with Battn in Div! Reserve + at FORT REGINA relieved. 2150 rounds fired from Fme D'HOINO + YOUNG ST. at usual targets. | FCWJ AL |

Instructions regarding War Diaries and Intelligence Summaries are contained in F. S. Regs., Part II. and the Staff Manual respectively. Title Pages will be prepared in manuscript.

# WAR DIARY
*or*
# INTELLIGENCE SUMMARY
*(Erase heading not required.)*

Army Form C. 2118

| Place | Date | Hour | Summary of Events and Information | Remarks and references to Appendices |
|---|---|---|---|---|
| KEMMEL | 23.8.16 | 12 noon | Transport, consisting of 1 limber and 2 mules, in connection with 2 guns in Div¹ Reserve, moved into transport lines of 7 R. Lanc. R. | A.L. |
| | | 6 pm. | 2/Lt. SMART, J.E. evacuated to 7 F.A. | |
| | 24.8.16 | | 2250 rounds fired along enemy roads & C.T.'s. Work on emplacements proceeded with. Div¹ General visited our positions in both sectors. | A.L. |
| | 25.8.16 | 8 pm | Section relief. Indirect fire along roads & CT's. Artillery on both sides fairly active. Completed 2 dugouts at L.S.1. | A.L. |
| | 26.8.16 | 10.15 am | Ground near Coy HQ shelled with whizz-bangs (about 8 in number). Indirect fire opened on roads & CT's on right of our Bde¹ front from Fme D'HOINO. Bn. relief during the night. | A.L. |
| | 27.8.16 | 10 am | About 6 small shells fell near Coy HQ on slope of KEMMEL HILL. Indirect fire proceeded with. | A.L. |
| | 28.8.16 | 4 pm | Guns in Div. Reserve relieved. Indirect fire more active. 3500 rounds fired. Enemy m.g's traversed YOUNG ST. searching for our guns. No damage done. Minnenwerfer fell near L.S.1, where we are taking out a sap. | A.L. |
| | 29.8.16 | | Telephone communication established between L.S.3 & R.S.3 (L. & R. HQ respectively). Great artillery activity in morning & afternoon from our own guns. Very wet weather prevented work during the day. | A.L. |
| | 30.8.16 | 11 pm | Heavy rain prevented an operation on the right in which our indirect fire guns were to take part. Our fire was active during the whole night. | A.L. |

1875 Wt. W593/826 1,000,000 4/15 J.B.C. & A. A.D.S.S./Forms/C. 2118.

Instructions regarding War Diaries and Intelligence Summaries are contained in F. S. Regs., Part II. and the Staff Manual respectively. Title Pages will be prepared in manuscript.

# WAR DIARY
*or*
# INTELLIGENCE SUMMARY
*(Erase heading not required.)*

Army Form C. 2118

| Place | Date | Hour | Summary of Events and Information | Remarks and references to Appendices |
|---|---|---|---|---|
| KEMMEL | | | | |
| | 31.8.16 | 8 pm | Lt. ~~K.M.~~ P.A. [AL] FORSTER joined for duty and took over command of the Coy. vice Capt. C.G. FANE evacuated sick. | AL |
| | | 11 pm | Two extra guns were taken to YOUNG ST. + Fme D'HOINO to assist in an operation carried out by the Right (57th) Bde. Cancelling orders were received early on 1st Sep. | |

No 56 COY. 24.8.16 MACHINE GUN CORPS

WD

Copy No. 2

SECRET.

56 Coy. Machine Gun Corps.

24 · Aug. 1916

Operation Order No. V. 95.

1. Nos. 3 & 4 sections will relieve Nos. 1 & 2 in the Left and Right Sectors respectively on the 25th inst. Relief to be completed by 8 p.m.

2. Arrangements for handing over tripods &c. to be made by officers concerned. Receipts for stores handed over to be brought to Orderly Room by officer relieved on reporting relief.

3. The two guns under Sergt. Waldren in Divl. Reserve will be relieved by two guns of No. 1 Sect. under Sergt. Miller. Transport to be arranged by O.C. No. 3 Section.

4. The gun at FORT REGINA will be relieved by a gun of No. 1 Sect. under Corpl. Gordon.

5. A statement showing work done and in progress will be handed to the relieving officer in each sector.

A. Lomax 2/Lt.
a/Adjt. for O.C.

Issued at 2 p.m.

Copy No. 1. Brigade
2. 7. N. Lan. R. ✓
3. 7. E. Lan. R.
4. 7. S. Lan. R.
5. to 8. O's. C. Sections.
9. Transport Officer.
10. 2/Lt. WALL.
11. O.C.

— CONFIDENTIAL —

# WAR DIARY

of

## 56TH M. G. Coy.

from

1 · 9 · 16

to

30 · 9 · 16

No 56 COY. MACHINE GUN CORPS
30 · 9 · 16

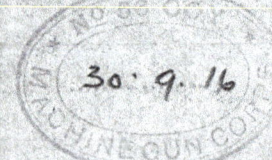

F.W. Taylor Lt
for O.C. Coy

Instructions regarding War Diaries and Intelligence Summaries are contained in F. S. Regs., Part II. and the Staff Manual respectively. Title Pages will be prepared in manuscript.

# WAR DIARY
*or*
# INTELLIGENCE SUMMARY
*(Erase heading not required.)*

Army Form C. 2118



Vol 10

| Place | Date | Hour | Summary of Events and Information | Remarks and references to Appendices |
|---|---|---|---|---|
| KEMMEL | 1 Sep 1916 | 10.0 am | Half the 12th Canadian M.G. Coy arrived for instruction. Our guns were active with indirect fire at night. 14374 Pte TAYLOR T. 7 S.Lan R att'd 56th M.G. Coy awarded the Military Medal. | T.W.T. |
| do | 2.9.16 | | Instructions received that ½ the 12th Can. M.G. Coy would relieve the Coy to-morrow. All Canadians withdrawn from the line | T.W.T. |
| do | 3.9.16 | | Relieved by half the 12th Can. M.G. Coy. Relief complete by 4 pm. Coy marched via DRANOUTRE, NEUVE EGLISE to camp near ROMARIN, arriving at 8.0 pm. | T.W.T. |
| PLOEGSTEERT | 4.9.16 | 9.0 am | Coy less transport moved up to line in front of PLOEGSTEERT WOOD relieving 14 guns of the 69th M.G. Coy. 2 in front system, 7 in support and 5 in reserve system; 2 guns remaining with transport which moved later in the day to B10b5.2 [Sheet 36 NW]. Relief complete by 2 pm. Coy H.Q. established at SOMERSET HOUSE, PLOEGSTEERT WOOD. | T.W.T. |
| do | 5.9.16 | | No operations by our guns. Two men wounded. | T.W.T. |
| do | 6.9.16 | | O.C. Coy 2/Lt Sheffield & 2 N.C.O.s attended lecture & demonstration on new box respirator at Div'l Anti Gas School. 1 Gun in Reserve fired indirect at MESSINES. | T.W.T. |

1875 Wt. W593/826 1,000,000 4/15 J.B.C. & A. A.D.S.S./Forms/C. 2118.

Instructions regarding War Diaries and Intelligence Summaries are contained in F. S. Regs., Part II. and the Staff Manual respectively. Title Pages will be prepared in manuscript.

# WAR DIARY
*or*
~~INTELLIGENCE SUMMARY~~
*(Erase heading not required.)*



Army Form C. 2118

| Place | Date | Hour | Summary of Events and Information | Remarks and references to Appendices |
|---|---|---|---|---|
| PLOEGSTEERT ~~T4~~ | 7.9.16 | | 11 men returned from Div! M.G. School. All had good reports with one exception. | |
| | | | Two guns used for Indirect Fire on ~~points~~ "tender spots" behind enemy's line from 9 pm – 12 mn | F.C.W.T. |
| | 8.9.16 | | Issue of new box respirator begun. Indirect Fire as before. | F.C.W.T. |
| | 9.9.16 | | 2/Lt. Smart relieved 2Lt. Rose as O.C. No. 4 Section. Indirect fire as usual. One man wounded by A.A. shrapnel; remained at duty. | |
| | | | 14374 Pte TAYLOR T att^d from 7 S. Lan. R. received Military Medal ribbon from the Corps Commander. | F.C.W.T. |
| | 10.9.16 | | 2Lt. Rose + 1 N.C.O. to Div! School. 5 O.R. to Div! M.G. School | |
| | | | Section relief complete by 6 pm. One gun taken from OXFORD CIRCUS into Brigade Reserve at Transport. | |
| | | | Inspection of Transport by O.C. Coy. | F.C.W.T. |
| | | | One gun only doing indirect fire. | |
| | 11.9.16 | | 1500 rounds fired at usual targets. | F.C.W.T. |
| | 12.9.16 | | 7500 rounds indirect at usual targets. ~~Two~~ New overhead fire emplacements built. | F.C.W.T. |

1875 Wt. W593/826 1,000,000 4/15 J.B.C. & A. A.D.S.S./Forms/C. 2118.

Instructions regarding War Diaries and Intelligence Summaries are contained in F. S. Regs., Part II. and the Staff Manual respectively. Title Pages will be prepared in manuscript.

# WAR DIARY
*or*
~~INTELLIGENCE SUMMARY~~
*(Erase heading not required.)*

Army Form C. 2118



| Place | Date | Hour | Summary of Events and Information | Remarks and references to Appendices |
|---|---|---|---|---|
| PLOEGSTEERT WOOD | 13/9/16 | | Two men surplus to establishment returned to Base Depot. Gun moved from support line to position nearer front line. U22 c 0.12 [S. YVES Sheet] 7250 rounds Indirect Fire on Tender Spots 150 rounds at enemy parapet | FCWT |
| | 14.9.16 | | 5000 rounds Indirect Fire on usual targets. | FCWT |
| | 15.9.16 | | 5750 rounds at usual targets in conjunction with T.M.B. + Artillery to support raiding party + inflict casualties on enemy supports. C.S.M. Elsbury reported. | FCWT |
| | 16.9.16 | | Section Relief complete at 7.45 pm. 750 rounds Indirect on U29b 75.35 [S. YVES Sheet] | FCWT |
| | 17.9.16 | 3.0pm | O.C. Coy inspected Transport 2000 rounds Indirect Fire. | FCWT |
| | 18.9.16 | | 3500 rounds Indirect Fire. Informed of forthcoming relief on 21st | FCWT |
| | 19.9.16 | | 4750 rounds Indirect Fire. O.C. 22nd M.G. Coy at Coy H.Q. & made preliminary arrangements for taking over. 4289 Cpl Alexander sent to Base Authority A.G. GHQ. A 5856. | FCWT |
| | 20.9.16 | | 3250 rounds Indirect Fire. Section Officers + Sergts of 22nd Coy visited guns they were to relieve. | FCWT |

1875 Wt. W593/826 1,000,000 4/15 J.B.C. & A. A.D.S.S./Forms/C. 2118.

Army Form C. 2118

# WAR DIARY
or
~~INTELLIGENCE SUMMARY~~
(Erase heading not required.)

Instructions regarding War Diaries and Intelligence Summaries are contained in F. S. Regs., Part II. and the Staff Manual respectively. Title Pages will be prepared in manuscript.



| Place | Date | Hour | Summary of Events and Information | Remarks and references to Appendices |
|---|---|---|---|---|
| PAPOT | 21/9/16 | | Coy was relieved by the 22nd M. G. Coy. Relief complete at 1.30 pm. Coy moved into billets at LE VEAU. | F.C.W.J. |
| OULTERSTEEN | 22.9.16 | | Coy marched via BAILLEUL STATION to billets at OULTERSTEEN arriving at 2.0 pm. 2Lt. Price + Cpl. Greaves returned from M G. School G.H.Q. | F.C.W.J. |
| do. | 23.9.16 | | Inspections of Guns + Equipment. Baths. | F.C.W.J. |
| do | 24.9.16 | | Church Parades. | F.C.W.J. |
| do | 25.9.16 | | Physical train. Arms Drill. Gun Drill. Lectures to N.C.O.s + Sections. | F.C.W.J. |
| do | 26.9.16 | | Parades according to programme. Two re-inforcements from Base. Pte. Harrison proceeded on special leave. Four men proceeded to DHQ for course of signalling. | F.C.W.J. |
| do | 27.9.16 | | Parades according to programme. All officers + N.C.O's attended a lecture on Bayonet Fighting by Capt. Betts 2nd A. G. S. 4306 Pte Beard sent to Base. under age | F.C.W.J. |
| do | 28.9.16 | | Inspection by 2nd Army Commander. 5 O.R. proceeded to Div! M G School | F.C.W.J. |

1875 Wt. W593/826 1,000,000 4/15 J.B.C. & A. A.D.S.S./Forms/C. 2118.

Instructions regarding War Diaries and Intelligence Summaries are contained in F. S. Regs., Part II. and the Staff Manual respectively. Title Pages. will be prepared in manuscript.

# WAR DIARY

*or*

~~INTELLIGENCE SUMMARY~~

*(Erase heading not required.)*

Army Form C. 2118



| Place | Date | Hour | Summary of Events and Information | Remarks and references to Appendices |
|---|---|---|---|---|
| OUTTERSTEEN | 29/9/16 | | 1 Reinforcement from Base Depot. Parades according to programme from 7.15 am – 3.30 pm. | FCWJ |
| | 30.9.16 | | Parades according to programme. Tactical Scheme – consolidation of village of OUTTERSTEEN. 2/Lt Flood proceeded on special leave. | FCWJ |

1875 Wt. W593/826 1,000,000 4/15 J.B.C. & A. A.D.S.S./Forms/C. 2118.

Instructions regarding War Diaries and Intelligence Summaries are contained in F. S. Regs., Part II. and the Staff Manual respectively. Title Pages will be prepared in manuscript.

# WAR DIARY
*or*
# INTELLIGENCE SUMMARY
*(Erase heading not required.)*

56th M.G. Company

Army Form C. 2118

Vol 13

| Place | Date | Hour | Summary of Events and Information | Remarks and references to Appendices |
|---|---|---|---|---|
| OUTTERSTEEN | 1/10/16 | | Church Parades. | F.W.J. |
| | 2.10.16 | | Route March & Scheme. Baths. | F.W.J. |
| | 3.10.16 | | Return of Lt. Rose NCO's & men from Div! School. Immediate Action. Mechanism. Lectures in afternoon. | F.W.J. |
| | 4.10.16 | | Return of 4 men from Div! Signalling Course. Cleaning of Guns & Gun Equipment. Packing of Limbers. No parades p.m. | F.W.J. |
| COIGNEUX | 5.10.16 | | Coy left OUTTERSTEEN at 4.30 am & 6.0 am. and entrained at BAILLEUL MAIN STN moving off at 9.0 am. Coy detrained at DOULLENS and marched to COIGNEUX arriving at 8.30 pm. Accommodation was found in huts and tents. 2/Lt. PRICE proceeded to U.K on special leave | F.W.J. |
| | 6.10.16 | | Gun and gun equipment cleaning | F.W.J. |
| SAILLY-AU-BOIS | 7.10.16 | | Coy relieved 2 guns of 152nd Coy near HEBUTERNE. Remainder of Coy less transport moved up to SAILLY AU BOIS | |
| | 8.10.16 | | No firing done. Billets cleaned up. Gun cleaning. | F.W.J. |

1875 Wt. W593/826 1,000,000 4/15 J.B.C. & A. A.D.S.S./Forms/C. 2118.

Instructions regarding War Diaries and Intelligence Summaries are contained in F. S. Regs., Part II. and the Staff Manual respectively. Title Pages will be prepared in manuscript.

# WAR DIARY
*or*
# INTELLIGENCE SUMMARY
*(Erase heading not required.)*

Army Form C. 2118

| Place | Date | Hour | Summary of Events and Information | Remarks and references to Appendices |
|---|---|---|---|---|
| SAILLY-AU-BOIS | 9/10/16 | | Route March by Sections out of line. No firing done owing to patrols | FCWJ. |
| | 10.10.16 | | Physical and Arms Drill. Officers inspect line. | FCWJ. |
| | 11.10.16 | | Working party sent up to trenches to prepare assembly trench. Officers attend lecture on "Tanks" by O.C. D Coy H.S. M.G.C. | FCWJ. |
| | 12.10.16 | | Two guns of No. 4 Sectn relieved by No. 2 Sectn. Working party not sent owing to operations on front. Gun cleaning. 2/Lt. J Lood returned from leave. 4000 rounds fired at enemy C.T.'s | FCWJ |
| | 13.10.16 | | No firing done | FCWJ |
| | 14.10.16 | | 2000 rounds fired in conjunction with artillery at enemy C.T's | FCWJ. |
| | 15.10.16 | | 2/Lt. Loman proceeded to M.G School. G.H.Q. Information - to be relieved by 57th Coy. - cancelled. To be relieved by 92nd Coy. O.C. 92nd Coy came to make arrangements. No firing | FCWJ |

Instructions regarding War Diaries and Intelligence Summaries are contained in F. S. Regs., Part II. and the Staff Manual respectively. Title Pages will be prepared in manuscript.

# WAR DIARY
or
~~INTELLIGENCE SUMMARY~~
*(Erase heading not required.)*

Army Form C. 2118

| Place | Date | Hour | Summary of Events and Information | Remarks and references to Appendices |
|---|---|---|---|---|
| COIGNEUX | 16.10.16 | | Relieved by 92nd Coy. Coy moved to billets at ROSSIGNOL FM. Relief complete by 4.0 pm. | F.W.S. |
| VADENCOURT | 17.10.16 | | Coy moved by route march to billets at VADENCOURT arriving at 6.0 pm. 2/Lt. Price returned from leave. | F.W.S. |
| | 18.10.16 | | Gun and equipment cleaning. Brigade attack scheme practised. | F.W.S. |
| | 19.10.16 | | Coy moved off at 10.0 am to proceed to new area. After proceeding ¼ mile, Coy was instructed to return to billets. | F.W.S. |
| AVELUY (Blighty Wood) | 20.10.16 | | ~~Lt~~ Lay Capt Peaves Coy for Grantham Coy moves to Albert. Bouzincourt Rd. 2nd Lt. Smart as Temp. Adj. 2nd Lt. Price acting second in Command | [illegible] |
| | | | 2nd Lt. Blackwood joins Coy from Base. | [illegible] |
| | 21.10.16 | | Coy moves into Line just south of THIEPVAL. Position taken up by 2½ Sections | |
| | 22.10.16 | | one man wounded. 2nd Lt. Sheffield wounded at Duty. Order for 2nd Lt. Lomare to join 98th Coy as 2nd in command. Coy. H.Q at AVELUY. | [illegible] |
| | 23.10.16 | | 2 men wounded. 2nd Lt. Sheffield again wounded. | [illegible] |

1875 Wt. W593/826 1,000,000 4/15 J.B.C. & A. A.D.S.S./Forms/C. 2118.

Instructions regarding War Diaries and Intelligence Summaries are contained in F. S. Regs., Part II. and the Staff Manual respectively. Title Pages will be prepared in manuscript.

# WAR DIARY
or
# INTELLIGENCE SUMMARY
*(Erase heading not required.)*

Army Form C. 2118

| Place | Date | Hour | Summary of Events and Information | Remarks and references to Appendices |
|---|---|---|---|---|
| | 24.10.16 | | 2 men wounded. Inter section relief. | H.W.P. |
| AVELUY | 25.10.16 | | 2nd Lt. Price as Adjt. 2nd Lt. Smart becomes shell shocked, his place in front line taken by 2nd Lt. Blackwood. | H.W.P. |
| | 26.10.16 | | 3 men wounded. Enemy attacked our part of the front line at 6 a.m. driven off with much loss chiefly inflicted by the four guns of No 2 Section. Relief ~~with~~ of Company with exception of 4 guns in reserve line by 58 Coy. | H.W.P. |
| | 27.10.16 | | Company in rest with exception of No 3 section who are in reserve. | H.W.P. |
| | 28.10.16 | | Company resting. No 3 employed in cleaning ammunition and forming a dump in the line. | H.W.P. |
| | 29.10.16 | | 2nd Lt. Doherty arrives from 123rd Coy to take over second in Command and Adjutant. | H.W.P. |
| | 30.10.16 | | Coy Relief of 58th M. G. Coy in the front line, positions taken over by No 1 and half No 4 under 2nd Lts Blackwood and Rose. No 3 relieved by No 2. Arrival of 2nd Lts Hutty and Havell from Base as reinforcements. ~~The~~ Rain and the resulting thick mud have been prevalent for the last week, preventing active operations. 8 O.R. reinforcements from Base Depot | |
| | 31.10.16 | | L/Cpl Pennington accidentally wounded (Self inflicted) | H.W.P. |

1875 Wt. W593/826 1,000,000 4/15 J.B.C. & A. A.D.S.S./Forms/C. 2118.

VOLUME NO. 10.

# WAR DIARY of 56 Machine Gun COY. for NOVEMBER 1916

Army Form C. 2118

~~INTELLIGENCE SUMMARY~~

(Erase heading not required.)

Instructions regarding War Diaries and Intelligence Summaries are contained in F. S. Regs., Part II. and the Staff Manual respectively. Title Pages will be prepared in manuscript.

| Place | Date | Hour | Summary of Events and Information | Remarks and references to Appendices |
|---|---|---|---|---|
| AVELUY | 1.11.16 | | Intersection Relief. No 3 Sect & 2 guns of No 4 sect. relieved No 1 sect. & other 2 guns of No 4 sect. in front line. Trenches over the knees in mud & water. Casualties Pte Plumbridge killed | RWO |
| | ~~2.11.16~~ | | Sgt Brocklebank wounded Ptes. Lord, Barber, Clarke Whiteside & Ball wounded. Trenches heavily shelled with shrapnel. | |
| | 2.11.16 | | Relief of front line guns by 58th M G C. Trenches again heavily shelled by shrapnel. Casualties. 2 Lt Price wounded. Ptes Keeble, Howes, Allday wounded | RWO |
| | 3.11.16 | | No 2 Sect. at Thiepval. Sections 1, 3 & 4 cleaning guns & equipment. | RWO |
| | 4.11.16 | | No 4 Sect relieved No 2 Sect at Thiepval. Sections Nos 1, 2, & 3 had baths at Aveluy | RWO |
| | 5.11.16 | | Coy relieved 58 Coy in front line. Coy H.Q moved from AVELUY WOOD to X 2 a 5.6. No 1 Sect 4 guns in front line. No 3 Sect. 4 guns in front line. No 2 Sect 2 guns in support line 1 gun CHQ 1 gun deficient. No 4 Sect 2 guns in support line 2 guns at Thiepval. Relief complete by 6.30 pm. | |
| | 6.11.16 | | No change 2 teams of No 2 sect. took rations up to Hessian. | RWO |
| | 7.11.16 | | Intersection relief. No 2 Sect relieved No 3 sect in front line. No 4 Sect. relieved No 1 Sect in front line. Trenches in bad condition. Communication trenches impassable. Casualties Cpl Gordon killed Pte Young wounded | |
| | 8.11.16 | | Coy relief by 57th M.G.C. Coy moved into billets in AVELUY. Casualties Pte Keith killed Pte Leslie wounded 2 Lt Oakes joined Coy from Camiers. | RWO |
| | 9.11.16 | | Coy cleaned guns. Rifle & Gun inspection by Sect. Officers. 2 Lt Cooper joined Coy from Camiers | RWO |
| | 10.11.16 | | Coy inspection. Gun drill. Belt filling. Kit & clothing inspection | RWO |
| | 11.11.16 | | Coy drill. Rifle inspection. Belt filling & advanced drill. | RWO |
| | 12.11.16 | | Sections Nos 1 & 2 and 2 teams of No 4 section relieved ~~57~~ Coy in front line. No 3 section & ½ No 4 section in reserve at AVELUY. O.C. Coy moved his H.Q. to Stuff Trench | RWO |

1875 Wt. W593/826 1,000,000 4/15 J.B.C. & A. A.D.S.S./Forms/C. 2118.

VOLUME NO 10 (ii)

Instructions regarding War Diaries and Intelligence Summaries are contained in F. S. Regs., Part II. and the Staff Manual respectively. Title Pages will be prepared in manuscript.

# WAR DIARY
*or*
~~INTELLIGENCE~~ SUMMARY
*(Erase heading not required.)*

56 COY. M. G. CORPS. for NOVEMBER 1916.

Army Form C. 2118

| Place | Date | Hour | Summary of Events and Information | Remarks and references to Appendices |
|---|---|---|---|---|
| STUFF TRENCH | 13.11.16 | | Attack by 19 + 39 Divisions on line running from O.G.1 across LUCKY WAY + along HANSA line to river ANCRE in conjunction with V Corps attack north of the river. Hour of attack 5.45 a.m. All objectives gained including the capture of ST PIERRE DIVION by 39th Div. Whole attack on 19th Divisional front made by 56th Brigade with 7 E/Lanc Regt on right and 7th N/Lanc Regt on left. Disposal of Machine Guns:— 2 Guns No 1 Section under 2/Lt OAKES take up point 50 yds in front of STUFF TRENCH prior to zero hour to cover infantry advance. 2 Guns of same section under 2/Lt BLACKWOOD in position to fire down O.G.1 on flank of attack. 2 Guns No 2 Section under 2/Lt SOPER to accompany attack of 7 E/LANC REGT. 2 Guns same section under 2/Lt MURRAY to accompany attack of 7 N/LANC REGT. 1 Gun of each BATTN reached correct posn and consolidated. 1 Gun support of 7 N/LANC REGT destroyed during advance. 1 gun support 7 E/LANC REGT lost direction took up posn in line of 7 N/LANC REGT and consolidated. ~~1 Gun support~~ Position originally allotted to these 2 guns subsequently taken up by 2 guns from No 1 section. 1 gun from No 4 Section moved up from reserve to posn in O.G.1. Casualties:— 3 wounded 1 gun No 2 section destroyed and 1 damaged in water-jacket but not put out of action. 1 gun No 1 destroyed and 1 damaged. Very misty during morning little enemy activity after capture of posn. During the afternoon STUFF TRENCH heavily shelled by enemy. | app. 1<br>2.<br>3<br>4<br>5.<br>6.<br>7<br>8.<br>T. W. |
| ST PIERRE DIVION | 14.11.16 | | Relief during early morning of all guns of No 1 Section and 2 guns of No 2 Section by all guns of No 3 Section and 2 guns of No 4 Section. Raid on enemy posn by 7 N/LANC and 7 S/LANC. Consolidation of position continued. Enemy snipers active on right. Enemy artillery active searching for new line. Casualties 1 killed 5 wounded | T. W. |

1875 Wt. W593/826 1,000,000 4/15 J.B.C. & A. A.D.S.S./Forms/C. 2118.

VOLUME No 10 (iii)

Instructions regarding War Diaries and Intelligence Summaries are contained in F. S. Regs., Part II. and the Staff Manual respectively. Title Pages will be prepared in manuscript.

# WAR DIARY ~~or~~ ~~INTELLIGENCE~~ SUMMARY of 56 M. G. COY for NOVEMBER. 1916.

(Erase heading not required.)

Army Form C. 2118

| Place | Date | Hour | Summary of Events and Information | Remarks and references to Appendices |
|---|---|---|---|---|
| ~~[illegible]~~ ST PIERRE DIVION | 15/11/16 | | Partial relief during early hours, of 56 BDE by 58 BDE and subsequent relief of 118th BDE in HANSA line by 56 BDE. 8 guns in front line 1 on left flank firing across river. Enemy infantry very quiet. Enemy artillery quiet during day but very active during night, searching for new line. Casualties 1 killed, 2 wounded. 1 Gun on extreme right damaged + put out of action by shell fire. | T. W. |
| " | 16/11/16 | | Capt FORSTER relieved in command by Capt PURVIS. 2/Lt DOHERTY departed to 123 Coy. Damaged gun replaced in line. Enemy artillery quiet during the day. One M. Gun in front line employed in intermittent during afternoon + evening on enemy BRIDGEHEAD across the river ANCRE. | T.W. |
| " | 17/11/16 | | Capt FORSTER departed for M.G.T.C. GRANTHAM. No III Section under 2/Lt WALL relieved 4 guns on rt of HANSA line under 2/Lts COOPER and FLAVELL | T. W. |
| " | 18/11/16 | 2 A.M. 6.10 AM. | 4 guns under 2/Lt WALL relieved by 58 BDE. Attack on GRANDCOURT began at 6.10 AM. 2 Guns under 2/Lt MURRAY with 7 S./LANC REGT advanced along HANSA ~~Rd~~ 4 Guns under 2/Lt OAKES proceeded to high ground above battery valley + fired on GRANDCOURT during attack. All these 4 guns were put out of action by shell fire + were replaced by 3 guns from Coy H.Q. On attempting to get these guns back to previous posns 2/Lt OAKES and his teams were held up by snipers and M.Gun fire. 2 Guns under 2/Lt FLAVELL reported to 7E/LANC REGT for attack on BAILLESCOURT FARM. | Appendix 9. |

1875 Wt. W593/826 1,000,000 4/15 J.B.C. & A. A.D.S.S./Forms/C. 2118.

VOLUME No 10 (iv)

Instructions regarding War Diaries and Intelligence Summaries are contained in F. S. Regs., Part II. and the Staff Manual respectively. Title Pages will be prepared in manuscript.

# WAR DIARY of 56 COY. M. G. CORPS for NOVEMBER '16.

or

~~INTELLIGENCE~~ SUMMARY

(Erase heading not required.)

Army Form C. 2118

| Place | Date | Hour | Summary of Events and Information | Remarks and references to Appendices |
|---|---|---|---|---|
| ST PIERRE DIVION | 18/11/16 | | on 2/Lt FLAVELL becoming a casualty 2/Lt COOPER took charge. These 2 Guns advanced along RAILWAY and HANSA RD respectively. Attack on BAILLESCOURT FM was held up by M.Gun fire. The gun on railway formed a strong point at R.8.c.5.7. [Sheet 57 D.S.E.]. The gun on road dug in at R.8.d.4.4. The 2 guns under 2/Lt MURRAY formed a strong point in GRANDCOURT village. The guns under 2/Lt OAKES were 2 guns + teams under 2/Lt WALL who took up a posn at R.14.b.3.2 under cover of darkness. Casualties 2/Lt FLAVELL wounded 3 guns out of action. | T.W. |
| | 19/11/16 | | Enemy made counter-attack on GRANDCOURT repulsed by our M.Gun fire. 2/Lt MURRAY and 1 O.R killed 2 O.R wounded in the gun teams by enemy bombs. 2/Lt BLACKWOOD and 2 teams relieved teams in GRANDCOURT. Casualties 1 officer 1 O.R killed 2 O.R wounded 1 gun out of action. | T.W. |
| | 20/11/16 | | 2/Lt OAKES relieved 2 guns + teams under 2/Lt WALL in BATTERY VALLEY at 6 p.m. The guns in GRANDCOURT and on railway under 2/Lt's COOPER + BLACKWOOD returned to Coy H.Q. a new line being formed in rear preparatory to handing over to a new division | T.W. |
| AVELUY | 21/11/16 | | Dull day 3 sections at Coy H.Q move to AVELUY in afternoon 2 guns in BATTERY VALLEY relieved by 2 Lewis Guns 9th SHERWOODS | T.W. |
| WARLOY | 22/11/16 | 4. A.M | Remaining section returns to AVELUY 4.A.M. 9 A.M. The company marches to WARLOY where they spend the night in tents | T.W. |
| VADENCOURT | 23/11/16 | | Coy march from WARLOY to VADENCOURT spending night in huts in VADENCOURT WOOD | T.W. |
| BEAUVAL | 24/11/16 | | Coy marched to BEAUVAL billeted in town fine day | T.W. |
| LA VACQUERIE | 25/11/16 | | Coy marched to LA VACQUERIE billeted in village very wet day | T.W. |
| DOMMESMONT | 26/11/16 | | Coy marched to DOMMESMONT billeted in village. Fine day | T.W. |

RET. C.O APP. 3.



1. 11. 16.

56 Coy M. G. Corps.

OPERATION ORDER No. 115A. War Diary Copy No. 1

Reference B.O. No. 116

I. The dispositions of for the Coy are as follows:-

a). Prior to Zero hour under cover of darkness O.C. Coy will push 8 guns out in front of STUFF TRENCH into shell holes to cover the advance of the troops to attack line A. As soon as line A is taken, he will push forward these 8 guns & take up positions about the 120 contour line. From these positions fire will be kept up as far as possible on the following objectives

(1.) Any likely M.G. Positions on the slopes N of the River Ancre

(2.) Enfilade fire on PUIZIEUX TRENCH to assist 5th Corps attack.

(3.) Any target which presents itself on the opposite slopes

(4.) The line of trench in front of line C until the attack on it is pushed home.

(5) Any counter attack which may develop.

b.) O.C. Coy will detail 3 guns, 1 each to operate under the orders of O.C. 7 E. Lan. R. 7 S. Lan. R. & 7 N. Lan. R. respectively. One officer will supervise the 2 guns operating under the orders of 7 E. Lan. R. & 7 S. Lan. R. These guns will report to O.C. concerned 2 hours before Zero hour.

c) O.C. Coy will retain the remaining 5 guns in hand ready to push them up to hold the line which is finally consolidated. These guns will assemble in the 130 yds. of BAINBRIDGE TRENCH immediately E of its junction with BULGAR TRENCH & C.T. at R.20. c.7.2.

II. a) No. 1 Section (2Lt Blackwood) & No. 3 Section (2Lt Wall) will supply the 8 guns detailed under Para. I a.) No. 1 Section will be on the left & will assemble in STUFF TRENCH between R.19. d.9.9 & R. 20. b.3.2. No. 3 Section will be on the right & will assemble in STUFF TRENCH between R. 20. b.3.2 & R. 21. a.7.3. Arrangements have been made for O.C. of Battn concerned to have sufficient accomodation for these guns. No. 3 Section will detail 1 gun to fire on PUIZIEUX TRENCH in accordance with Para I a.(2).

b). O.C. No. 1 & 3 Sections will observe the following time table after Zero 1.30 they will NOT fire on any point South of the

trench mentioned in Para I a(ii). 1.45 They will NOT fire on any point E of the quarry at R.8.a.2.0. 3.15 They will NOT fire on any point E of BOIS d'HOLLANDE. 3.25 They will NOT fire on any point South of the 100 contour line North of the River Ancre. 3.40 They will ~~cease~~ fire NOT fire on any point E of RIVER TRENCH
4.10 They will cease fire

III. No 2 Section will supply the 3 guns detailed under Para I(b). 2Lt Soper will supervise the 2 guns operating under the orders of 7 E. Lan. R. & 7 S. Lan. R. 2Lt Murray will supervise the gun operating under the orders of 7 N. Lan. R. These guns will report to O.C. concerned in accordance with Para I b)

IV. No. 4 Section with the remaining gun of No 2 Section will supply the 5 guns detailed in Para I c). 2Lt [illegible] & 2Lt Hewitt will accompany these guns. They will assemble in the 150 yds of [illegible] TRENCH specified in Para I c. Thirty minutes after Zero these guns will move forward to report to O.C. Coy at Coy H.Q. at the point mentioned in Para VII.

V. The following Officers, W.O. N.C.O. & men will not be taken into the attack. They will report to Brigade Transport Lines by 1 AM on the morning of Zero day. 2Lt Doherty. 2Lt Rice. 2Lt Hand. CSM Eleby. Sgt Green, & Pte Thackeray.

VI. Prior to assembly each section will detail 2 men to act as carriers. These will report to Sgt Matthews at the Co. dump in HESSIAN TRENCH & will be under his orders.

VII. Coy H.Q. will be at the Visual Signalling Station in STUFF TRENCH at R.20.0.3.3. O.C. Coy will be accompanied by the Coy Runners & Signallers detailed under Para XI.

VIII. In addition to the guns & gun equipment the following will be carried on the men. Iron rations & the unexpended current days ration. Equipment. Water bottle full. Box Respirator. Haversack with spare pair of socks. Waterproof Sheet. Mess tin. Yellow patch, 2 Sandbags rolled. Men with rifles 50 Rounds S.A.A. Men with Revolvers, 12 Rounds of Revolver ammunition. All available regimental periscopes will also be carried forward.

IX. Mark IV tripods will NOT be taken forward with the 3 guns detailed in Para. III. Auxiliary mountings will be carried on all guns.

X. Officers will wear trousers & puttees similar to the men. They will avoid wearing Burberry or similar type overcoats in the actual attack.

XI. The Signal Section will detail:-

1 Signaller to accompany No. 1 Section

1 Signaller to accompany No. 3 Section

2 Signallers to accompany O.C. Coy

XII. The CAREFUL ATTENTION of all Sections is drawn to the timings of the V Corps attack from W to E:—

| Troops due to arrive in line | at. | and advance again at |
|---|---|---|
| a) W edge of BEACOURT - L36 Central - SERRE. | 1·50 | 2·20 |
| b.) Quarry R.8.a.2.0 - L32.c.0.0 - L25 a.4.9. | 3·20 | 3·40 |
| c). RIVER TRENCH (support trench to PUISIEUX TRENCH) with left flank thrown back to L25.a.4.9 | 4·20 | 4·50 |

ISSUED AT 8·30 P.M.

COPIES TO:-

Nos 1 - 10 Company Officers
11 Sgt Major
12 File
} NOT to be taken in advance of present Coy H.Q.

13 Brigade H.Q.
14 4 S.Lan.R.
15 4 E.Lan.R.
16 4 N.Lan R.

1. 11. 16

[signature]

Captn

Commdg 56 Coy M.G. CORPS.

M.G.C.

[illegible] Copy No. 17.

Order No. 114 [illegible] Order No. 116.



War diary

APP. 4.

[illegible]

[illegible]

[illegible] Trench Map

[illegible] (BEAUMONT)

1. [illegible] to [illegible] the operation [illegible] [illegible] will attack with the 57th Bde. on the RIGHT and the 56th Bde. on the LEFT. 58th Bde. will be in Reserve.

2. [illegible] following are the objectives of the 56th Bde:

[illegible] [illegible] 6 1. – R.15 c. 05.95. – R.14.b.90.15 – R.14.b. [illegible].05. approximately R.14.b.3.3. – R.14.a.2.5.

(b) LINE B. [illegible] line running from R.9.a.7.2. to R.8.c.4.5. [illegible] thence S.W. to a point R.8.c.2.0.

(c) LINE C. [illegible] of MIRAUMONT – BEAUCOURT – Road from R.3.c.7.3. to R.8.a.2.[illegible] thence to R.8.c.2.0.

[illegible] The objectives are divided into 3 Sub sectors:-

RIGHT – 7. E. LAN. R.

CENTRE – [illegible]

LEFT. – 7. N. LAN. R.

The 7. R. LANC. R. will provide clearing up parties for each Sub-Sector which will work under the orders of O.C. the sector to which they are allotted.

3. The boundaries of the [illegible] Sub-sector are as:-

RIGHT

O.G.1. from R.20.b.8.5. to junction of 130 contour line and trench at R.15.c.05.95. – entry of STUMP ROAD into [illegible] at R.9.c.2.5. – point where [illegible] bends N.E. from Railway embankment at R.9.a.20.15. thence to MIRAUMONT Road at R.3.c.2.0. (All exclusive)

LEFT.

R.20.b.25.20. – to Road junction R.20.b.2.7. thence [illegible] road to R.8.d.50.35. – R.8.d.80.95. – line of trench at R.8.b.8.2. – MIRAUMONT Road at R.8.b.7.7. (All EXCLUSIVE)

The dividing line between the left and right coys. of the Batt. is a line drawn from [illegible] TRENCH at R.20.b.5½.4. – R.14.d.5½.9½ – trench junction R.14.[illegible].8.½. – R.8.b.9.9. – R.8.b.8.9½.

4. (a) The attack on line 'A' between the boundaries mentioned in para. 3. will be delivered in two waves by 'A' Coy. on the right and D. Coy. (in two platoons) plus [illegible] Bombing Platoon of R.LANC.R. on [illegible] Coy.

N.B. The Bombing Platoon 7. R. LANC. R. will be equipped and work as an ordinary platoon with only the usual complement of men armed as Bombers viz:- 8.

(b) No. 16 Platoon 7. R. LANC. R. (Commander 2Lt. [illegible]) will be attached to A. Coy.

No. 13 Platoon 7. R. LANC. R. (Commander 2Lt. [illegible]) will be attached to D. Coy.

OVER

4. (continued) These platoons will form a third wave 30 yds behind the Coys. to which they are attached and will be responsible for "cleaning up" between our present front line and line 'A'.

These platoons should be equipped with the necessary bombs, bomb carriers, 'P' Grenades, torches, revolvers, cards for marking dug-outs, etc.

A sniper with a telescopic sighted rifle should accompany each platoon.

As soon as line 'A' is captured Coys will reorganize and prepare for a further advance.

(c.) The attack on line 'B' between the boundaries mentioned in para. 3. will be delivered by "C" Coy. on right and 'B' Coy. on the left.

These Coys. with attached troops (vide 'd') will move into our present front line immediately A & D Coys are clear.

At one hour after ZERO they will move forward, in Artillery formation until the leading line is close behind line 'A' where they will halt. When the barrage again becomes intense they will move forward and advance in 4 waves, i.e assaulting troops in two waves and clearing up troops in two waves.

3. H.Q. Lewis Guns will be distributed in the second wave on arrival at line 'B' they will push forward and take up positions covering the bridges over the ANCRE.

The Battn Bombers will move behind the troops detailed for line 'B' to line 'A'. They will remain in line 'A' until the troops for line 'C' advance.

They will move with these troops to the objective, clear trench running N.W. from R.8.b.9.9. and road running N.W. from R.9.a.0.9. for at least 40 yds and establish and hold posts at these points.

(d) B Coy. 7. R. LANC. R. (less two platoons) Commander Capt. HOYLE will be attached to 'C' Coy.

Nos ? & ? platoons B Coy 7. R. LANC. R Commander 2Lt. OLIVER will be attached to "B" Coy.

This Coy. will clean up between line 'A' and southern edge of village and also the village itself.

The instruction in (b) re equipment etc. apply to this Coy.

50% of the Coy. should carry 10 bombs each and only 50 rounds of S.A.A.

Coy. Lewis Guns should be sent one with each ½ Coy.

(e) As soon as the cleaning up of the village is completed – B Coy. 7. R. LANC. R. will re-organize on the line of the road running E. and W. on the ~~Western~~ Northern side of the village.

(f.) The attack on line 'C' will be carried out by the troops detailed for the attack on line 'A' (less any parties attached who may not have completed their duties)

They will move in artillery formation from line 'A' and arrive at line 'B' half an hour after that objective is taken.

When barrage again becomes intense they will advance – cross the ANCRE and assault line 'C'.

5. Timings of the "Rolling" barrage will be issued separately.

5. (continued) On reaching a [illegible] 200 yds [illegible] objective [illegible] the barrage will remain stationary and become [illegible] for ONE HOUR [illegible] time of lifting off the objective [illegible] will then become [illegible] again remaining stationary for [illegible] minutes and then move forward.

When line 'B' is taken the above applies except that the barrage will be from 200 to 250 yds in advance to enable the R.E. to bridge the river at any point 150 yds from the railway.

N.B. The importance of the leading waves for each objective keeping right up to the barrage MUST be instilled into all ranks.

6. 81st Fd. Coy. R.E. and 1 Coy. 5. S.W.B. (Pioneers) for bridging and consolidating strong points will move in rear of the troops attacking line 'B'.

7. 4 Tanks will assist the attack.

8. 56th Coy. M.G.C. will, prior to ZERO hour, have guns in front of STUFF TRENCH to cover the attack on line 'A'.

After the capture of line 'A' one gun will be sent to O.C. 7. S. Lan. R.

5 Guns will be available for holding the line which is finally consolidated.

9. Two guns from 56th T.M.B. will co-operate with the 7. S. Lan. R. against any strong points in the village. They will move in rear of B. and C. Coys.

10. The Battn. will assemble on the night prior to the attack as under:

A. Coy. and attached Platoon in Stuff Trench from R.20.b.[illegible] to R.20.b.[illegible] inclusive;

[illegible] Coy. and attached Platoon in STUFF TRENCH from R.20.b.5.4. to R.20.b.2.3. (exclusive)

C. Coy. in BAINBRIDGE TRENCH from R.20.b.85.60. to R.20.b.5.[illegible]

D. Coy. in BAINBRIDGE TRENCH from R.20.b.6.6. to R.20.b.[illegible]

H.Qrs. in HESSIAN TRENCH about R.20.d.[illegible]

B Coy. 7. S. LANC.R. in HESSIAN TRENCH from R.20.d.4.1. to R.20.d.3.1.

11. Regtl. aid post will be in BAINBRIDGE or HESSIAN trench. F.A. collecting post will be at R.26.[illegible]

12. Bde. Battle H.Q. will be at R.26.[illegible] [illegible] advanced [illegible] will be at R.[illegible]

Details of [illegible] arrangements will be [illegible]

14. Reports in assembly position: to Battn. H.Qrs. about R.20.d.6.1.
From ZERO hour until 1 hour after ZERO to front line about R.20.b.4.3.
From there report centre will move to the centre of line 'A' and then to about R.14.b.9.2.
After the village is ~~taken~~ cleared reports will be sent to centre of objective 'B'.

N.B. It should be impressed on all ranks that messages and reports are to be taken to Report Centres and not individuals who may be moving about anywhere far from the report centre.

NOTE These orders are not to be taken into the front line before the day of assembly.

B.W. Ridley
Capt a/Adjt
7. S. Lan. R.

29-10-16
Issued at:- 5. p.m.

Copies to:-

1. War Diary
2. File
3. O/C A. Coy.
4. O/C B. Coy.
6. O/C C. Coy.
7. O/C D. Coy.
8. Officer Commanding
9. 2nd in Command.
10. Medical Officer
11. Signalling Officer
12. Bombing Officer.
13. Quartermaster
14. Transport Officer
15. R.S.M.
16. 7. R. Lanc. R.
17. 56th Coy. M.G.C.
18. 56th Inf. Bde.

——— 11 ———

NO. 56 COY. MACHINE GUN CORPS.

APP. 5.   WAR DIARY

## 56th INFANTRY BRIGADE ORDER No. 123.

Reference – Sheet 57D S.E. 1/20.000.   7th Nov. 1916.

1. The major operations are postponed indefinitely, and all efforts are now to be directed towards consolidation of the front system of trenches and improvement of accommodation and communication.

2. The 56th Bde. will be relieved by the 57th Bde. in the line tomorrow – 8th inst.

3. All reliefs will be carried out in accordance with the attached table. Any details not laid down herein will be settled between C.O.'s concerned.

4. Battalions will detail advance parties consisting of 1. officer and 16. O.R. to take over camps and dug-outs from the battalions which they are relieving. These parties will arrange to guide battalions into camp on completion of the relief.

5. Trench stores will be carefully checked and receipts taken on handing over. These receipts to be forwarded to Bde. H. Qrs. by 6 p.m. 9th inst. All trench boots and petrol tins will be taken out of the line, and not handed over to incoming battalions.

6. Battalions will find guides (1 officer and 17. O.R. each) as laid down in the table attached.

7. 20 pack animals per battalion will report to Battn. Transport Officers under arrangements to be made direct between these officers and the Staff Captain.

8. Brigade H. Qrs. will close at X. 2. a. 9. 8. on completion of the relief, and open at BONNET POST.

9. Reports on completion of the relief by wiring the word "DOUBLE".

10. ACKNOWLEDGE.

E. O. Sewell.
Captain
Brigade Major
56th Infantry Brigade.

Issued at 9.30. p.m.

Copies to :-

| | | | |
|---|---|---|---|
| 1. 19th Divn. 'G'. | 6 117th Infy. Bde. | 11. 56th M.G. Coy. | 16. G.O.C. |
| 2. 19th Divn. 'Q'. | 7. 7. R. LANC. R. | 12. 56th T.M.B. | 17. Staff Captain |
| 3. 56th Infy. Bde. | 8. 7. E. LAN. R. | 13. Signals | 18. Capt. HASSALL. |
| 4. 57th Infy. Bde. | 9. 7. S. LAN. R. | 14. 81st Fd. Coy. R.E. | 19. War Diary |
| 5. 58th Infy. Bde. | 10. 7. N. LAN. R. | 15. 82nd Fd. Coy. R.E. | 20. File. |

## TABLE of RELIEFS. Appendix to 56th Infy. Bde. Order No. 123.

| Unit. | From. | On relief by. | To. | Taking over from. | Guides. | Remarks. |
|---|---|---|---|---|---|---|
| 7. R. LANC. R. | Trenches (right subsector) | 10th WORCESTERS. | OVILLERS POST. | 10. R. WARWICKS. | GRAVEL PIT. R.27(c) centre at 5.30 p.m. | . |
| 7. E. LAN. R. | Trenches (right centre subsector) | 8th N. STAFFORDS. | Dugouts about X.2. a. and c. | 8th N. STAFFORDS. | Same place at 7.30. p.m. | . |
| 7. S. LAN. R. | Trenches (left centre subsector). | 10. R. WARWICKS. | GRAVEL PIT (R.27.c. central) ZOLLERN REDOUBT - JOSEPH, DANUBE and CONSTANCE trenches. | 10. WORCESTERS. | Junction of Road and Tramway, R.32. b.8.7. 2. Coys in SCHWABEN and BAINBRIDGE trenches at 5 p.m. 2 Coys f. front line 7 p.m. | This battalion will on completion of relief be at the disposal of G.O.C. 57th Bde. for tactical purposes. |
| 7. N. LAN. R. | Trenches (left subsector) | 8th. GLOUCESTERS. | NISSEN HUTS (W.13 a. 8.5.) | 8. GLOUCESTERS. | Same place. 3 Coys. in RANSOME - SPLOTTER and BAINBRIDGE TRENCHES at 5.30 p.m. 1 Coy. in Front line at 8. p.m. | . |
| 36th M.G. Coy. | Trenches. | 57th M.G. Coy. | Dugouts CRUCIFIX CORNER | 57th M.G. Coy. | .. | All details to be fixed by O.C.'s concerned. Reliefs to be completed by 6 p.m. |
| 56th T.M.B. | Trenches. | 57th T.M.B. | Dugouts. CRUCIFIX CORNER. | 57. T.M.B. | .. | |

[illegible]
Captain
Brigade Major
56th Infantry Brigade.

SECRET

Copy No: 10

No 56 COY. MACHINE GUN CORPS

56th Infantry Brigade Order No: 124.

Supplement to 56th Infantry Brigade Order No: 116 A.

11.11.16.

Reference:- 1/5,000 Special Sheets.
1/10,000 Special Map.
issued with Operation Order No: 116.A.

WAR DIARY. APP. 6.

1. Whilst the ultimate scope of the contemplated operations of the Fifth Army remains approximately the same, the attack will now be undertaken in stages.

2. The first stage only will take place on "zero" day which will be communicated separately. Zero hour will be notified later.
The second stage will take place subsequently, weather permitting, on Z plus 2 day, but the 1st Cavalry Division is not to take part.

3. The first stage consists of the capture by the II Corps ( 19th and 39th Divisions) of the line R.21.a.0.6½. (actually shown as '0.8' in 1/5,000 Map) - R.20.b.4.9. - R.14.c.9.0. - R.20.a.54 96. - HANSA Line.
In the case of the V Corps the first stage is the capture of BEAUCOURT SUR ANCRE and the high ground N.N.W. of that village.

4. The 56th Brigade will carry out the attack in the first stage of that portion of the above mentioned line which lies between our present front line at R.21.a.0.6½. and R.14.c.2.1.
The attack will be made by 7/E.Lan.R. and 7/N.Lan.R. the former being on the right.
7/E.Lan.R. will attack the line between R.21.a.0.6½. and track junction at R.20.b.05.92. inclusive and will, at the same time, establish posts in advance of this line as under:-

| | |
|---|---|
| O.G. 1<br>O.G. 2<br>LUCKY WAY | As far forward as possible and at least 100 yards in advance. |

7/N.Lan.R. will attack the portion of the line between R.20.b.05.32.(exclusive) to R.14.c.2.1.(inclusive) and will, at the same time, establish posts in advance of this line as under:-

| | |
|---|---|
| BATTERY VALLEY | Any convenient distance but as far forward as possible. |
| Trench leading North from R.20.a.54.96. | NOT more than 100 yards to the front. |

In both cases the attack will be delivered in two waves at an interval of 50 yards. "Cleaning up" parties will be detailed by Os.C. concerned from the troops under their Command.

5. Details of the artillery barrage programme will be communicated as soon as settled.

6. The Strong Point about R.20.a.6.2. which is too close to our present front line to be dealt with by the artillery will be subjected to a STOKES Mortar hurricane Bombardment immediately before the assault. O.C. 56th T.M.B. will arrange to construct the necessary platforms and register two guns by 4 p.m. to-morrow 12th inst., The hour of opening fire will be notified to O.C. 56th T.M.Bty. as soon as the barrage programme is fixed.

7. O.C. 56th M.G.Coy. will push 8 guns out in front of our present front line prior to zero hour, to cover the advance of the assaulting troops. As soon as the objective is gained, O.C. 56th M.G.Coy. will detail two guns each to report to Os.C. 7/E.Lan.R. and 7/N.Lan.R., and move under their orders. Each of these pairs of guns will be under the command of an officer.

8. Flares will be shown at the following times:-
Zero plus 35 minutes, Zero plus 1 hour.
They will NOT be shown on reaching the objective.

9. The captured line will be consolidated by the assaulting Battalions as far as possible during the hours of daylight.

Two Companies 5th S.W.B.(Pioneers) are allotted to the Brigade to assist in consolidation.

As soon as it is dark one Company will report to O.C. 7/E.Lan.R. with a view to digging a trench across the gap between R.21.a.0.6½. and R.20.b.4.9.

One Company will report to O.C. 7/N.Lan.R. and will similarly dig a trench across the gap between R.14.c.9.0. and R.20.a.54.96.

Os. C. the respective Coys will report to H.Qrs. 7/E.Lan.R. and 7/N.Lan.R. respectively, not later than 2-30 p.m. in order that they may receive instructions as to the details of the work to be executed.

Communication with the new line will be opened up as far as possible, via O.G.1 on the right, and either the trench running N.N.W. from R.20.a.6.2. or that leading down BATTERY VALLEY on the left.

10. Strong Points will be constructed in the sector allotted to 7/E.Lan.R. at or near the junction of the new trench with O.G.1 and LUCKY WAY. In the sector allotted to 7/N.Lan.R. at or near the junction of the new trench with BATTERY VALLEY and about R.14.c.3.0.

O.C. 81st Fd. Coy. will detail one section to report to 7/E.Lan.R. and 1 section to 7/N.Lan.R.. The Officers in command of these sections will report to H.Qrs. the resp ective Battalions not later than 6 p.m. to-morrow 12th inst..

11. The 56th Infy Bde will relieve the two Battalions of the 57th Infy Bde now holding the left and left-centre subsectors, on the night prior to zero day in accordance with orders to be issued separately. When this relief has been completed, troops will be assembled as under:-

7/E.Lan.R. First wave: In front of STUFF TRENCH between R.21.a.0.6½. and R.20.b.1.2½.(inclusive)
Second wave: Immediately in rear of STUFF TRENCH between the same two points.

7/N.Lan.R. First wave: In front of STUFF TRENCH between R.20.b.1.2½.(exclusive) and R.20.a.½.1. (inclusive)
Second wave: Immediately in rear of STUFF TRENCH (AND 7/N.Lan.R.) between the same two points.

Os. C. 7/E.Lan.R./will arrange to leave room in front of STUFF TRENCH for the M.Gs. referred to in para: 7.

7/R.Lanc.R. will be in reserve:-
2 Coys: in BAINBRIDGE TRENCH 2 Coys in SCHWABEN TRENCH.
Battn H.Qrs. in ZOLLERN TRENCH WEST at R.26.1.0.3.

7/S.Lan. R., 56th M.G.Coy.(less the 8 guns referred to in para: 7) and remaining guns of 56th T.M.B. will remain in their present positions but will be in a state of readiness to move as required after zero hour.

12. The Tanks allotted to 19th Division will be reserved for use in the second stage of the operations.

13. With the exception of this Brigade and attached troops mentioned above, no troops of the 19th Division are to be moved up to places of assembly.

At same time, should a favourable situation arise on Zero day, it is the intention of the II Corps to take advantage of it. The 56th Brigade will be prepared to make a further advance and the 57th Bde. to carry out original programme of 57th Brigade in conjunction with the Divisions on the right at a later hour on "Z" day, should orders be issued for this advance.

14. The instructions, previo usly issued as to equipment, liaison, (so far as 7/N.Lan.R. is concerned), and administration will continue to apply, so far as the modification of the scheme admits.

Armlets will not now be worn.

15. Watches of assaulting troops will be synchronised from Bde: H.Qrs. at 12 midnight Y/Z days and 3 a.m. Z morning, under arrangements of the Brigade Signalling Officer.

16. Brigade Battle H.Qrs. will be at R.26.b.3.3. A visual station and relay post for runners will be established at R.20.b.3.3. in STUFF TRENCH at 1 hour before zero.

17. <u>ACKNOWLEDGE</u>.

Captain.
Brigade Major.
56th Infantry Brigade.

Issued at 7 pm

Copies to:-

1. 19th Division "G"
2. 19th Division "Q"
3. 57th Infy Bde.
4. 58th Infy Bde.
5. 118th Infy Bde.
6. 7/R.Lanc.R.
7. 7/E.Lan. R.
8. 7/S.Lan. R.
9. 7/N.Lan. R.
10. 56th M.G.Coy.
11. 56th T.M.Bty.
12. 81st Fd. Coy. R.E.
13. A.D.M.S. 19th Division.
14. 5th South Wales Borderers.
15. Signals.
16. C.R.A. 19th Division.
17. G.O.C.
18. Staff Captain.
19. Captain Hassall.
20. War Diary.
21. File.

**SECRET** Addendum to 56th Infantry Brigade Order No: 124. COPY NO: 10
12th November 1916

"Artillery Barrage Arrangements"

1. The timing of the barrage will be exactly the same in the initial stages as laid down for the original plan of operations under 19th Division No: G.54/4/16, of 28th October.

2. That is to say, that up till 0.24, the barrage along the whole Divisional front will roll back as before and then remain stationary on the line of the original "first objective".

3. In addition, however, six extra 18-pr batteries of the 11th Divisional Artillery have been allotted to the 19th Division. These batteries will at zero hour form standing barrages on various trenches in or near the objective. As the rolling barrage reaches these points, the standing barrages will join it and roll back with it until a line of 300 yds North of the objective is reached. They will then form a protective barrage on this line for half an hour, i.e. till 0.42, after which there will be a further lift of 300 yds.

4. The Warwick Battery R.H.A. will enfilade the LUCKY WAY keeping 100 yds in advance of the rolling barrage and subsequently continuing to enfilade this trench (outside the limits laid down for the protective barrage in para: 3) and the trench - R.15.a.95.40. - R.15.b.4.6½ - R.15.b.70.95.

5. The 56th T.M.B. will open fire at zero hour on the point R.20.a.6.2. at the rate of 15 rounds per gun per minute and will continue for two ~~four~~ minutes. At zero plus ~~four~~ two minutes ~~when the artillery barrage begins to roll back~~ the T.M.B. will cease fire and the Infantry will rush the strong point.

Captain.
Brigade Major.
56th Infantry Brigade.

Issued at 11 a.m.

(Distribution as fo r Order No: 124)

WAR DIARY. APP. ~~6~~ 7

**SECRET**

Copy No. 10.

56th Infantry Brigade Order No: 125
11th November 1916.

NO 56 COY. MACHINE GUN CORPS.

Reference:- BEAUMONT Trench Map 1/5,000.

1. The 56th Infantry Brigade will relieve the two Battalions of the 57th Infy Bde in the left-centre and left subsectors of the Divl: front, R.21.a.3.7. to R.20.a.1 to-morrow night 12th inst.

2. Moves will take place in accordance with the attached table. All details other than those laid down herein will be settled between C.Os. concerned. On completion of the moves the Brigade will occupy the positions of assembly laid down in Bde. Order No: 124, para: 11. In the case of 7/E.Lan.R. and 7/N.Lan.R., men will on no account enter the trenches with the exception of the men detailed by O.C. 7/E.Lan.R. ________________, to hold the line between his right at R.21.a.3.7. and the right of his advance at R.21.a.0.6½.

3. C.Os. concerned will impress on all ranks the importance of absolute silence during the advance to, and when in occupation of, the position of assembly. Bayonets will not be fixed until the artillery barrage opens.

4. Os.C. 7/E.Lan.R. and 7/N.Lan.R. will push forward small parties with LEWIS Guns to c over their front during the night. These will be withdrawn under cover of darkness not less than 45 minutes before zero hour.

5. Guides for Battalions going into the line will meet them at the junction of the Road and Tramway R.32.b.7.8. as under:-

| Guides for: | From: | Time: |
|---|---|---|
| 7/N. Lan. R. | 8th Gloucesters | 5-0 p.m. |
| 7/E.Lan. R. | 10th R.Warwicks: | 5-30 p.m. |

6. 15 pack animals each for 7/E.Lan.R. and 7/N.Lan.R. will be at CRUCIFIX CORNER at 3-30 p.m. to-morrow 12th inst, to convey stores to the line. Guides will be sent to meet these animals and lead them to the respective Headquarters.
Transport Officers of 7/E.Lan.R. and 7/N.Lan.R. will arrange to convey 17 "hot boxes" per battalion to the H.Qrs. of their respective Battalions in the line at about midnight. These hot boxes will be filled with the "OXO" which has already been issued, and which will be distributed to the men prior to zero hour.
8 pack animals for 7/R.Lanc.R. will be at CRUCIFIX CORNER at 12 midnight 12th/13th inst., a guide should be sent to meet them.

7. Seperate instructions have already been issued as to the equipment and stores to be carried on the man.
Ankle boots and not gum boots will be worn during the operation.

8. Reports to present Brigade H.Qrs. up to 5 p.m. after that hour to Brigade Battle H.Qrs. R.26.b.3.3.

E. O. [signature]
Captain.
Brigade Major.
56th Infantry Brigade.

Issued at 10-30 p.m.

| Copy No: | To: | Copy No: | To: |
|---|---|---|---|
| 1 | 19th Division "G" | 12 | 81st Fd. Coy. R.E. |
| 2 | 19th Division "Q" | 13 | Signals. |
| 3 | 57th Infy Bde | 14 | 5th S.Wales Borderers. |
| 4 | 58th Infy Bde | 15 | C.R.A. 19th Division. |
| 5 | 118th Infy Bde | 16 | A.D.M.S. " |
| 6 | 7/R.Lanc.R. | 17 | G.O.C. |
| 7 | 7/E.Lan. R. | 18 | Staff Captain. |
| 8 | 7/S.Lan. R. | 19 | Captain Hassall. |
| 9 | 7/N.Lan. R. | 20 | War Diary |
| 10 | 56th M.G.Coy. | 21 | File. |
| 11 | 56th T.M.Bty. | | |

# TABLE OF MOVES. Appendix to 56th Bde ORDER No. 125.

| Unit | From | Handing over to | To | Taking over from | Remarks |
|---|---|---|---|---|---|
| 7. E. Lan. R. | OVILLERS POST HUTS. | 7. S. Lan. R. | Trenches (left centre sub-sector) R. 21. a. 5 ? to R. 20. b 1. 2½ | 10. R. Warwicks (part of). | Battalions of 57th Bde are adjusting their frontages under arrangements of G.O.C. 57th Bde. prior to relief |
| 7. N. Lan. R. | DONNET POST. Nissen Huts | 'A' Bn: 57th Infy: Bde. | Trenches (left sub-sector) R. 20. b. 1. 2½ to R. 20. a. 1. 1. | 8. Gloucesters. 10. R. Warwicks (part of) | |
| 7. S. Lan. R. | OVILLERS POST Road Nissen Huts. | "B" Bn: 57th Infy: Bde. | OVILLERS POST HUTS. | 7. E. Lan. R. | Move to be completed by 5.30 p.m. |
| 7 R. Lanc. R. | WOOD POST and LEIPZIG REDOUBT. | — | BAINBRIDGE and SCHWABEN Trenches. | — | Move to be completed by 5.15 a.m. on the morning of ZERO day. O/c 7 R. Lanc. R. will arrange to have breakfast before moving off from WOOD POST. |
| 56th M. G. Coy. | AVELUY. | — | Trenches | 57th M. G. Coy | Details to be fixed between C.O.'s concerned. |
| 56th T. M. B. | CRUCIFIX CORNER dug-out | — | Trenches | 57th T. M. B. | |
| 2 Sections 81st Field Coy. R.E. | Dug-outs in W. 12. a | — | Trenches | — | These sections will move into positions of assembly as ordered by O.C. 7 E. Lan. R. and 7 N. Lan. R. in accordance with Bde. Order No 124 para 10. |

All movement during hours of daylight to be by platoons at 200 yards interval.

[illegible] Captain.
Brigade Major.
56th Infantry Brigade

Copy No 5

# 7th East Lancashire Regiment

## Operation Order No 5

WAR DIARY

12/11/16



APP. 8.

Ref Grandcourt Map 1/5000 Edit 4

(I) INFORMATION (a) The original programmes issued with Operation Order No 4 of 31/10.16 will now be undertaken in stages

(b) The first stage will take place on ZERO DAY. ZERO hour to be notified later.

(c) In the event of a decisive success as regards operation by V Corps on our left it is possible that this success may be exploited by further action on that day.

(II) OBJECTIVES. (a) In the first stage the BRIGADE less 7/Kings Own & 7th S. Lancs. objective is (RIGHT) R21.a.0.8 – (LEFT) R14.c.2.1 (off the Map) 7th EAST LANCS. on the right 7th NORTH LANCS on the left

(b) The Battalion objective being (right) R21.a.0.8 – (left) track junc. R20.b.½.9 both inclusive, with advance POSTS along O.G.1 and LUCKY WAY.

(c) 6th Wilts Regt co-operates with rifle & Lewis Gun action on our right from STUFF TRENCH

(d) The attack will be carried out by D. C & B Coys. A Coy will remain in STUFF TRENCH between R21.a.0.8 and R20.b.1.2½ (both inclusive)

(III) DISPOSITIONS D Coy to attack in one line disposed in groups of platoons; each platoon extended to one pace. Right Platoon with its right on O.G.1 to reach about R20.b.8.9 (200 yards North of STUFF TRENCH) Two centre platoons to occupy incomplete trench which extends from (roughly) R20 b.7.8 to R20 b 5.7½ (175-200 yds NORTH of STUFF TRENCH)

Left platoon with its left on LUCKY WAY to reach junction of LUCKY WAY and C.T. R20.b.4.9 inclusive.

'C' Coy to pass over LUCKY WAY and occupy Communication Trench from R20 b.4.9 — track junction (probably not recognisable on the ground) R 20 b.½ 9 both inclusive; and to be extended on this frontage (i.e 200 YDS)

'B' Coy in rear of 'C' Coy at a distance of 30 y... will advance with its right directly behind that of C Coy and its left approximately behind the centre of that Coy. (frontage 100 YDS roughly)

Then dropping into LUCKY WAY it will clear that sunken road from R20.b.2.7 North eastwards whilst taking due precautions to clear it also to the south west.

NOTE In all cases any unknown dugouts or trenches not hitherto detected must be dealt with on the initiative of Company or other Commanders

REGIMENTAL BOMBERS 2 squads will advance in file astride 'C' Coy with head immediately behind the right flank of D Coy clearing that C.T en route and making it their object to gain the trench junction with LUCKY WAY at R14.d.8.2

2 squads to advance extended at one yard interval simultaneously with and on the immediate right of B Coy and on arrival in LUCKY WAY to precede that Coy whilst clearing up LUCKY WAY North eastward to trench junction R 14 d.8.2 (i.e joining hands there with the other two squads

Blocks will be at once established in either case at the furtherest point gained but no advance should be made beyond that junction

LEWIS GUNS of

A Coy one about R ~~14~~ 21.a.0.8 the other about R20 b 1.2½

D Coy one immediately in rear of and to co-operate with Regimental Bombers along O.G, one with 2 centre platoons and one at disposal of O.C. Coy

'C' Coy guns to be equally distributed along the Company front.

B Coy. One on right of Company to co-operate with Regimental Bombers up LUCKY WAY the other being left at disposal of O.C Coy

(V)

CO-OPERATION of OTHER ARMS

(a) Artillery Barrage will be notified later

(b) Machine Guns will be pushed out in advance of STUFF TRENCH prior to ZERO hour and thence will move at first opportunity one to O.G1, R20 b.8.5½ where it is intended to establish a strong point. The other to drop into LUCKY WAY at R20.b.2.7 and later to gain the trench junction R20 b.4.9 where another strong point will be established

(c) R.E section prior to ZERO hour will be accommodated in STUFF TRENCH in immediate vicinity of Battalion H.Qrs dugout R20 b.5½.5 in order to establish after dark strong points in O.G1 at R20 b.8.7½ and in LUCKY WAY R20.b.4.9

(d) PIONEERS. 1 Coy S.W.B (pioneers) will immediately after a tk assist D Coy in digging a trench across the gap between R21.a.0.8 and LUCKY WAY

(V) CONSOLIDATION

(a) The captured line is to be consolidated as far as feasible during hours of day light

(b) All consolidation will be protected by covering parties thrown forward to a distance of at least 30 yards.

(VI) On night Y/Z the Battalion will take over trench line from R21 a.3.7 to R20.b.1.2½ in order from Right to left A.D.C.B. Movements immediately prior to ZERO hour will be notified later

(VII) Capt Palmer and 2 runners from "A" Coy will report to O.C 7/North Lancs Regt tomorrow for instructions by 12 noon.

(VIII) TIME

Watches will be synchronized at 12 midnight Y/Z days and 3AM Z [illegible] morning

(IX) Flares — Flares will be shown at the following times only (ZERO + 35 minutes) and (ZERO + 1 hour)

They will not be shown on reaching the objective

(X) REPORT CENTRE — Reports to Battalion H.Q in dug out off STUFF TRENCH at R 20 b. 5½. 5

(XI) ACKNOWLEDGE

(Sd) T. G. J. TORRIE Lt Colonel
CMDG. 7th EAST LANC REGT

Issued at 8 AM to

(1) 56th Infantry Bde
(2) 6th Wilts (thro 58th Infy Bde)
(3) 7th North Lancs Rgt
(4) 5th South Wales Brdrs
(5) 56th M. G. Coy } thro 56th Infy Bde
(6) 81 Field Coy R E }
(7) Captain Palmer
(8) A Coy
(9) B Coy
(10) C Coy
(11) D Coy
(12) Bombing Officer
(13) Headquarters
(14) WAR DIARY

"A" Form. Army Form C.2121 (in pads of 100).

## MESSAGES AND SIGNALS.

No. of Message ..............

| Prefix ........ Code ........ m. | Words | Charge | This message is on a/c of: | Recd. at ........ m. |
|---|---|---|---|---|
| Office of Origin and Service Instructions. | Sent | | ........ Service. | Date ........ |
| | At ........ m. | | | From ........ |
| | To ........ | | | |
| | By ........ | | (Signature of "Franking Officer.") | By ........ |

NO 56 COY. MACHINE GUN CORPS

TO: 7 E. Lan. R. | 7 S. Lan. R. | 56 M.G. Coy. | 56 T.M.B. | 2/7th Worcesters.

| Sender's Number. | Day of Month. | In reply to Number. | AAA |
|---|---|---|---|
| * BM. 715/3. | 18. 11. 16 | | |

Ref.ce orders No 132(1) the scope of ~~[illegible]~~ frontage is now extended. After 1½ hours halt after gaining objective further advance is to be made in an Easterly direction through GRANDCOURT by 56th & 57th Bdes the second objective being the line of road running from R.9 c 9½.0 to R.9 b.20.25

(2) The dividing line between Bdes will be the same road.

(3) The attack on the first objective will now be carried out by 7 S. Lan. R. complete. One platoon will move by the cutway as already detailed. One company will now be employed on carrying. The original orders will be amended in respect to these alterations.

(4) The attack on the second objective will also be carried out by 7 S. Lan. R. in accordance with detailed instructions

From

Place

Time

*The above may be forwarded as now corrected.* (Z)

*Censor.* Signature of Addressor or person authorised to telegraph in his name.

* This line should be erased if not required.

750,000. W 2186—M509. H. W. & V., Ld. 6/16.

"A" Form.

# MESSAGES AND SIGNALS.

No.

Prefix ............ Code ............ m. | Words | Charge

Office of Origin and Service Instructions.

Sent

At ............ m.

To ............

By ............

*This message is on a/c of:*

............ *Service.*

(Signature of "Franking Officer.")

Recd. at ............ m.

Date ............

From ............

By ............

TO

| Sender's Number. | Day of Month. | In reply to Number. | AAA |
|---|---|---|---|
| * BM 715/3 | (continued) | | |

being carried out verbally

(5) The attack on BAILLESCOURT FARM will be carried out by 7th E. Lanc. R. in accordance with verbal instructions already issued

(6) The attack mentioned in paras 4 and 5 above will be carried out by infantry and in conformity with the artillery barrage programme which will be as under

Zero + 1.55 all guns firing on GRANDCOURT will cease fire

2.00 Standing barrage on the line R.9.c.3.3 – R.9.a.0.0 will open [illegible] for 4 minutes, then will creep forwards off the village at the rate of 50 yards in 4 minutes till on line 200 yds East of

From

Place

Time

*The above may be forwarded as now corrected.*

(Z)

*Censor.*

Signature of Addressor or person authorised to telegraph in his name.

* This line should be erased if not required.

750,000. W 2186—M509. H. W. & V., Ld. 6/16.

"A" Form.
Army Form C.2121
(in pads of 100).

# MESSAGES AND SIGNALS.

No. of Message..................

| Prefix ........ Code ............ m. | Words | Charge | This message is on a/c of: | Recd. at .............. m. |
|---|---|---|---|---|
| Office of Origin and Service Instructions. | Sent | | ............................ Service. | Date .................. |
| .................................... | At ................ m. | | | From .................. |
| .................................... | To .................. | | | |
| .................................... | By .................. | | (Signature of "Franking Officer.") | By .................... |

TO

| Sender's Number. | Day of Month. | In reply to Number. | AAA |
|---|---|---|---|
| * BM 715/S (contd) | | | |

the objective which it will hold for 1 hour
2 sections of [illegible] trench mortar battery will
be formed at BAILLESCOURT FARM which
with help of 4 [illegible] 7 E Lan R will
attack and mop up the Farm

7. O C 56 M G Coy will detail 2 guns
to report to O C 7 E Lan R prior to
zero hour and operate under his
orders. These guns will not be taken
from the 4 guns detailed under para 11
of Bde order No 132 for forward work

8. O C 56 T M B will as far as possible
avoid any expenditure of ammunition
prior to the attack on the 2nd objective.
During the attack he will detail the
two guns already placed under orders of
O C 7 S Lan R to come under his
orders.

9. 82nd Fd Coy R.E. will [illegible]
after the capture of the final objective

From
Place
Time

The above may be forwarded as now corrected. (Z)

.................................... Censor. Signature of Addressor or person authorised to telegraph in his name.

* This line should be erased if not required.

750,000. W 2186—M509. H. W. & V., Ld. 6/16.

"A" Form.

**MESSAGES AND SIGNALS.**

Army Form C.2121
(in pads of 100).
No. of Message ..........

| Prefix ........ Code ........ m. | Words | Charge | This message is on a/c of: | Recd. at ........ m. |
|---|---|---|---|---|
| Office of Origin and Service Instructions. | | | .................... Service. | Date .......... |
| | Sent | | | From .......... |
| | At ........ m. | | | |
| | To .......... | | | |
| | By .......... | | (Signature of "Franking Officer.") | By .......... |

TO

| Sender's Number. | Day of Month. | In reply to Number. | AAA |
|---|---|---|---|
| * BM 715/S | continued | | |

and bridge the river in R 9 for the attack on BAILLESCOURT FARM.

10 Tanks are to be used for the attack on 2nd and 3rd objectives.

11 HQ 7 E Lan R will now be established with HQ 7 V Lan R at R 13 b 6½ ½

[illegible signature]
Capt.
Brigade Major 56th Inf Bde

Issued at 3.15 am

Copies to. 7 E Lan R — 56 M G Coy
7 V Lan R — 56 T M B
2/7 Worcesters

| From | | | |
|---|---|---|---|
| Place | | | |
| Time | | | |

*The above may be forwarded as now corrected.* — (Z)

Censor. — Signature of Addressor or person authorised to telegraph in his name.

* This line should be erased if not required.

750,000. W 2186—M509. H. W. & V., Ld. 6/16.

**Secret.** 56th Infantry Brigade Order No. 132.

Reference 1/10.000. Operation Map issued 31/10/16.



WAR DIARY. No 9.

1. The II Corps is now to capture O.G.1, O.G.2. and DESIRE TRENCHES at a zero day-hour to be notified separately.

2. The 19th Division is to capture the line R.15.c.8.8 (exclusive) - R.15.a.5.1. - R.15.a.1.0 - R.8.d.5.1. - R.8.d.7.2. - R.8.d.6.4 - R.8.d.4.8.

3. The 18th Division is attacking on the right and V Corps on the left of the 19th Division.

4. The attack of the 19th Division is to be carried out by the 57th Brigade and 1 battalion 56th Brigade. This Battn. will be 7.S.LAN.R (less 1 Coy.).

5. The 57th Brigade is to form up on the frontage STUMP ROAD (exclusive) to R.14.c.0.1. The right boundary of their attack will be STUMP ROAD (exclusive) - R.15.c.5½.4½. - R.15.c.8.8. (exclusive)

6. The objective allotted to 7.S.LAN.R is the line R.8.d.6½.4 (exclusive) - R.8.d.4.8. inclusive.

7. The attack of 7.S.LAN.R will be carried out as under:-

(a) Two Coys. will attack up the line of the HANSA ROAD and establish themselves on their objective.
One platoon will advance along the line of the railway from BEAUCOURT MILL to R.8.d.4.8. and will gain touch at that point with the V. Corps on the left.
Three platoons will furnish a carrying party in accordance with para.9

(b) The rolling barrage will open at zero on a line 200 yards in front of the line held by 57th Brigade. The left flank of this barrage will be on the approximate line R.14.c.4.4 - R.8.c.4.8.
The barrage will remain stationary for four minutes and then role forward at the rate of 100 yards every two minutes.

On reaching the line of DESIRE TRENCH and a continuation of that line Westwards - i.e. about 400 yards in front of the 57th Brigade line - the barrage will pause for six minutes, when it will go forward at the same pace as before.
It will lift off the large dug.out at R.14.a.4.8 at 0.24.
It will roll on to the railway and will then cease.

There will in addition be a standing barrage on supposed dug-out at R. 14. a. 4 8, which will last at zero and lift off with a rolling barrage at 0.24.

(c) The two Coys. of 7 S. LAN. R. will advance in platoon waves at 50 yards distance – so that the leading platoon reaches a point 200 yards West of the dug-out referred to above at 0.24. When the barrage lifts off that point – these Coys. will advance and seize their objective.

(d.) The platoon moving up the railway embankment will advance so as to be 200 yards W. of the railway bridge at R. 8. c. 4. 6 at 0.32. As soon as the barrage ceases – this platoon will advance to the point R. 8. d. 4 8 and gain touch at that point in accordance with (a) above.

8. The captured line will be consolidated by 7. S. LAN. R when gained. Strong points will be established at R. 8. d. 6. 4. and at R. 8. d. 8. 8. Two sections 81st F.T Coy R.E. will assist 7. S. LAN. R. in this work. One section will move up the railway in rear of the platoon detailed to move along the embankment – the other section following in rear of the last wave of the two Coys. on HANSA ROAD.

A switch line is to be dug on the night after the attack from about R. 13. b. 9. 8 to R. 14. b. 5½. 3½. This work will be done by 24th MANCHESTER Regt. All ranks will be warned that this Battalion is attached to the Divn. for this purpose.

9. The 3 platoons 7 S. LAN. R. for carrying will be formed up at the dump at R. 13. c. 7. 7. at ZERO. Twelve mules will be at the same point. The whole of this party will move under the directions of Capt. A. B. HASSALL – 9th CHESHIRE Regt: and will establish a dump of Mills grenades and Stokes mortar bombs at the Western entrance to GRANDCOURT VILLAGE.

10. Two guns of 56th T.M.B. with spare teams in addition will move in rear of 7. S. LAN. R. As many rounds as possible will be carried by these teams. O/c. 56. T.M.B. will cooperate with 7. S. LAN R. on the left of 57th Brigade as the situation demands.

11. O/C 56th M.G. Coy. will detail two guns to report to O/C 7. S. LAN. R. at his H.Q. by 5.30. a.m. and move under his orders.

4 guns of 56. M.G. Coy. now in the line will move forward to the crest of the ridge immediately E. of their present emplacements as soon as the barrage clears these advance points, and will cooperate under arrangements of O/C 56. M.G. Coy. in covering the advance of the 57th Brigade and 7. S. LAN. R.

12. Troops for the attack will assemble by 5.30. a.m. as under:-
2 coys. 7. S. LAN. R. on HANSA ROAD about R. 13. b. 3. 5.
1 platoon 7. S. LAN. R at BEAUCOURT MILL.
56. T.M.B. and 81st Fd. Coy. in rear of 7. S. LAN. R. as detailed above.
Carrying party and mules at the Brigade dump.

13. Flares will be shown at ZERO + 1 and ZERO + 2, and also at any other time when demanded by the contact patrol aeroplane.

14. Cleaning-up parties should be warned to search for GERMAN listening apparatus in any deep dug-outs which may be captured.

15. Tanks are being used to assist the attack of the 57th Bde.

16. Brigade H.Q. will remain as at present (Q. 24. b. 9. 9.)
An advanced visual signalling station and relay post for runners will be established at R. 13. b. 1. 2 about 100 yards South of HANSA Road. This will be manned under orders of 2/Lt. RIDGWAY half an hour before ZERO.

H.Q. 7. S. LAN. R. – dug-out in HANSA LINE at R. 13. b. 6½. ½.
Regtl. Aid Post - 7. S. LAN. R – Q. 18. d. 9½. ½.

17. Reports to Bde. H.Q. or advanced report centre as above.

18. ACKNOWLEDGE.

Issued at 11.15 p.m.

E. Atwell. [signature] Captain
Brigade Major
56th Infantry Brigade

Copies to :-

| | | | |
|---|---|---|---|
| 1. 19th Divn. "G". | 7. 7. R. Lanc. R. | 13. No. 4. M.M.G.B. | 19. Capt. Hassall. |
| 2. " "Q". | 8. 7. E. Lan. R. | 14. 2/7 Worcesters. | 20. War Diary |
| 3. 57th Infy. Bde. | 9. 7. S. Lan. R | 15. Signals. | 21. File |
| 4. 63rd Infy. Bde. | 10. 7. N. Lan. R. | 16. 81st Fd. Coy. R.E. | |
| 5. C.R.A. 18th Divn. | 11. 56th M.G. Coy. | 17. G.O.C. | |
| 6. C.R.A. 19th Divn. | 12. 56th T.M.B. | 18. Staff Captain | |

**WAR DIARY**
~~or~~
~~**INTELLIGENCE SUMMARY**~~.
*(Erase heading not required.)*

Instructions regarding War Diaries and Intelligence Summaries are contained in F. S. Regs., Part II. and the Staff Manual respectively. Title pages will be prepared in manuscript.

Army Form C. 2118.

56 M G Coy

Vol 15

| Place | Date | Hour | Summary of Events and Information | Remarks and references to Appendices |
|---|---|---|---|---|
| DOMESMONT | 1-12-16 | | Progressive training begun, in conjunction with sports & recreation | mg |
| Do. | 2-12-16 | | Continued | mg |
| Do | 3-12-16 | | Do Lieut M. JOSEPH (from 10th Coy) takes over as 2nd in command | mg |
| Do | 4-12-16 | | Training continued; shortage of men renders this difficult | mg |
| Do | 5-12-16 | | Do | mg |
| Do | 6-12-16 | | Do. (6-12-16 to 10-12-16) | mg |
| Do | 7-12-16 | | | mg |
| Do | 8-12-16 | | | mg |
| Do | 9-12-16 | | | mg |
| Do | 10-12-16 | | | mg |
| Do | 11-12-16 | | Reinforcements - three drivers; Company in training | mg |
| Do | 12-12-16 | | Reinforcements 14 other ranks. do. | mg |
| Do | 13-12-16 | | | mg |
| Do | 14-12-16 | | | mg |
| Do | 15 | | | mg |
| Do | 16 | | Corps M. G. Officer (Lt Col. BADHAM) inspects the Company at work and on the range. | mg |
| Do | 17 | | Training continued and intersection football | mg |
| Do | 18 | | do. very cold day | mg |
| Nr. BERNEVIL | 19 | | Company inspected with 7 L.N.L Regt. by the Corps Commander | mg |

A5834 Wt. W4973/M687 750,000 8/16 D. D. & L. Ltd. Forms/C.2118/13.

Instructions regarding War Diaries and Intelligence Summaries are contained in F. S. Regs., Part II. and the Staff Manual respectively. Title pages will be prepared in manuscript.

# WAR DIARY

~~or~~

~~INTELLIGENCE SUMMARY.~~

*(Erase heading not required.)*

Army Form C. 2118.

| Place | Date 12-16 | Hour | Summary of Events and Information | Remarks and references to Appendices |
|---|---|---|---|---|
| DOMESMONT | 20 | | Training and recreation continued; inclemency of weather hampers progress: (32 other ranks reported for duty on the 19th) | MJ |
| do | 21 | | | MJ |
| do | 22 | | Training<br>do | MJ |
| do | 23 | | do | MJ |
| do | 24 | | do<br>do | MJ |
| do | 25 | | Christmas day spent quietly 2/Lt. BONNYMAN reports for duty | MJ |
| do | 26 | | Company canteen started. | MJ |
| do | 27 | | Three other ranks report for duty Company now at full strength. | MJ |
| do | 28 | | Training (advanced) and football | MJ |
| do | 29 | | do | MJ |
| do | 30 | | do | MJ |
| do | 31 | | do | MJ |

A5834 Wt. W4973/M687 750,000 8/16 D. D. & L. Ltd. Forms/C.2118/13.

Army Form C. 2118.

56 M Gun Coy

Vol 16

Instructions regarding War Diaries and Intelligence Summaries are contained in F. S. Regs., Part II. and the Staff Manual respectively. Title pages will be prepared in manuscript.

# WAR DIARY

~~or~~

~~INTELLIGENCE SUMMARY.~~

(Erase heading not required.)

| Place | Date JAN 17 | Hour | Summary of Events and Information | Remarks and references to Appendices |
|---|---|---|---|---|
| DOMESMONT | 1 | | Advanced training continued in conjunction with recreation | MG |
| " | 2 | | Do | MG |
| " | 3 | | Do | MG |
| " | 4 | | Do | MG |
| " | 5 | | Do | MG |
| " | 6 | | Do | MG |
| " | 7 | | Do | MG |
| " | 8 | | Preparations made for moving up to the line | MG |
| " | 9 | 7.30 am | Company marched to BEAUQUESNES: in billets for the night | MG |
| BEAUQUESNE | 10 | – | Marched via AUTHIE & ST LEGER to COIGNEUX: Company in huts. | MG |
| COIGNEUX | 11 | | Company in Divl Rese: improvements on camp &c begun | MG |
| " | 12 | | Company carried on with work and as far as possible training | MG |
| | 13 to 21 | | Do. | MG |
| | | | Preliminary reconnaissance of trenches in HEBUTERNE Sector | MG |
| HEBUTERNE and BAVENCOURT | 22 | | Marched from COIGNEUX to BAVENCOURT and took over from 57 M. G. Coy* in the HEBUTERNE Sector: Coy Hq. at BAVENCOURT, Adv. Hq. in HEBUTERNE. | MG |
| | 23 | | Company in the trenches; situation fairly quiet: 16 guns in the line | MG |
| " | 24 | | Do | MG |
| " | 25 | | Intersection Relief: No 3 Section relieved No 4 Section | MG |
| " | 26 | | Indirect fire carried out by night on tracks behind enemy lines. | MG |
| " | 27 | | Do: Situation normal: weather during this period very cold dry & fine | MG |
| " | 28 | | Intersection Relief: No 2 Section relieved No 1 Section. | MG |
| " | 29+30 | | Situation normal: indirect fire continued: weather still very cold: frosty | MG |
| " | 31 | | Intersection Relief: No 1 Section relieved No 4 Section | MG |

* See APPENDIX A and Operation Order 1A dated 21-1-17

A5834 Wt. W4973/M687 750,000 8/16 D. D. & L. Ltd. Forms/C.2118/13.

APPENDIX A W.D. JAN 17.

9.

# 56 COY M.G. CORPS

2[illegible] 1. 17

## OPERATION ORDER NO. 1A

References { Sheet 57.D. N.E. 1/20,000
{ Trench Map HEBUTERNE 1/10,000

1. RELIEF 56 Coy M.G. Corps will relieve 57 Coy M.G. Corps in Trenches & billets during the 22nd inst.

2. PARADE The Company will parade for trenches at 11 AM. Packs will be taken into trenches but no Blankets. Belt Boxes & belts will be taken over from 57 Coy. Guns, Tripods, Spare Parts & cleaning material will be the only gear taken into the trenches. Guns will be two thirds filled with a mixture of Water & Glycerine before parade. Each Group will pack all gear on to one limber & march as a unit. On leaving SAILLY Groups will move off at 3 minutes intervals. H.Qrs & Remainder of No. 4 Sect. Cooks etc will parade separately & march to BAYENCOURT (which will be Coy. H.Qrs) leaving at 11.30.

3. GUIDES Guides one per Gun will be met at the Cross Roads, HEBUTERNE & will guide Guns to their positions.

4. GROUPING OF GUNS.

| | |
|---|---|
| Left Group | Nos. 1, 1A, 2, 3 & 4 under 2Lt BLACKWOOD. Four guns of No. 1 Sectn & 1 gun of No. 3 Sectn |
| Centre Group | No. 5, The KEEP (2 Guns) & KELLERMAN under 2Lt FLAVELL with No. 4 Sect. |
| Right Group | Nos. 6 & 8, HOPE & PELLISIER under LT COOPER with No. 2 Sectn. |

5. GUMBOOTS Sectns will call at Divl Gum Boot Store in SAILLY & draw Gum Boots.

6. STORES Team commanders will check trench stores & sign for same afterwards sending down a list of all stores taken over.

ISSUED AT 3.P.M.

COPIES.

1. 57 Coy M.G. CORPS
2. LT. COOPER
3. LT. FLOOD
4. 2LT. FLAVELL
5. -do- BLACKWOOD
6. C.S.M.
7. C.Q.M.S.
8. FILE
9. WAR DIARY

G. B. Purvis CAPT.
56 COY M.G. CORPS

Army Form C. 2118.

56 M G Coy

Vol 17

Instructions regarding War Diaries and Intelligence Summaries are contained in F. S. Regs., Part II. and the Staff Manual respectively. Title pages will be prepared in manuscript.

# WAR DIARY

~~or~~

~~INTELLIGENCE SUMMARY.~~

*(Erase heading not required.)*

| Place | Date FEB. | Hour | Summary of Events and Information | Remarks and references to Appendices |
|---|---|---|---|---|
| HEBUTERNE + BAYENCOURT | 1 | | Company in the line in HEBUTERNE sector; situation normal | MG |
| | 2 | | weather very cold; indirect fire carried on tracks behind enemy lines | MG |
| — " — | 3 | 11a.m. | Intersection relief situation normal | MG |
| — " — | 4 5 & 6 | | Indirect fire continued HEBUTERNE intermittently shelled. | MG |
| — " — | | | Intersection relief on 6th. | MG |
| | 7 to 9 | | Situation normal | MG |
| | | | Intersection relief | MG |
| | 10 11 | | — | MG |
| | 12 | | Intersection relief weather continues very cold. | MG |
| | 13 14 | | Normal | MG |
| | 15 | | Intersection relief. | MG |
| | 16 | | Normal weather misty and cold | MG |
| | 17 | | Captain Purvis proceeds on special leave. Weather dull & misty. | MG |
| | 18 | | Intersection relief. | MG |
| | 19 | | Preparation for relief No 2 Section sent to Bois du WARNIMONT | MG |
| | 20 | | Rain and slight mist. | MG |
| | 21 | | Relief arranged direct with O.C. 93rd M.G. Coy. Relief commenced 3pm Company march from BAYENCOURT at 8pm & arrive at BUS at 9.0pm. Operation Orders for relief are attached with amendments etc. | MG [illegible] appendices |
| | 22 | | No 2 Section join the Coy in NISSEN huts at J 19 d 9.8 (57D N.E. 1/20000) | MG |
| | 23 | | Cleaning up sorting out guns etc settling down generally | MG |
| | 24 | | Advanced training commenced. Weather dull. | MG |
| | 25 | | Company under 1 hours notice to move. Enemy reported retiring along V Corps front Miraumont Pys and Serre reported in our hands. | MG |
| | 26 | | Weather improving training continued as far as possible | MG |
| | 27 | | | MG |
| | 28 | | Puisieux reported fallen Company still at J 19 d 9.8 (BUS) | MG |

A5834 Wt. W4973/M687 750,000 8/16 D. D. & L. Ltd. Forms/C.2113/13.

Copy No. 6

Operation Order No. 3A.

Reference: 1/20,000 Sheet 57D.N.E.
1/10,000 HEBUTERNE Map.

1. 56 Machine Gun Company will be relieved by 93 Machine Gun Company tomorrow 21st inst the relief commencing at 9 a.m.

2. Guides from each gun team will report at Add Hq. at a time which shall be notified later.

3. Trench Stores including maps will be handed over on relief & receipts obtained.

4. Company Trench Stores viz Small Box Respirators & P.H. Helmets will not be handed over.

5. Guns, tripods, spare parts cases etc will not be handed over. Further instructions follow with regard to belt boxes.

6. Gun teams will be relieved independently & each gun team commander will obtain receipts for all stores handed over. All receipts must be handed in to Orderly Room by 12 noon 22nd inst.

7. As soon as each Section relief is complete, the section relieved will

Operation Order No. 3A.
continued

7. (ctd) proceed to Coy. Hq at BAYENCOURT.
Sections will move off at not less than 5 minute intervals from HEBUTERNE.

8. Fighting Limbers will report to O.C. Adv. Hq at a time to be notified later.

9. Gum Boots will be handed in to Fyg Boot Store SAILLY by sections and receipts obtained.

10. Billeting party already detailed will report to the Staff Captain at 9.30 am. on the Wat. crnt at J. 19. d. 7.7.

11. From BAYENCOURT the Company will proceed direct to YEW + JUNIPER Camps BUS J 19 b. and d.

12. Amendment to this Operation Order follows.

13. Acknowledge.

M Joseph
Lt for O.C.
56 M.G. Coy

Copy No 1. O.C. Adv. Hq.
No. 2 2Lt. BLACKWOOD
No 3 O.C. Transport
No 4 O.C. 93 M.G. Coy.
No 5 File
No 6 War Diary.

Copy no 5

AMENDMENT I

to Operation Orders 3 A

MG/a/31
21-2-17.

Reference 1/20,000 57 D.N.E.
1/10000 HEBUTERNE

1. The relief will commence at 3 p.m and not at 9 a.m.
2. Guides from each gun team will report to Adv. Hq. by 2.45 p.m.
3. Fighting limbers will report to O.C. Adv. Hq at 4 p.m.
4 No 4 Section 56 M.G. Coy will be relieved by no. 1 Section 93 M.G. Coy no 1 Section 56 M.G. Coy by no 2 Section 93 M.G. Coy and no 3 Section by no 3 Section 93 M.G. Coy
5 The order of arrival in HEBUTERNE of relieving sections will be at 15 min. intervals no 1, no 2 and no 3.
6 Completion of relief will be reported in writing and handed in at BAYENCOURT on arrival.
7 Acknowledge

Copy no 1 O.C. Adv. Hq
no 2 O.C. Transport
no 3 O.C. 93 M.G. Coy
no 4 File
no 5 War Diary
~~no 6~~

M Joseph
Lt for O.C.
56 M.G. Coy

Copy No 5

AMENDMENT II

Operation Orders 3 A

Reference 1/20000 57 D.N.E.

1/10 000

MG/a/32

21. 2. 17.

1. Belt Boxes will be handed over and receipts obtained. 94 belt boxes are being taken over by us from 93 M.G. Coy

Copies as Amendment I

M Joseph
Lt for O.C.
56 M.G. Coy.

Instructions regarding War Diaries and Intelligence Summaries are contained in F. S. Regs., Part II. and the Staff Manual respectively. Title pages will be prepared in manuscript.

# WAR DIARY
or
~~INTELLIGENCE SUMMARY.~~
*(Erase heading not required.)*

56 M.G. Co
Vol 18

Army Form C. 2118.

| Place | Date | Hour | Summary of Events and Information | Remarks and references to Appendices |
|---|---|---|---|---|
| BUS | 1.3.17 | | Training. Baths | [illegible] |
| " | 2.3.17 | | Training 1 Reinforcement joined | [illegible] |
| " | 3.3.17 | | Training | [illegible] |
| " | 4.3.17 | | Moved to VAUCHELLES | [illegible] A1 |
| VAUCHELLES | 5.3.17 | | Advanced gun drill & cleaning guns | [illegible] |
| " | 6.3.17 | | No 3 section co-operated with 7 S. LANCS RGT for a scheme. Training for remainder of Coy | [illegible] |
| " | 7.3.17 | | Training | [illegible] |
| " | 8.3.17 | | Preparations for move | [illegible] A2 |
| " | 9.3.17 | | Moved to LONGUEVILLETTE | [illegible] A3 |
| LONGUEVILLETTE | 10.3.17 | | Moved to LIGNY-SUR-CANCHE | [illegible] |
| LIGNY-S-CANCHE | 11.3.17 | | Cleaning guns & equipment | [illegible] |
| " | 12.3.17 | | Moved to ~~Rethon~~ BETHONVAL | [illegible] |
| BETHONVAL | 13.3.17 | | Moved to SACHIN | [illegible] A4 |
| SACHIN | 14.3.17 | | Cleaned guns & equipment | [illegible] A4 |
| | 15.3.17 | | Moved to LAIRES | [illegible] |
| LAIRES | 16.3.17 | | Training | [illegible] A5 |
| " | 17.3.17 | | Washing limbers & training | [illegible] |
| | 18.3.17 | | Moved to Cohem | [illegible] |
| COHEM | 19.3.17 | | Moved to SERCUS | [illegible] A6 |
| SERCUS | 20.3.17 | | Moved to LA RECOUSSE | [illegible] A7 |
| LARECOUSSE | 21.3.17 | | Cleaning guns & training | [illegible] A8 |
| " | 22.3.17 | | Scheme | [illegible] |
| " | 23.3.17 | | Combined Drill | [illegible] |
| " | 24.3.17 | | Immediate Action & Gas drill. Summer time commenced at 11PM (Winter Time) | [illegible] |
| " | 25.3.17 | | Firing | [illegible] |
| " | 26.3.17 | | Tactical scheme for No 1, 2 & 3 section. No 4 co-operated with 7 L.N. LANCS R. | [illegible] |
| " | 27.3.17 | | Training | [illegible] |
| " | 28.3.17 | | Action from limbers | [illegible] |
| " | 29.3.17 | | Action from limbers | [illegible] |
| " | 30.3.17 | | Action from limbers & training Coy specialists | [illegible] |
| " | 31.3.17 | | No 2 & 3 sections co-operated with 7 E. LANCS RGT & 7 S LANCS respectively. Remainder Training | [illegible] |

A5834 Wt. W4973/M687 750,000 8/16 D. D. & L. Ltd. Forms/C.2118/13.

Instructions regarding War Diaries and Intelligence Summaries are contained in F. S. Regs., Part II. and the Staff Manual respectively. Title pages will be prepared in manuscript.

NO 56 COY. MACHINE GUN CORPS.

# WAR DIARY
## 56th M. ~~or~~ G. Coy.
## ~~INTELLIGENCE SUMMARY.~~
(Erase heading not required.)

Vol 19

Army Form C. 2118.

| Place | APRIL Date 1917. | Hour | Summary of Events and Information | Remarks and references to Appendices |
|---|---|---|---|---|
| LA RECOUSSE | 2nd | 9.40 am | Company march to WIZERNES according to 56th Inf Bde Order No 59 of 1-4-17 | MG |
| WIZERNES | 3rd | 8.0 am | Company march to SCHERPENBERG camp (M 17 b 7.3) | MG |
| SCHERPENBERG | 4.5.6 | — | Various company parades, inspections etc prior to going into the line. | MG |
| —— | 7 | | Reserve line (DIEPENDAAL sector) reconnoitred by O.C. + 1 officer per section. | MG |
| —— | 8 | | Four NCO instructors detailed + sent to the battalions to train 10 men per bn in the Vickers gun. Courses to last 6 days. | MG |
| —— | 9-13 + 14 | | Training carried on. Bombing, bayonet fighting, n claiming, immediate action, stripping, route marches etc etc. | MG |
| —— | 15th | | Reconnaissance of trenches by five officers. Inoculation of company begun. | 10th April No 3 Sec returned from anti aircraft duty at CAESTRE |
| —— | 16th | | Working party supplied by the Company to R.E. (HALLEBAST) dump. This is continued nightly until the end of the month under review. | |
| —— | 17th | | The Company relieve 58 M.G Coy in the DIEPENDAAL SECTOR: vide attached Operation Order No 6A. 9 guns + 2 officers in the line. Coy Hq at Camp North LA CLYTTE. | |
| Trenches LA CLYTTE | 18-22 | | Coy in the line. Situation normal. Indirect fire carried on by night. | MG |
| —— | 23 | | Intersection relief. Situation normal. Cpl Dunford Killed 1 man wounded in VIERSTRAAT. | MG |
| —— | 24-28 | | Indirect fire continued. Enemy activity lessens. | MG |
| —— | 29 | | Intersection relief: Nos 1+2 relieve 3+4 sections. | MG |
| —— | 30 | | O.C. No 49 M.G Coy at Coy Hq to arrange relief. 56th Inf Bde Order No 78 states 56 M.G Coy will relieve 194 M.G Coy in HILL 60 + HOOGE sector on night of the 2nd/3rd MAY. | MG |
| | | | Day occupied preparing to move. | MG |
| General | | | Inoculation of all ranks almost complete by the end of the month. Sickness decrease: 2 casualties. 5 O.R. reinforcement. | MG |

A5834 Wt. W4973/M687 750,000 8/16 D. D. & L. Ltd. Forms/C.2118/13.

Appendix A
W.D. April

# 56 COY M.G. CORPS.

Operation Order No. 6A.



Copy No. 8

Refs. French Map FRANCE SH. 28. S.W. 1: 20,000

The 56 M.G. COY will relieve 58 M.G. COY in Trenches & Billets on April 17th

REVEILLE 6.30 AM. BREAKFAST 7 AM.

Nos. 1 & 2 Sections will relieve 9 teams in the Trenches

No. 1 Sectn. with 2Lt. OAKES will relieve 4 teams in the Right Sector. No. 2 Sectn. with Lt. COOPER will relieve 5 teams in the Left Sector, dividing up into teams of 4 men & 1 N.C.O. each for this purpose. These sectns. will parade in Fighting Order with Greatcoats & Capes at 8.30 AM. No packs will be taken. These will be left in the Huts in a pile, each pack being marked with owners name in indelible Pencil. One limber per Sectn. will be packed at the Transport Lines, with Guns, Tripods, Spare Parts, Condensers, Belt Box Carriers etc. No ammunition will be taken as this is being handed over. The unconsumed portion of the days ration must be taken.

GUIDES. will be met at LONE HOUSE at 10 AM.

RECEIPTS. Signed receipts for Trench Stores will be sent down to Coy. H.Q. LA CLYTTE as soon as possible.

SIGNALLERS. One Signaller & one Runner will live at Right Sector H.Q. All Officers of Nos. 1 & 2 Sectns will go up to Trenches to superintend relief. The 2 Officers not remaining in Trenches will return to Coy. H.Q. after relief is complete. Horses to be borrowed by these Officers.

Remainder of Company. Immediately after Breakfast, Huts to be cleaned, blankets rolled in bundles of 10. Gun equipment ready for loading. Packs & Steel Helmets to be carried. Five limbers will be fetched by hand from T. Lines and packed with all stores at the Camp. Anything which cannot be taken in these Limbers to be stacked in No. 1 hut, with a guard, & collected in next load. Company will parade in Marching Order with these 5 Limbers at 9.30 AM. Remainder of Transport will be picked up on passing T. Lines. Huts, T. Lines & Tents to be left perfectly clean & a certificate to that effect received from 58 Coy. Lt. JOSEPH will leave camp at 9.0 AM to take over 58 Coy. Camp, Maps, Stores etc.

Copies. No. 1. 58 M.G. COY
2. O.C. No. 1 Sect. 56 M.G. COY.
3. " " 2 " " "
No. 4. O.C. No. 4 Sect. 56 M.G. COY
No. 5. T. Officer 56 M.G. COY
No. 6. Adjutant
No. 7 FILE.
No. 8 WAR DIARY
No. 9 C.S.M.
No. 10. C.Q.M.S.

G. B. Kerrovis Capt

# 56th M.Gun Company

Instructions regarding War Diaries and Intelligence Summaries are contained in F. S. Regs., Part II. and the Staff Manual respectively. Title pages will be prepared in manuscript.

**WAR DIARY**
*or*
**~~INTELLIGENCE~~ SUMMARY.**
*(Erase heading not required.)*

Army Form C. 2118.

Vol 20

| Place | Date | Hour | Summary of Events and Information | Remarks and references to Appendices |
|---|---|---|---|---|
| In the line | 1.5.17 | | No 1 & 2 Sections relieved in the line by part of 49 Coy. The Coy moved to SCHERPENBERG. | WSLG Appen 1 |
| SCHERPENBERG | 2.5.17 | | The Coy moved up to relieve the 194th Coy in the HILL 60 - HOOGE sector | WSLG Appen 2 |
| In the line | 3.5.17 | | 4 men killed and L.G. alternate emplacement blown in. Night firing from VALLEY COTTAGES on CORNER HOUSE | WSLG |
| — | 4.5.17 | | The emplacement RUDKIN HOUSE SOUTH occupied. Night firing continued. Enemy M.G. fire swept ZILLEBEKE | WSLG |
| — | 5.5.17 | | Enemy aeroplane fell near the MOUND. Enemy artillery very active during the night | WSLG |
| — | 6.5.17 | | Inter Coy relief. Enemy M.G. fire again swept ZILLEBEKE | WSLG |
| — | 7.5.17 | | RAILWAY DUG-OUTS heavily shelled. Night firing continued | WSLG |
| — | 8.5.17 | | Night firing continued. Enemy quiet | WSLG |
| — | 9.5.17 | | Enemy artillery put up barrage to assist raid at 9.0 p.m. and 3.30 A.M. Coy relieved by 194 Coy on night 9/10 May and returned to IX Corps | WSLG |
| LACLYTE | 10.5.17 | | We relieved 49th Coy in the DIEPENDAL SECTOR. Night firing from MANTHORPE POST on HOSPICE. | WSLG Appen III |
| In the line | 11.5.17 | | Night firing carried on on the road from NORTHERN BRICKSTACKS to HOSPICE and from BEGGARS REST on ONRAET WOOD | WSLG Appen III |
| — | 12.5.17 | | LT COOPER relieved 2nd LT DUMMETT in the line. Night firing continued | WSLG |
| — | 13.5.17 | | Inter Coy relief night firing continued | WSLG |
| — | 14.5.17 | | Enemy T. Ms active. No night firing | WSLG |
| — | 15.5.17 | | Wire cutting started. M.Gs kept gaps open by Indirect fire. | WSLG |
| — | 16.5.17 | | No 3 section relieved No 2 section in the line. Indirect fire continued on Gaps. Emplacement at S.P. 7 taken over in place of TELFORD POST. | WSLG |
| — | 17.5.17 | | Gaps kept open by Indirect Fire | WSLG |
| — | 18.5.17 | | Night firing on gaps continued | WSLG |
| — | 19.5.17 | | Gaps kept open by Indirect Fire | WSLG |
| — | 20.5.17 | | Coy relieved in line and billets by 57 Coy. Coy moved to SCHERPENBERG | WSLG |
| SCHERPENBERG | 21.5.17 | | Instruction in Barrage Work given. | WSLG |
| — | 22.5.17 | | Re-fitting out of Coy and Training | WSLG Appen IV |
| — | 23.3.17 | | Practiced attacking from Trenches | WSLG |
| — | 24.3.17 | | Moved to WESTOUTRE. | WSLG |
| WESTOUTRE | 25.3.17 | | Practice Bde Attack | WSLG |
| — | 26.3.17 | | Practice Bde attack | WSLG Appen V |
| | 27.3.17 | | | WSLG |

A5834 Wt. W4973/M687 750,000 8/16 D. D. & L. Ltd. Forms/C.2118/13.

Instructions regarding War Diaries and Intelligence Summaries are contained in F. S. Regs., Part II. and the Staff Manual respectively. Title pages will be prepared in manuscript.

# WAR DIARY
*or*
~~INTELLIGENCE~~ SUMMARY.

(*Erase heading not required.*)

Army Form C. 2118.

| Place | Date | Hour | Summary of Events and Information | Remarks and references to Appendices |
|---|---|---|---|---|
| WESTOUTRE | 28.3.17 | | Practice Bde Attack | WSLB |
| " | 29.3.17 | | Relieved 57 Coy in the line & billets. Moved to LA CLYTTE | WSLB. APPEN VI |
| In the line. | 30.3.17 | | Fire on gaps made in enemy wire by Artillery | WSLB |
| " | 31.3.17 | | Fire on gaps continued. Enemy artillery active. Working party on Barrage Emplacement during night 31st Mar/1st [illegible] | WSLB<br>WSLB |

Instructions regarding War Diaries and Intelligence Summaries are contained in F. S. Regs., Part II. and the Staff Manual respectively. Title pages will be prepared in manuscript.

# WAR DIARY
or
~~INTELLIGENCE SUMMARY.~~

(Erase heading not required.)

Army Form C. 2118.

56 M G Coy
Vol 21

| Place | Date | Hour | Summary of Events and Information | Remarks and references to Appendices |
|---|---|---|---|---|
| LA CLYTTE | 1.6.17 | | Coy. training. Indirect Fire at night on Saps made in the enemy wire by Artillery. | SWG3 |
| " " | 2.6.17 | | Coy. training with sections out of the line. No. 1 and 2 Sections on working party in the New Reserve Line at 8.30 pm. Casualty 1 O.R. Shell Shock. Lt. M. JOSEPH to FLD. AMBL. | SWG3 |
| " " | 3.6.17 | 2pm | Relief of No. 4 Section in the line by No. 2 Section under 2Lt DUMMETT. Indirect Fire carried out on the enemy wire as before. | SWG3 APPX. I |
| " " | 4.6.17 | | Sect. training. Practise Attack from trenches. No. 3 Sect. on working party at night. Indirect Fire carried out as before. | SWG3 |
| " " | 5.6.17 | | Sect training. Explanation of Scheme for the forthcoming operations. No. 1 and 4 Sections on working party at 8.30pm. 4 Guns under 2Lt DUMMETT cooperate with Infantry in a raid, placing a barrage of indirect fire behind enemy support line. | SWG3 APP II |
| " " | 6.6.17 | 8pm | The 3 sections in reserve move up to the line. Nos 1 and 4 Sections under 2/Lts. OAKES and BONNYMAN take up positions ready for the attack. No. 1 Sect. being attached to the 7th K.O.L. Rgt and No. 4 Sect. to the 7th N. LANC'S RGT. Nos. 2 and 3 Sections take up their positions in the New Reserve Line, their emplacements for the Barrage Scheme. 25% Officers and O.R. stay behind at LA CLYTTE in reserve. List of Targets engaged in the Barrage Scheme attached APP. IV | SWG3 APP III APP IV APP V |
| " " | 7.6.17 | 3.10am | At Zero hour the 2 sections advanced with the Infantry, their objectives being the RED, BLUE, GREEN and BLACK. 2 Guns of No. 1 Sect under Sgt Scully consolidated the RED LINE. 2 Guns of No. 4 SECT under 2Lt BONNYMAN consolidated the GREEN LINE. The 4 guns of No. 1 SECT under 2Lt OAKES consolidated the GREEN LINE at this point 2Lt OAKES was wounded 2Lt JONES assumed command of the section. The Barrage Guns No. 2 and 3 Sect under 2Lt WALL and 2Lt DUMMETT opened fire at Zero hour on their Barrage Lines, when the objectives had been carried they moved forward and consolidated the GREEN LINE. Nos 1 and 4 Sections moved forward and consolidated the BLACK LINE. | |

A5834 Wt. W4973/M687 750,000 8/16 D. D. & L. Ltd. Forms/C.2118/13.

Army Form C. 2118.

Instructions regarding War Diaries and Intelligence Summaries are contained in F. S. Regs., Part II. and the Staff Manual respectively. Title pages will be prepared in manuscript.

# WAR DIARY
*or*
## ~~INTELLIGENCE SUMMARY.~~
*(Erase heading not required.)*

| Place | Date | Hour | Summary of Events and Information | Remarks and references to Appendices |
|---|---|---|---|---|
| LA CLYTTE | 7.6.17 | | (Continued). these sections now consisted of 7 guns one of No 1 Sects guns having been knocked out. During the action the Company suffered the following casualties. Officers wounded 2Lt WALL 2Lt OAKES. 2Lt DUMMETT (remained at duty). 5 O.R. wounded 2 O.R. wounded remained at duty. Lt CAMPBELL joins from 19th Coy as O.C. | RWG |
| " | 8.6.17 | | This day was spent in consolidating the GREEN and BLACK LINES, at night the Company moved up to the MAUVE LINE the last objective taken by the 57th Inf Bde and relieved the 57th M.G. Coy. All the guns of the company were now in the MAUVE LINE the consolidation of which was carried on. No 1 + 2 Sections were under the command of 2Lt JONES & DUMMETT No 3 and 4 under 2Lt BONNYMAN. During the day CAPT E. B. PURVIS was killed in action. | RWG APP VI |
| " | 9.6.17 | | Consolidation was carried on, 2 guns under 2Lt DUMMETT were pushed forward into a new front line dug immediately in front of the MAUVE LINE, this took place in the left SECTOR. also 2 guns on the RIGHT SECTOR were sent forward into the front line the same way. The guns were now arranged as follows. LEFT SECTOR under 2Lt DUMMETT 7 guns 5 in the MAUVE LINE 2 in the FRONT LINE. RIGHT SECTOR under 2Lt BONNYMAN and 2Lt JONES 8 guns. 6 in the MAUVE LINE 2 in the FRONT LINE. During the night 2Lt DUMMETT was wounded. 2Lt BONNYMAN took command of the LEFT SECTOR, also the teams were reduced 50% to enable a inter-team relief to take place at an early date. | RWG APP VII |

A5834 Wt. W4973/M687 750,000 8/16 D. D. & L. Ltd. Forms/C.2118/13.

3

Army Form C. 2118.

Instructions regarding War Diaries and Intelligence Summaries are contained in F. S. Regs., Part II. and the Staff Manual respectively. Title pages will be prepared in manuscript.

# WAR DIARY
*or*
# INTELLIGENCE SUMMARY.
*(Erase heading not required.)*

| Place | Date | Hour | Summary of Events and Information | Remarks and references to Appendices |
|---|---|---|---|---|
| La CLYTTE | 10.6.17 | 9am. | LT. FLAVELL relieved 2LT. JONES in the RIGHT SECTOR. LT FLOOD takes over duties of 2nd in Command from LT FLAVELL. During the night the Brigade Frontage was readjusted. 7 guns in the RIGHT SECTOR relieved 7 guns of the 58th M.G Coy in their LEFT SECTOR. | EWG APP III |
| " | 11.6.17 | 9am | 2LT BLACKWOOD relieved 2LT BONNYMAN in the LEFT SECTOR. 4 guns did Indirect Fire behind the enemy FRONT LINE, cooperating with the 7th K.O.R.L.Rgt who were raiding VAN HOVE FARM. 12 gun teams were relieved at 10.30pm by the men at Coy HDQ. | EWG APP IV APP V |
| " | 12.6.17 | | The 4 guns in Reserve on the LEFT SECTOR were laid for a Barrage Scheme in case of a counter-attack. Casualty. 1 O.R. killed. | EWG APP VI |
| " | 13.6.17 | 10.30pm | Indirect Fire was carried out on suspected enemy M.G. Position between O.22.A.3.8 and O.16.C.3.0. 2 sections are withdrawn from the FRONT SYSTEM. 1 Section under Cpl Dawson in support at the GREEN LINE. 1 Section in RESERVE at the OLD BRITISH FRONT LINE, leaving 8 guns in the line, 4 in the LEFT SECTOR, 4 in the RIGHT SECTOR. | EWG APP XII |
| " | 14.6.17 | | 4 guns cooperate with the 7th E.LANCS raid, by putting up a barrage behind the enemy front line. 1 gun was pushed out on the extreme RIGHT FLANK to protect the retirement after the raid. Casualties 2LT BLACKWOOD wounded. 1 O.R. killed and 1 O.R. wounded. [illegible] to Field Ambulance. LT FLAVELL assumes command of the Company. 2LT BICKERTON and 2LT ECKERSLEY join from the BASE DEPOT. 2LT JONES takes command of the 8 guns in Front System | EWG |
| VIERSTRAAT | 15.6.17 | | 2LT BONNYMAN takes over command of the RIGHT SECTOR, leaving the LEFT to 2LT JONES. | |
| | | 6pm | The Company is relieved in the line by the 57th M.G Coy. 11pm march to KLONDYKE FARM CAMP. 2nd ECHELON is relieved at LA CLYTTE by 57th M.G.Coy. | EWG APP XIII |
| KLONDYKE FARM, KEMMEL | 16.6.17 | | Company resting. 2LT. JONES. E.D. joins from BASE DEPOT. | EWG |

A5834 Wt. W4973/M687 750,000 8/16 D. D. & L. Ltd. Forms/C.2118/13.

Instructions regarding War Diaries and Intelligence Summaries are contained in F. S. Regs., Part II. and the Staff Manual respectively. Title pages will be prepared in manuscript.

# WAR DIARY
*or*
# INTELLIGENCE SUMMARY.
*(Erase heading not required.)*

Army Form C. 2118.

| Place | Date | Hour | Summary of Events and Information | Remarks and references to Appendices |
|---|---|---|---|---|
| KLONDYKE FARM. KEMMEL | 17.6.17 | | Company Resting. | EWGF |
| " " | 18.6.17 | | Company Resting. | EWGF |
| " " | 19.6.17 | 9am | Attached men returned to their BATTALIONS. 1 Officer and 50 men working party for STEENBECQUE 12 O.R working party STRAZEELE RAILHEAD. 8 O.R working party CAESTRE RAILHEAD. Remainder of Company inspection by the O.C. | EWGF |
| " " | 20.6.17 | | Company moves to new camp at LOCRE. | EWGF |
| LOCRE | 21.6.17 | | Coy training. 2Lt HODGSON joins from BASE DEPOT | EWGF |
| " " | 22.6.17 | | Coy training 2Lt HODGSON relieves 2Lt JONES on working party at STEENBECQUE RAILHEAD | EWGF |
| " " | 23.6.17 | | Coy training. | EWGF |
| " " | 24.6.17 | | Coy training. working parties at STRAZEELE and CAESTRE relieved by men of No 4 Section. | EWGF |
| " " | 25.6.17 | | Coy training. 2Lt JONES promoted LT. | EWGF |
| " " | 26.6.17 | | Coy training. TRANSPORT takes part in DIVISIONAL HORSE SHOW. | EWGF |
| " " | 27.6.17 | | Coy training. | EWGF |
| " " | 28.6.17 | | 2Lt BICKERTON and 20 men on BRIGADE FATIGUE. Company takes part in 58th BDE. Sports 2Lt. BLACK joins from BASE DEPOT. | EWGF |
| " " | 29.6.17 | | Coy training. Working parties at STEENBECQUE, CAESTRE and STRAZEELE relieved and rejoin Company. | EWGF |
| " " | 30.6.17 | | Coy training. | EWGF |

EWG Flavell Lt
56th M G Coy.

A5834 Wt. W4973/M687 750,000 8/16 D. D. & L. Ltd. Forms/C.2118/13.

APPEN I | SECRET.

Relief Orders.

No 2 Section under 2/Lt 3.6.17
DUMMETT will relieve No 4
Section in trenches tomorrow leaving
Coy H.Qrs as soon after 2 pm as possible.
No 2 Section will take in their own guns
and spare parts & No 4 bring theirs out.
A half limber will be at Coy H.Qrs
at 2 pm to take guns up and will
wait near ~~[illegible]~~ to bring back
SWAN EDGAR
No 4 section guns. No 4 will hand over
the two guns of No 1 which are in the line.
2nd Lt Jones will remain in the line
for instruction
Trench stores will be handed over
correctly and all dugouts & emplacements
left clean by No 4 Secn.

[illegible] B Purvis Capt
56 MG Coy.

# APP. II

To
2nd Lt Dummett.
56 MG Coy.

MG/3/250.
5.6.17.

Herewith Operation Order re Raid.
Zero is 3pm.
Get all guns on to barrage. Take guns out of S.P. 7. and GORDON'S POST and fire them from Breastworks.
Fire far enough back to clear our troops
~~After Barrage keep [illegible] the [illegible]~~
Send 2nd Lt Jones "out" after lunch so that he can have a decent night tonight he will probably have to go over the top.
~~[illegible]~~ top.
~~[illegible]~~ Bab code received.

G. B. Purvis Capt.
56 MG Coy.

APP. III

# BARRAGE SECTIONS

## Preliminary Operation Orders

**GUNS IN THE LINE.**

Two Guns of No. 3 Sectn will relieve the two guns of No. 1 which are at BEGGARS REST at 5 P.M. No. 1's guns moving to MANTHORPE POST. No. 2 Sectn will carry out their relief & man guns. The Section in the line on Y day will move the Guns from GORDON POST & S.P. 4 with all Belt Boxes (full) into Barrage Positions No. 7 & 8 i.e. on the extreme left at 10.30 p.m. Y. day.

The remaining 4 guns are to do indirect fire as usual, only more intense on Y night. At Zero less two hours these four guns will pack up & move down to Nos. 3. 4. 5. 6 Emplacements, No. 3 Sctns guns being in emplacements 3 & 4. The guns at BEGGARS REST will be the last to leave & will continue firing as long as possible.

**GUNS OUT OF THE LINE.** The Sectns out of the line will move up to Gun positions leaving Coy. H.Qrs at 8 P.M. They will take all spare Barrels & Condenser Tubes obtainable. All Spirit Levels to be taken. Men who are to be left behind will not parade. Q.M. Stores & Orderly Room will not move. On arrival of above Sectn at Emplacements they will mount Gun in Nos 1 & 2 Emplacements & take over Nos. 3 & 4 Guns on arrival. Fill Petrol Cans with Water fix condensers etc. There must be a supply of oil in each position. A hot meal will be prepared at MANTHORPE POST & served about midnight if possible. All surplus men will remain at MANTHORPE POST position in BREASTWORKS & behind Hedge. 3 men will be on each gun & 10 men in Belt Filling Depot.

**SECOND BARRAGE.** At Zero plus 3.40 the first Barrage will cease. Guns will be cleaned, fresh water put in, Belts filled, triangles & aiming sticks taken out & everything got ready for the advance. The 8 Pack Mules which will be waiting behind MANTHORPE position, & the spare men from there will come up to REDOUBT FARM as soon as possible. The Mules will be loaded with 6 Belt Boxes, Gun Tripod, & other Belt Boxes, Spare Parts, Petrol Tins etc will be carried by Teams. The Teams will move forward in file to a position behind MARTENS FARM & after laying out aiming sticks will open on Barrage lines, not however before Zero plus 5 hours. At Zero plus 11 hours the second Barrage will cease and guns will come under control of G.O.C. Brigade. Belts will be refilled etc. so as to be complete once more.

**Coy. H.Qrs.** will be at BEGGAR'S REST position to which all messages should be sent.

G.B. Purvis Capt

APP. IV

# 56 Coy. M. G. Corps.

LIST of TARGETS to be engaged on 'Z' day

These targets have been chosen on account of their having direct observation on to the various objectives and thus beable to turn long range M. G and Rifle fire on to attacking troops without themselves being under the BARRAGE Fire from Artillery.

I have purposely kept away from Farms etc as the artillery will be paying suffitient attention to them, and, unless there are trenches round them M. G. fire would have very little effect.

| TIME TABLE. | No. of GUN. | Fisced TARGET. | Remarks. |
|---|---|---|---|
| 0 – 10 minutes. | No. 1 | ONRAET FARM. | |
| | No. 2 | TRENCH in front of ZERO HOUSE 0.14.a.3.8 – 0.14.a.5.8½. | Traverse. 5°. |
| | No. 3 | ENTRANCE to OBTUSE KEEP. 0.14 a.2½.7 – 0.14 a 3½.6. | Vertical Search. |
| | No. 4 | RENTY FARM. | |
| | No. 5 | EVANS FARM. | |
| | No. 6 | OBTUSE CRESCENT. 0.14.a.8½.9. | |
| | No. 7 | PART of OBSTINATE TRENCH. 0.8.c.8¼.8 – 0.8.c.9½.2. | |
| | No. 8. | CATTEAU FARM. | |
| 10 – 35 minutes. | No 1. | DUGOUTS at back of ONRAET wood 0.14.c.6.6½. | Spray area. |
| | No 3 | OBTUSE KEEP | |
| | No 6 | OBTUSE AVENUE 0.14.b.6.3. | |
| | No 8. | MARTEN's FARM. | |
| — | — | — | — |
| 35 – 69. | No 5 | EVANS FARM | Spray area. |
| | No 6. | Trenches near BONDULLE Fm. 0.14.b.8.5 – 0.15.b.0.6. | Traverse |
| 69 – 100 | No fixed Targets. All guns helping in Barrage. | | |

G. B. Purvis Capt
56. MG Coy.

2.6.17.

Instructions regarding War Diaries and Intelligence Summaries are contained in F. S. Regs., Part II. and the Staff Manual respectively. Title pages will be prepared in manuscript.

# WAR DIARY
*or*
# INTELLIGENCE SUMMARY.

*(Erase heading not required.)*

Army Form C. 2118.

[illegible] Co.
[illegible]
Vol 22

| Place | Date | Hour | Summary of Events and Information | Remarks and references to Appendices |
|---|---|---|---|---|
| LOCRE | 1-7-17 | | Company Training. [illegible] | [illegible] |
| " | 2-7-17 | | Company [illegible] | [illegible] |
| " | 3-7-17 | | Company Training [illegible] ART-LY [illegible] | [illegible] |
| " | 4-7-17 | [illegible] | Company relieved [illegible] Companies in the line [illegible] DAMMSTRASSE. Transport lines at SIEGE FARM. [illegible] under [illegible] COOPER and [illegible] BICKERTON [illegible] JONES and [illegible] 500 [illegible] | [illegible] |
| SIEGE Farm | 5-7-17 | | Company in the line. [illegible] | [illegible] |
| " | 6-7-17 | 10 pm | [illegible] | [illegible] |
| " | 7-7-17 | [illegible] | [illegible] 1500 [illegible] | [illegible] |
| " | 8-7-17 | [illegible] | [illegible] carried out [illegible] | [illegible] |
| " | 9-7-17 | 9 pm | [illegible] ceased at [illegible] firing about [illegible] yds. 1 O.R. Casualty. | [illegible] |
| " | 10-7-17 | 1 pm | [illegible] SIEGE FARM [illegible] under [illegible] COOPER [illegible] BICKERTON [illegible] established at SIEGE FARM [illegible] DAMMSTRASSE [illegible] | [illegible] |
| " | 11-7-17 | 10.30 pm | Orders received for [illegible] | [illegible] |
| " | 12-7-17 | | [illegible] Sections [illegible] | [illegible] |
| | | 3 pm | [illegible] DRANOUTRE [illegible] | [illegible] |

A5834 Wt. W4973/M687 750,000 8/16 D. D. & L. Ltd. Forms/C.2118/13.

Instructions regarding War Diaries and Intelligence Summaries are contained in F. S. Regs., Part II. and the Staff Manual respectively. Title pages will be prepared in manuscript.

# WAR DIARY
*or*
# INTELLIGENCE SUMMARY.
*(Erase heading not required.)*

Army Form C. 2118.

| Place | Date | Hour | Summary of Events and Information | Remarks and references to Appendices |
|---|---|---|---|---|
| SIEGE FM | 13-7-17 | | Nos 3 & 4 Sections training. No 1 & 2 [illegible] [illegible] 2 Gun [illegible] SPANBROEK [illegible]. Lt FLOOD returns from leave. No 2 Section [illegible] [illegible] during the night. [illegible] | [illegible] |
| " | 14-7-17 | 10 pm | Nos 3 & 4 Sections training. [illegible] in the [illegible] [illegible] 2 [illegible] [illegible] no casualties. | [illegible] |
| " | 15-7-17 | 9 pm | Nos 3 & 4 Sections relieve Nos 1 & 2 [illegible] [illegible] of [illegible] 16th Division [illegible] [illegible] relieves [illegible] of No 4 Section at DRANOUTRE [illegible] [illegible]. [illegible] relieves Lt FRAVELL in command [illegible] line. 2Lt BONNYMAN returns from leave. No 4 [illegible] [illegible] 2Lt BONNYMAN [illegible] [illegible] Section under Lt JONES RN. [illegible] [illegible] [illegible] [illegible] night. | APP [illegible] |
| | 16-7-17 | | Nos 1 & 2 Sections training at SIEGE [illegible] [illegible] 2/Lt ECKERSLEY to [illegible] [illegible] Regt. | [illegible] |
| | 17-7-17 | | Nos 1 & 2 Sections training. Night firing carried out by guns in the line. Lt [illegible] to UK on leave. | [illegible] |
| " | 18-7-17 | | Nos 1 & 2 Sections training. Night firing carried out [illegible] [illegible] 3 [illegible] [illegible] [illegible] | [illegible] |
| " | 19-7-17 | | 2 Teams of No 2 Section [illegible] [illegible] [illegible] [illegible] [illegible] remainder of Nos 1 & 2 sections training. | [illegible] |
| " | 20-7-17 | 10 pm | Company relieved in the line by [illegible] [illegible] and moved to billets at KEMMEL | [illegible] |
| KEMMEL | 21-7-17 | | Company training. | |
| " | 22-7-17 | | Company training. 2 Teams of No [illegible] [illegible] [illegible] [illegible] [illegible] [illegible]. | [illegible] |
| | 23-7-17 | | Company training. 2 Teams of No 2 Section [illegible] [illegible] [illegible] relieved. | |
| " | 24-7-17 | | Company training. | [illegible] |
| | 25-7-17 | | Nos 2, 3 & 4 Sections [illegible] [illegible] [illegible] Battalions for [illegible] | [illegible] |
| | 26-7-17 | | Company training. | |

A5834 Wt. W4973/M687 750,000 8/16 D. D. & L. Ltd. Forms/C.2118/13.

Instructions regarding War Diaries and Intelligence Summaries are contained in F. S. Regs., Part II. and the Staff Manual respectively. Title pages will be prepared in manuscript.

# WAR DIARY
*or*
# INTELLIGENCE SUMMARY.
*(Erase heading not required.)*

Army Form C. 2118.

| Place | Date | Hour | Summary of Events and Information | Remarks and references to Appendices |
|---|---|---|---|---|
| | | | Operations commence. All Objectives gained & held. Defensive flank formed in conjunction with Infantry on our right. Casualties. Lt. R.H. JONES killed. 2Lt. J. BONNYMAN wounded. O.Rs. 4 Killed. 15 Wounded. 3 Guns of No. 4 Section knocked out. | |

A5834 Wt. W4973/M687 750,000 8/16 D. D. & L. Ltd. Forms/C.2118/13.

Company Operation Orders No. 1.
By Capt. R.L. HARTLEY APP I

Reference MAP WYTCHAETE. 1/10,000

<u>Secret</u>. 9 - 7 - 17 Copy No. 5

1/. The 57th Inf Bde will attack and occupy the following line this night 9th/10th July — O.23. a 5.4. thence North to include the buildings at O.23 a.5 5. and O.23. a 4.7. — TOOL FARM thence to join up with the present line of posts at O.17.a 3.4

2/. The attack will take place at Zero hour when the assaulting troops will ~~leave~~ leave the assembling trenches and will be made in 3 waves.

3/. The 56th M. G. Coy will cooperate by placing a Barrage of Indirect Fire on a line from O.11.d.45.00. due South to O.17 b 4.08. South west along ROAD to TOOL FARM. O.17.c 3.4. No. 4 Section taking a line from O.11 d. 45 00. to ROAD O.17 b.4.08. No. 3 Section the remainder from O.17. b 4.08 to TOOL FARM O.17.c 3.4.

4/. Firing will commence at Zero hour and for the first 15 minutes will be intense. Guns will fire approximately 100 rds per minute. At Zero + 15 minutes the Barrage will lift. No. 4 Section

Para 4 (Cont)

No 4 Section on a line approximately from O.18.a.8.7. to O.18.c.65.65.
No 3 Section O.18.c.80.95. to O.18.c.5.0. and search all tracks and areas likely to be used by the enemy.

5. The following rate of fire per gun will be kept up.

| | |
|---|---|
| Zero to Zero + 15 minutes | = 1500 rds |
| Zero + 15 to Zero + 60 " | = 1000 " |
| Zero + 60 to Zero + 3 hrs. 0 " | = 2000 " |
| Zero + 3 hrs to Zero + 5 hrs 0 " | = 1000 rds. |

6. 4 Belt Boxes per gun will be borrowed by Nos 3 + 4 Sects from No 1 + 2 Sects, these will be returned complete at the earliest opportunity.

7. Casualties + Reports will be sent to Coy: Hdq as soon as possible after completion of the operations.

8. Zero hour will be 9 pm.

Issued at 5 pm.

P Hart Capt
Comdg 56th M.G. Coy.

Copies to

No 1. O.C. No 1 Sect
2 " No 2 "
3 " No 3 "
4 " No 4 "
No 5. War Diary
" 6 File.

Coy Operation Orders No. 2
By Captain R. L. Hartley.
Reference Map 28. S.W. 2 1/20,000 APP II

**Secret.** Issued at 11.30.

1. Nos. 3 and 4 Sections and Coy Headquarters will be withdrawn from the line on the 11th/7/17.

2. All guns, spare parts, and Belt Boxes will be at Company Hdq by 1pm ready to load the limbers, which will be at the RATION DUMP by 2pm. SAA. will not be taken out.

3. On completion of the loading Sections will proceed to the TRANSPORT LINES at SIEGE FARM N.16.c.3.9, marching with a 20 minutes interval between Sections 200 yds between Subsections and Limbers. Headquarters will march with No 4 Sect.

4. The following on Headquarters will not be withdrawn at present. 4 Signallers, O.Room Clerks, and Officers Mess Staff.

5. Coy Hdq will be established at SIEGE FARM N.16.c.3.9. from 12 noon 12/7/17.
Advance Coy Hdq from 12 noon 12/7/17 at O.9.a.8.1.

6. The 8 guns remaining in the line will be distributed as already ordered

2.

7/. The S.A.A. at present with Nos 3 & 4 Sections will be handed over to Nos 1 & 2 Sections.

8/. Great care must be taken to show the least possible movement during the relief.

9/. The Transport Sgt will detail Nos 3 & 4 Section Fighting limbers to be at the Ration Dump by 2pm.

10/. Acknowledge.

E.W.C. Howard Lt. Adjt
56th M. G. Coy

11-7-17

Copies to

| | | | | |
|---|---|---|---|---|
| No 1. | to | O.C. No 1 Sect. | No 7 | C.Q.M.S |
| " 2 | " | O.C. No 2 " | 8 | War Diary |
| " 3 | " | O.C. No 3 " | 9 | File. |
| " 4 | " | O.C. No 4 " | | |
| " 5 | " | C.S.M. | | |
| " 6 | " | T. Sgt | | |

56 COY. M.G. CORPS. APP II

Company Orders by CAPT R.L. HARTLEY

| | |
|---|---|
| ORDERLY OFFICER | 2ND LT BONNYMAN. |
| NEXT FOR DUTY | LT JONES R.M. |
| ORDERLY SERGEANT | CPL CORNELL |
| NEXT FOR DUTY. | CPL GALLAGHER. |

REVEILLE 6.30 AM. BREAKFAST 7.30 am LIGHTS OUT 10.15 pm.

| | | |
|---|---|---|
| PARADES. | 7-7.30 am. | Saluting and Arms Drill. Dress. Drill Order. |
| | 9-10 AM | Gun Cleaning. |
| | 10-11 AM | Overhaul and check all Gun Stores and Spare Parts. |
| | 11.15 am-12.15 pm | Gun Drill. |
| | 12.15-12.45 pm | Lecture on Anti-aircraft mounting and firing. |
| | 3.0 PM | The sub-section of No 4 Sec will parade at 3-0 pm to relieve remainder of section at Dranoutre. The sub-section will be in charge of 2ND LT JONES E.D. |
| 12.7.17. | | |

R L Hartley Capt

"A" Form.

**MESSAGES AND SIGNALS.**

Army Form C.2121
(in pads of 100).
No. of Message

| Prefix ... Code ... m. | Words | Charge | This message is on a/c of: | Recd. at ... m. |
|---|---|---|---|---|
| Office of Origin and Service Instructions. | Sent | | ... Service. | Date |
| D. R. L. S. | At ... m. | | | From |
| Sent. | To | | | |
| | By | | (Signature of "Franking Officer.") | By |

TO 56th M. G. Coy

APP. IV

| Sender's Number. | Day of Month. | In reply to Number. | AAA |
|---|---|---|---|
| *BM. 385/S | 13 7 17 | | |

Ref. my BM 367/S. The intention of your company in A. A. Defence Work at CRUCIFIX Corner will be relieved by 14th Division by 6 pm on 15th inst.

From 56th Inf Bde

Place

Time 3. 45 p.m.

The above may be forwarded as now corrected. (Z) L. O. Serwell Capt.

Censor. Signature of Addressor or person authorised to telegraph in his name.

* This line should be erased if not required.

750,000. W 2186—M509. H. W. & V., Ld. 6/16.

RELIEF ORDERS by CAPT R.L. HARTLEY

MAP REFERENCE 28 S.W. 1/10,000 APP. IV A

1. 2 Teams of No. 1 Sectn will relieve 2 Teams of No. 2 Sectn employed on A.A. duties with the Divisional Artillery tonight 22/4/17

2. Teams will parade at 5.30 pm in fighting order, taking provisions for the 23rd

3. Guns, spare parts, belt boxes & ammunition will be taken over. Receipts for same will be given

4. 2Lt BLACK will accompany the teams and is responsible that the relief is correctly carried out. On completion of relief he will hand over the command to SGT MATTHEWS.

5. Relief will be reported complete by 2Lt BLACK to Coy H.Qrs. on his return

6. C.Q.M.S. will arrange to have a hot meal ready for the teams being relieved on their arrival in camp.

ACKNOWLEDGE.

Copies.

1. 2Lt BLACK
2. O.C. No 2 Sect.
3. C.S.M.S.
4. C.S.M.
5. WAR DIARY.

22.4.17

R.L. Hartley Capt.

Comdg. 58 COY. MACHINE GUN CORPS.

APP. V

56 COY. M.G. CORPS

Operation Orders by CAPTN. R.L. HARTLEY

ORDERLY OFFICER 2LT. E.D. JONES
" SGT. CPL. CORNELL
REVEILLE 7 AM. BREAKFAST 7.30

| | |
|---|---|
| PARADES | 9 am Packing Limbers ready for the line<br>11 am. Inspection in Fighting Order.<br>11.30am Gas Drill<br><br>The Coy will proceed to the line tomorrow at times arranged with Battns. to which they are affiliated<br>Nos. 1 & 2 Sectns at 5 pm.<br>No 3 & H.Q. at 3 pm<br>No. 4 Sectn at 8 pm.<br>1 Fighting limber will accompany each section.<br>8 Belt Boxes, 1 Petrol Tin per gun team will be taken.<br>All surplus Belt Boxes 16,000 SAA, Sandbags, Oil, 1 spare Parts case per Sectn. 4/2, packing armourers equipment with H.Q. Limber<br>Bombs, Spades, Very Lights, Flares will be drawn from Brigade H.Q. DAMSTRASSE.<br>Coy H.Q. & surplus personnel will leave at 6 pm for SIEGE FARM |
| 28.7.17 | R.L. Hartley |

56 COY M G CORPS. APP VI

GENERAL SCHEME. OPERATION ORDERS NO. 9 B. Copy No. 14.

I. The 19th Division is attacking a portion of the BLUE LINE from HOUSE O.23.a.65.65 to ROAD at O.11.b.55.00. on Zero day and time to be notified later. The attack will be carried out by the 56th Inf. Bde. The 56 M.G. Coy will conform and its instructions [illegible] following [illegible].

II. Distribution of Guns. No. 1 Section under 2Lt BLACK will be in Reserve in O.B.L. under direct orders of G.O.C. 56th Inf. Bde. No 2 Section under 2Lt BICKERTON will be [illegible] to the 7th East Lancs. No. 3 Section under Lt R.N. JONES & 2Lt HODG[E] & affiliated to 7 North Lancs & No. 4 Secn. under 2Lt BONNYMAN & 2Lt E.D. JONES affiliated to 7th Royal Lanc. R.

III. The Boundaries between Battalions on the assembly position will be 7 R LANC. Right on [illegible] right boundary will be O.23.a.5.4. 7 EAST LAN. Right at S.E. [illegible] small wood at O.14.c.03.68 thence due westwards. 7 NORTH LAN. Right at junction of present front line and ROSEBEEK thence due westwards. Left on O.11.a.5.1 and thence westwards along the line of the Divisional [illegible] Boundary.

IV. The Objective of the Brigade is a line from On the right. The ROAD from O.23.a.3.3 to O.23.b.2.4 ([illegible] to 58th Inf. Bde). On the left. A line drawn from O.11.c.5.7 to O.11.a.55.0 — FORRET FARM being inclusive to the Brigade on the left.

V. Instructions for M. Guns. The purpose of the M.G's is to cover consolidation & repel counter attacks. No. 1 Secn. will remain in their position in O.B.L. about O.10.a.9.8. until required to move elsewhere. O.C. No. 1 Secn will [illegible] best runner forward to each sector. 2 Guns of Nos 2, 3 & 4 secns. will go forward at zero hour with the carrying platoons of 2 Coys. in each sector, one pair being pushed right forward the other pair placed in the support line but in such a position as to bring direct fire across the objective. Suggested localities for the guns are:-

Right Sector. 2 Guns. O.23.a.80.70 2 Guns O.17.d.30.30.

Centre Sector 2 Guns. O.17.b.35.30 2 Guns O.17.a.85.05

Left Sector 2 Guns. O.11.d.40.30. 2 Guns O.11.c.45.90.

These guns are under the orders of Os.C. Battalions but any changes of position will be reported at once to O.C. M.G. [illegible] as well as O.C. Battns. As soon as strong points are constructed some guns will be moved into these positions.

VI. Reports. Immediately gun positions are sited they will be marked + a report sent by 2 Runners to Coy. H.Q. via Battn H.Q. giving

1. Position of Gun
2. Field of Fire
3. Section H.Q.

also time, date, place + sender.

Intelligence + Casualty Reports will be sent to Coy. H.Q.

Any gun damaged will be reported at once, giving maker's no. of gun, extent of damage + position of gun team.

VII. Emplacements. Sections must build their own emplacements using the sandbags carried by each man. These emplacements should be marked by a board carried by the N.C.O. i/c of the team.

VIII. Equipment. Sections will be equipped in fighting order carrying 2 Sandbags per man. Each man carrying his own rations + waterbottle full.

Nos. 1. Tripod. Nos. 2 Gun + 1st Aid Case. Nos. 3. 2 Belt Boxes 1 Spade. Nos. 4. 2 Belt Boxes + 1 Spade. Nos. 5. 2 Belt Boxes. Nos. 6. 1 Petrol tin of Water + 1 Belt Box. Nos. 7. Bag of Bombs for 2 teams + 1 Belt Box.

IX. Supplies. A Brigade Reserve Water Supply will be established at O.16.a.4.9½. Supplies of the following will be kept at Advanced Coy H.Qrs under the C.S.M.

Sandbags. S.A.A. Lewis Spare Parts Water 4 by 2
Oil. Belt Boxes Rations Packing.

X. Runners. 2 Runners will be attached to Adv. Coy. Hdq. + to each section. Officers servants will also be used as Runners.

XI. Personnel. The following N.C.O.s will be left out of their sections for the operations.

| | | |
|---|---|---|
| No. 1 Secn. | Sgt. Matthews. | L/Cpl Gerrard. |
| " 2 " | Sgt. Smith | L/Cpl Thornton |
| " 3 " | Sgt. Pennington | L/Cpl Thackray |
| " 4. " | Sgt Honor | L/Cpl Young |

and 25% of the men of the Company already detailed.

XII Accomodation. Section Commanders will report to O.C. Battns to arrange for accomodation for their teams in the line.

XIII. <u>Regtl. Aid Posts</u> near H.Q. of 7th Royal Lanc. 7th East Lan. & 7th North Lan.

<u>Advanced Dressing Stations</u> DAMSTRASSE & ONRAET FARM

XIV. <u>Headquarters</u>.

Brigade. DAMSTRASSE. O. 9. c. 3. 8.

7th Royal Lanc. POLKA EST. O. 22. a. 3. 2.

7th East Lan. in O.B.L. west of RIDGE FARM. O. 6. d. 1. 6.

7th North Lan. in RAVINE O. 10. d. 15. 55

7th South Lan. (Support Bn.) S. edge ROSEWOOD O. 16. a. 8. 6.

56 Coy. M.G.C. at SIEGE FARM.

" " Adv. H.Q. ROSEWOOD O. 10. c. 40. 10

<u>ACKNOWLEDGE</u>

Copies:-

1. O.C. No. 1 Section
2. O.C. No. 2 "
3. O.C. No. 3 "
4. O.C. No. 4 "
5. 2Lt. HODGSON
6. 2Lt. JONES E.D.
7. Lt. FLOOD (T.O.)
8. O.C. 7th East Lan.
9. O.C. 7th North Lan.
10. O.C. 8th Kings Own.
11. O.C. 7th South Lan.
12. A.D.M.S.
13. D.D.M.S.
14. War Diary
15. File.

28. 7. 17.

56th M.G. Coy.

1

AUGUST - 1917.

56 M G Coy

Fredk Champion Captain
56 COY. MACHINE GUN CORPS

Army Form C. 2118.

Instructions regarding War Diaries and Intelligence Summaries are contained in F. S. Regs., Part II. and the Staff Manual respectively. Title pages will be prepared in manuscript.

# WAR DIARY
or
# INTELLIGENCE SUMMARY.

(Erase heading not required.)

Vol 23

| Place | Date | Hour | Summary of Events and Information | Remarks and references to Appendices |
|---|---|---|---|---|
| SIEGE Fm | 1·8·17 | | Consolidation of the line carried on. No.1 Section under 2/Lt Black moves up and reinforces No. 4. Section on the Right Sector | |
| " | 2·8·17 | | Capt Hartley and 2 O.R. missing. Lt Hazell assumes command of the Company. 2/Lt Eckersley proceeds to the line and assists. 1 O.R. wounded. Company's Dispositions: No.3 Section 4 guns under 2/Lt Hodgson on the left {Company front runs from 200 yards E of Forret Fm (O 11 b 50·05) to Road junction 200 yards S of Bee Fm (O 23 b 25·40)} to 100 yards SE of Gym Fm. No 2 Section 4 guns under 2/Lt BICKERTON Centre - to 250 yards E of road junction at GROENELINDE CABT (O 17 d 35·80). Nos 1 and 4 Sections 5 guns under 2/Lts BLACK and JONES E.D. | |
| " | 3·8·17 | | 2 guns of No.1. Section are withdrawn from the Right Sector and are sent to new positions under 2/Lt ECKERSLEY to a point 50 yards S. of GREEN Fm Only one gun reached that point the other being blown up and the No.1. of the team wounded. The one gun of No.4. Section under 2/Lt JONES is withdrawn to Company H.Q. Dispositions: No 3 Section 4 guns - 2 in new front line under 2/Lt HODGSON 2 in the Support Line (Old British Front Line) under Sgt WALDRE 1. 1 gun under 2/Lt ECKERSLEY in the Centre Sector S. of GREEN Fm 4 guns of No.2 Section in the front line Centre Sector. 2 guns of No.1 Section under 2/Lt BLACK S.W. of JUNCTION BUILDINGS on the Right Sector. 8 Reinforcements arrive from the Base. 56th Infantry Bde less 56th M.G. Coy is relieved in the line by 57th Inf. Bde. | App I |
| " | 4·8·17 | | 2 Guns under 2/Lt BLACK are withdrawn to Company H.Q. (O 10 c 40·10) 3 guns of 57th M.G. Coy under 2/Lt ROGERSON relieve 1 gun of 2/Lt ECKERSLEY and No.2. Section under 2/Lt BICKERTON who are withdrawn to Company H.Q. Lt COOPER with teams made up of reinforcements and men of No.1. Section relieves No.3 Section under 2/Lt HODGSON. Dispositions: 4 guns under Lt COOPER on the left sector (2 in front line and in O.B.F.L in support) 4 guns under 2/Lt BLACK in Barrage Positions at Company H.Q. - the remaining guns in reserve at Transport Lines (SIEGE FARM). Indirect Fire carried | |

A5834 Wt. W4973/M687 750,000 8/16 D. D. & L. Ltd. Forms/C.2118/13.

56th M.G. Coy — 2 — AUGUST - 1917

Instructions regarding War Diaries and Intelligence Summaries are contained in F. S. Regs., Part II. and the Staff Manual respectively. Title pages will be prepared in manuscript.

# WAR DIARY
*or*
# INTELLIGENCE SUMMARY.
(*Erase heading not required.*)

Army Form C. 2118.

Fred H Champion, Captain
56 COY. MACHINE GUN CORPS.

| Place | Date | Hour | Summary of Events and Information | Remarks and references to Appendices |
|---|---|---|---|---|
| SIEGE Fm | 4.8.17 | (Contd) | carried out on Barrage Lines in conjunction with guns of 57, 58, and 226 M.G. Coys. 4 O.R. wounded, 3 O.R. missing. | |
| " | 5.8.17 | | 2 Lt JONES relieves 2 Lt BLACK in command of the 4 Barrage Guns and the latter becomes Adjutant. Owing to reports of expected enemy counter-attacks harrassing fire is carried out throughout the night and day in front of HOLLEBEKE. Guns on left sector fired direct fire at the enemy during their attempts to recapture HOLLEBEKE. These attempts failed. Lt F.H. CHAMPION ~~the 90th M.G. Coy~~ appointed O.C. Company. | |
| " | 6.8.17 | | Intermittent Fire is carried out throughout the day and night on ground in front of HOLLEBEKE. 2 Lts ECKERSLEY, BICKERTON and HOBSON with 8 gun teams relieve the officers and teams in the line. Lt CHAMPION reports as O.C. 2 Lt GATENBY joins from Base also 12 O.R. as re-inforcements. 2/Lt JONES E.D. wounded and remains at duty. | |
| " | 7.8.17 | | Indirect Fire carried out during the night. Arrangements made for relief by 112 M.G. Coy | |
| " | 8.8.17 | | Company is relieved in the line by 112 M.G. Coy. 4 guns under 2 Lt ECKERSLEY only relieved. The 4 guns in Barrage Positions are withdrawn early in the evening under 2 Lts HOBSON and GATENBY proceed to Transport lines where lorries convey them to BERTHEN. 4 teams under 2 Lt ECKERSLEY stay the night at SIEGE FARM. | |
| BERTHEN | 9.8.17 | | 4 Teams under 2 Lt ECKERSLEY join the Company at BERTHEN. Company rest at BERTHEN | |

56th M.G. Coy

3

AUGUST - 1917

Army Form C. 2118.

# WAR DIARY
*or*
# INTELLIGENCE SUMMARY.
*(Erase heading not required.)*

Instructions regarding War Diaries and Intelligence Summaries are contained in F. S. Regs., Part II. and the Staff Manual respectively. Title pages will be prepared in manuscript.

Fred H Champion, Captain
56 COY. MACHINE GUN CORPS.

| Place | Date | Hour | Summary of Events and Information | Remarks and references to Appendices |
|---|---|---|---|---|
| BERTHEN | 9.8.17 | Contd | for the day. Total Casualties to date: Officers - 1 killed, 1 missing, wounded; O.R. - 4 killed, 16 wounded (2 at duty) 4 missing, 1 wounded and missing. Amongst the Infantry attached for carrying purposes the Casualties were: 5 killed 6 wounded, 4 missing. | FHC |
| " | 10.8.17 | | Company entrain at BAILLEUL for Rest Area with the exception of Transport who proceed under Lt. FLOOD and 2/Lt BLACK by road. Detrain at WIZERNES and march to WATTERDAL. Billeted for the night | APP. II FHC |
| WATTERDAL | 11.8.17 | | Company march to COLEMBERT in the Rest Area | FHC |
| COLEMBERT | 12.8.17 | | Company resting and cleaning up. | FHC |
| " | 13.8.17 | 6 pm | Transport join the Company. The Sections are reorganised re-inforcements being posted. Company attend Brigade Parade and are inspected by G.O.C. 2nd ARMY; they march past and are complimented on their smart bearing | FHC |
| " | 14.8.17 | | Company Training by Sections | FHC |
| " | 15.8.17 | | Company Training by Sections | FHC |
| " | 16.8.17 | | Company Training - Tactical Schemes. | FHC |
| " | 17.8.17 | | Company Training - Firing on the Range. | FHC |
| " | 18.8.17 | | Company Training by Sections. | FHC |
| " | 19.8.17 | | Church Parade at Brigade H.Q. Presentation of Medal Ribbons by G.O.C. 19th Division. Sgt SCULLY receives the Military Medal. Brigade Sports. | FHC |
| " | 20.8.17 | | Divisional Sports. Capt F.H. CHAMPION rejoins from leave and assumes command. | FHC |

56th M.G. Coy

4

AUGUST 1917

Instructions regarding War Diaries and Intelligence Summaries are contained in F. S. Regs., Part II. and the Staff Manual respectively. Title pages will be prepared in manuscript.

# WAR DIARY
*or*
# INTELLIGENCE SUMMARY.
*(Erase heading not required.)*

Army Form C. 2118.

Fred H. Chambers Captain
56 COY. MACHINE GUN CORPS

| Place | Date | Hour | Summary of Events and Information | Remarks and references to Appendices |
|---|---|---|---|---|
| COLEMBERT | 21.8.17 | | Company training and preparing to move. | |
| " | 22.8.17 | | Company move to WATTERDAL and take over from 57th M.G. Coy. Route taken LONGUEVILLE, QUESQUES, WATTERDAL | |
| WATTERDAL | 23.8.17 | | Company Training | |
| " | 24.8.17 | | Company Training. Practice Inspection for the Commander in Chief. Company Sports held in the afternoon. | |
| " | 25.8.17 | | Company inspected by the Commander in Chief and congratulated on their appearance and performances in recent operations. Brigade formed up in mass for inspection off the BOULOGNE-ST OMER Rd 1000 yards E. of HARLETTES. | |
| " | 26.8.17 | | Company Training | |
| " | 27.8.17 | | Company Training and preparing to move. 1st Line Transport leaves for new area by road under Lt FLOOD and 2 Lt BLACK. | |
| " | 28.8.17 | | Company Training. 2Lt HIGGSON leaves with an advance party to billet for the company in the new area. | |
| " | 29.8.17 | | Company Training. Company march to WIZERNES via LUMBRES, SETQUES and entrain. Detrain at BAILLEUL and march via ST JANS CAPPEL, BERTHEN, to Camp at N.13.b.9.9 near WESTOUTRE, arriving 3 a.m. 30.8.17 | |
| WESTOUTRE | 30.8.17 | | Company resting and cleaning up | |
| " | 31.8.17 | | Company Training. 14 reinforcements arrive from Base. Company provides a working party of 1 officer (2Lt BLACK) and 100 O.R. on the night of 31/8 – 1/9/17 for unloading purposes at R.E. PARK, ZEVECOTEN, G.36.c. returning to Camp at 6.30 a.m. 1/9/17. | |

Fred H. Chambers Captain
OC 56 M.G. Company.
1/9/17

C.C.

9.8.17

COMPANY OPERATION ORDERS by L^T E.W.C. FLAVELL.

REVEILLE . 6 am, BREAKFAST 6.30 am.

1. The Company will parade at 7.30 am. for the purpose of proceeding to BAILLEUL WEST Railway Station to entrain for Rest Area.

2. The C.S.M. will detail 10 men to act as Brakesmen. They will report to T. Sgt. at 7.30 am.

3. The Transport will move off according to orders issued with the exception of 1 Limber & 2 Officer's Chargers which will proceed with the Company by train.
2Lt BLACK is detailed to assist the Transport Officer.
2Lt JONES E.D. will be responsible that the Limber mentioned above is correctly loaded with the following:- Cook's Dixies, Officer's & Sgts Mess equipment, & Orderly Room Boxes. Nothing else is to be loaded on this Limber.

4. Company will parade in fighting order, each man carrying his Steel Helmet & Rations for the day. Men's packs & Officers Valises will be packed on Lorry by the Brakesmen. The storeman will accompany the Lorry, which is reporting to 56 T.M.B at 7 am. where it will be half loaded, the remaining space being available for Packs & Valises of this Coy.

5. On arrival at BAILLEUL WEST STN. 100 men or as many as possible will report under 2Lt JONES and 2Lt Gatenby to the R.T.O at 9. am for loading duties & on completion of their duties they will be entrained in No. 1 Train. The above mentioned Officers will report to Lt COOPER before entraining the men. Lt COOPER will find out the exact space & carriages allotted to the Coy for Officers, Men, & Animals & 1 Limber. He will have an entraining state prepared ready, showing exact number of Officers, O.Rs, animals & axles, so that it may be rendered immediately when called for.

6. On arrival at destination (WIZERNES) the unloading party mentioned above will be held in readiness to unload, should they be required.

7. Officer's servants, Cook & Mess Waiter & all Headquarters will parade with Coy. with the exception of Storeman who will accompany the Lorry.

W.S.L. Cooper
Lt for O.C.
56 Coy. M.G. Corps.

Copies. All Officers.
C.S.M.
C.Q.M.S.
T. Corpl.
War Diary.

56th M.G. Coy.

Instructions regarding War Diaries and Intelligence Summaries are contained in F. S. Regs., Part II. and the Staff Manual respectively. Title pages will be prepared in manuscript.

# WAR DIARY
*or*
# INTELLIGENCE SUMMARY.
*(Erase heading not required.)*

SEPTEMBER - 1917.

Army Form C. 2118.

Vol 24

| Place | Date | Hour | Summary of Events and Information | Remarks and references to Appendices |
|---|---|---|---|---|
| WESTOUTRE | 1.9.17 | | Company resting after being out on an all-night working party. Training in the afternoon. | |
| " | 2.9.17 | | Church Parade and baths. | |
| " | 3.9.17 | | Company Training - Tactical Scheme including practice on barrage lines. | |
| " | 4.9.17 | | Tactical Scheme in the morning. A working party of 1 Officer and 70 O.R. left at 2 p.m. and returned at 4 a.m. 5.9.17 | |
| " | 5.9.17 | | Company resting and overhauling equipment, gun stores, &c. O.C. and LTS FLAVELL and COOPER proceed up the line to reconnoitre the sector allotted to the Company. Transport Officer - LT. FLOOD - reports sick and is sent to C.C.S. | |
| " | 6.9.17 | | Company moves to LOCRE (YORK HUTS, M.23.C.4.9). An unloading party of 1 Officer and 75 O.R. leaves at 6.40 a.m. returning to new camp at 6 p.m. | |
| LOCRE | 7.9.17 | | A working party of 2 Officers and 75 O.R. leaves at 7 a.m. and returns at 5 p.m. | |
| " | 8.9.17 | | A working party of 2 Officers and 75 O.R. leaves at 7 a.m. and returns at 5 p.m. O.C. and LT. COOPER and 2/LT. BICKERTON proceed up the line to reconnoitre a site for barrage positions I.36.c.80.95 to I.36.b.10.25. | |
| " | 9.9.17 | | Nos. 1 + 2 Sections under LT. COOPER and 2/LT. BLACK proceed to establish an advanced camp at DEAD DOG Fm (N.6.b) and to work on the construction of barrage positions and dugouts. Church parade for Nos. 3 and 4 Sections. | |
| " | 10.9.17 | | Nos. 3 and 4 Sections fill belts and prepare for leading operations. Nos. 1 + 2 Sections work on the barrage positions | |
| " | 11.9.17 | | Nos 3 and 4 Sections fill belts, &c. LT. FLAVELL proceeds to U.K. on leave. | |
| " | 12.9.17 | | Nos 3 and 4 Sections fill belts &c. Camp at DEAD DOG Fm is transferred to BOIS CARRE (N.12.b) in 19th Divl. area. | |

Credit Champion Captain

A5834 Wt. W4973/M687 750,000 8/16 D. D. & L. Ltd. Forms/C.2118/13.

56th M.G. Coy.

Instructions regarding War Diaries and Intelligence Summaries are contained in F. S. Regs., Part II. and the Staff Manual respectively. Title pages will be prepared in manuscript.

# WAR DIARY or INTELLIGENCE SUMMARY.

2

(Erase heading not required.)

SEPTEMBER - 1917.

Army Form C. 2118.

Cecil H Champion Captain

| Place | Date | Hour | Summary of Events and Information | Remarks and references to Appendices |
|---|---|---|---|---|
| LOCRE | 13.9.17 | | No. 3 Section proceeds to relieve No. 1 Section on the work at the barrage positions, No. 4 Section fills belts &c. 2/LT VARLEY C.G. joins from the Base as re-inforcement. | |
| " | 14.9.17 | | No. 1 Section returns to LOCRE | |
| " | 15.9.17 | | No. 3 Section under 2/LTS BICKERTON and HODGSON and No. 4 Section under 2/LT VARLEY relieve 2 sections of 57 M.G. Coy in the line. The former takes over "D" group of guns and the latter "C" group. The relief was reported "complete" to Adv. Coy. H.Q. at the BLUFF (I.34.c.2.2) by 8 p.m. "C" group is in the vicinity of KLEIN ZILLEBEKE 400-500 yards behind front line - 1 gun at I.36.b.20.25; 2 guns at I.36.a.95.35; 1 gun at I.36.a.43.65. "D" group is just S. of "HILL 60" at I.35.a.95.65; I.35.b.00.68; I.35.b.13.90; and I.35.a.95.95. Guns are also mounted by day for anti-aircraft defence in I.36.a.6.5 and 2 others in vicinity of the CATERPILLAR at I.35.b.05.65 and I.35.b.12.85. A two Brigade front is being held by 111th Bde who relieved 57th and 58th Inf. Bdes less M.G. Coys. Harassing night fire is kept up on selected targets which are engaged by artillery during the day. An average of 10,000 rounds per night is fired by 56 M.G. Coy's guns. Capt. CHAMPION proceeds to Adv. Coy. H.Q. at the BLUFF with LT COOPER. The transport and No. 1 Section remain under 2/LTS ECKERSLEY and BLACK at LOCRE and No. 2 Section carries on with the work at the barrage positions. | |
| " | 16.9.17 | | Church Parade for No. 1 Section. O.C. and 2/LT BICKERTON returns to LOCRE leaving LT COOPER in charge of Nos 2, 3, and 4 Sections. | |
| " | 17.9.17 | | No. 1 Section proceeds to BOIS CARRE Camp and from there assist in carrying S.A.A. up to the barrage positions | |
| " | 18.9.17 | | First line transport proceeds to KLEINE VIERSTRAAT (N.10.b.2.8) under 2/LT BLACK, Company H.Q. remain at LOCRE. 2/LT GATENBY returns from BOIS CARRE camp to LOCRE for the night. | |
| " | 19.9.17 | | Company H.Q. proceed to join transport at KLEINE VIERSTRAAT and Capt CHAMPION and 2/LTS BICKERTON and GATENBY proceed to Adv. Coy. H.Q. in the line. | |

A5834 Wt. W4973/M687 750,000 8/16 D. D. & L. Ltd. Forms/C.2118/13.

56th M.G. Coy

Instructions regarding War Diaries and Intelligence Summaries are contained in F. S. Regs., Part II. and the Staff Manual respectively. Title pages will be prepared in manuscript.

# WAR DIARY 3
or
# INTELLIGENCE SUMMARY.
(Erase heading not required.)

SEPTEMBER 1917

Army Form C. 2118.

| Place | Date | Hour | Summary of Events and Information | Remarks and references to Appendices |
|---|---|---|---|---|
| KLEINE VIERSTRAAT | 19.9.17 (contd) | | An attack is to be made by the Second Army with the object of capturing the southern portion of the PASSCHENDALE RIDGE. The IX Corps is to secure the right flank of the X Corps. The 19th Divn is to attack from the front of IX Corps on the north of the YPRES Canal. The attack by the 19th Divn is to be carried out by the 57th and 58th Inf. Bdes, the 56th Bde less M.G. Coy being in Divl Reserve. The 56th M.G. Coy is detailed to assist in producing a M.G. barrage (See copy of operation orders by Capt CHAMPION and map attached) The Company accordingly assembles at the barrage positions, with Adv. Coy H.Q. at I.36.c.3.7. 2/Lt ECKERSLEY remains behind in charge of details, with 2/Lt BLACK acting as T.O. | App. I |
| " | 20.9.17 | | Operations commence at 5.40 a.m. All objectives are gained and held. The Company has 16 guns in position at I.36.c.8.9 – 200 yards S.W. of KLEINE ZILLEBEKE – in specially prepared emplacements. These guns opened fire at Zero in conjunction with the Artillery producing a barrage E. of BASSEVILLE BEEK. The enemy almost immediately opened his Artillery Barrage which came down heavily on and around the gun positions. In the first hour 2 officers and 12 OR became casualties and 3 guns were put out of action. The undamaged guns continued to fire well. Between 7 a.m. and 8 a.m. the enemy shelling was quieter but subsequently resumed in violence and continued incessantly for several hours. 4 more guns were knocked out by 10 a.m. and several more casualties occurred. The remaining 9 guns worked splendidly. Teams were re-organised and the rate of fire increased in order to search effectively the allotted barrage area. O.C. Company arranged with O.C. 246 Company to cover part of 56 Company's area. O.C. considered the necessity of moving the guns back on account of enemy shelling and reconnoitred with Section officers for positions 300 yards in rear and suitable for firing on S.O.S. lines later. Meanwhile the guns still fired well, officers and men behaving splendidly notwithstanding the trying conditions and heavy casualties. The D.M.G.O.'s assent to the withdrawal of the guns was obtained and as circumstances permitted later guns were withdrawn one by one to I.36.c.1.8 at the W. end of FUSILIER WOOD. About 1 p.m. 7 guns had been knocked out and 30 per cent of the personnel had become casualties. The battle died down to some extent during the afternoon. The abandoned emplacements were still shelled intermittently and it appeared probable that the enemy | |

A5834 Wt. W4973/M687 750,000 8/16 D. D. & L. Ltd. Forms/C.2118/13.

56th M.G. Coy

# WAR DIARY
*or*
# INTELLIGENCE SUMMARY.
(*Erase heading not required.*)

SEPTEMBER-1917

Army Form C. 2118.

Instructions regarding War Diaries and Intelligence Summaries are contained in F. S. Regs., Part II. and the Staff Manual respectively. Title pages will be prepared in manuscript.

Fred H Champion Captain

| Place | Date | Hour | Summary of Events and Information | Remarks and references to Appendices |
|---|---|---|---|---|
| KLEINE VIERSTRAAT | 20-9-17 (Contd.) | | Enemy were searching for the guns. Gun stores were salvaged with difficulty. The newly selected positions were practically untouched and the remaining 9 guns were in position by 7.10 p.m. At 7.25 p.m. the guns responded immediately to the S.O.S. signal in conjunction with Arty. The RAVINE in FUSILIER WOOD where Company H.Q. were situated was shelled considerably during the afternoon and evening. The D.M.G.O. reported that the Infantry were very pleased with the M.G. barrage which it was stated accounted for many enemy casualties and in which our guns greatly helped. One more of our guns was put out of action. The guns fired during the night on areas where it was reported enemy had collected in shell holes. Casualties: Killed, 2/Lt W. BICKERTON and 6 O.R.; Wounded 2/Lt M. HODGSON and 14 O.R.; Died of wounds, 1 O.R.; Wounded and at duty 1 O.R. 8 guns out of action. Ammunition expended: About 280,000 rounds | HS |
| " | 21.9.17 | | Guns fired on S.O.S. lines from 4.30 am. to 5.10 a.m. in conjunction with Artillery barrage. Enemy shelled FUSILIER WOOD and vicinity during the day. An inspection of the abandoned emplacements revealed all but 3 blown in. Extract from IX Corps Intelligence of 21/9/17: "Prisoners state that in the attack our M.G. barrage prevented almost all their Trench Mortars and M.G.s from coming into action." The Army Commander congratulates all ranks of the 19th Divn on the great success gained by them in the operations | HS |
| " | 22.9.17 | | Enemy's artillery active during the day. FUSILIER WOOD shelled between 12 noon and 2 p.m. Extract from IX Corps Intelligence of 22/9/17: "Prisoners state that during the last days previous to the attack ration parties and reliefs invariably had casualties from our shrapnel and in the forward area from our M.G. fire. Wounded of the 2nd Battalion to whom they spoke [illegible] that our M.G. barrage made it almost impossible to get either Trench Mortars or M.G.s into action." The Company relieves 57th M.G. Company in the line (8 Guns) and 246 M.G. Coy. relieves 58th M.G. Coy (8 guns). The 16 guns are under the command of Captain CHAMPION. [illegible] Gun Positions of 56 M.G. Coy: J.31.c.95.40 and 90.45 (STRONG PT); 2 guns at J.31.d.25.90 (STRONG PT); 2 guns at J.31.d.5.2 (WOOD FT); J.31.d.7.9 and J.31.c.65.20. Gun Positions of 246 M.G. Coy: I.36.d.75.40 and 75.50 (Old front line); P.1.a.8.7 and 87.73 (POTSDAM FT); 2 guns at O.6.b.90.45 (STRONG PT); O.6.c.7.8 (CEMETERY EMBT); O.6.a.6.4 (PAGUE WOOD). | HS |

A5834 Wt. W4973/M687 750,000 8/16 D. D. & L. Ltd. Forms/C.2118/13.

56th M.G.Coy. — 5 — SEPTEMBER-1917 — Fred H Champion Captain

Instructions regarding War Diaries and Intelligence Summaries are contained in F. S. Regs., Part II. and the Staff Manual respectively. Title pages will be prepared in manuscript.

# WAR DIARY
or
# INTELLIGENCE SUMMARY.
(*Erase heading not required.*)

Army Form C. 2118.

| Place | Date | Hour | Summary of Events and Information | Remarks and references to Appendices |
|---|---|---|---|---|
| KLEINE VIERSTRAAT | 23.9.17 | | Company H.Q. (Advanced) moved to HILL 60. Enemy shelled the forward area during the night and early morning. | FHC |
| " | 24.9.17 | | Hostile shelling on forward area, all guns report all fire. Emplacement at J.31.d.25.90 blown up and tripod damaged. Casualties: killed 1 O.R.; Wounded 1 O.R. | FHC |
| " | 25.9.17 | | Casualties: Wounded 4 O.R. Orders received to put up a barrage on following day, preparations made. LT FLAVELL returns from U.K. leave. | FHC |
| " | 26.9.17 | | In conjunction with guns of 41 M.G.Coy (37th Divn) and 246 M.G.Coy. 4 guns of 56 M.G.Coy. formed a barrage commencing at 5.50 a.m. in conjunction with Arty bombardment. The 4 guns at I.36.c.1.8 searched the area W. of the BASSEVILLEBEEK in J.32.b+d, J.33.c, and P.2.b. and P.3.a. Fire was continued throughout the day all guns firing well. Guns also opened on S.O.S. lines during the evening. Enemy's reply on forward area fairly heavy HILL 60 heavily shelled. No casualties. LT FLAVELL reports to O.C. at Adv. Coy H.Q. in the line. | FHC |
| " | 27.9.17 | | 4 guns fired in conjunction with Arty barrage on the same area W of the BASSEVILLEBEEK from 5 a.m. to 5.30 a.m. O.C. and 2/LT GATENBY return to transport lines leaving LT FLAVELL in command of the Company in the line. 4 guns are withdrawn from the forward area and utilized for night firing on enemy tracks approaches, to x from I.36.c.2.8 and I.36.d.2.6, in accordance with suggestions made by the O.C. to Brigade on the 26th Sept 17. The 5 guns of 56 M.G.Coy withdrawn were at J.31.d.7.9, J.31.c.95.40 + 90.45. 1 gun of 246 M.G.Coy withdrawn from P.1.a.8.7 | FHC |
| " | 28.9.17 | | Indirect fire carried out on various targets. 7000 rounds fired. | FHC |
| " | 29.9.17 | | 58th Inf Bde (less 58th M.G.Coy) relieves 56th Inf Bde (less 56 M.G.Coy) in the line. 2/LT JONES takes over command of the indirect fire guns from 2/LT BLACK who commands the 5 guns in the line. 2/LTS CARTER A.C., COCKER J. and SLACK J.G. report at the transport lines as re-inforcements from the Base. | FHC |
| " | 30.9.17 | | 2nd Lts CARTER + COCKER proceed to Hill 60 – 2nd Lt Cocker goes forward to Forward H.Q. to relieve 2nd Lt BLACK 3 forward guns relieved by 37 to carry out night firing with other guns at I.36.c.2.8 – [illegible] Casualties Wounded at duty 2nd Lt Black 1 O.R. | |

A5834 Wt. W4973/M687 750,000 8/16 D. D. & L. Ltd. Forms/C.2118/13.

Fred H Champion Capt
OC 56 M.G. Coy.

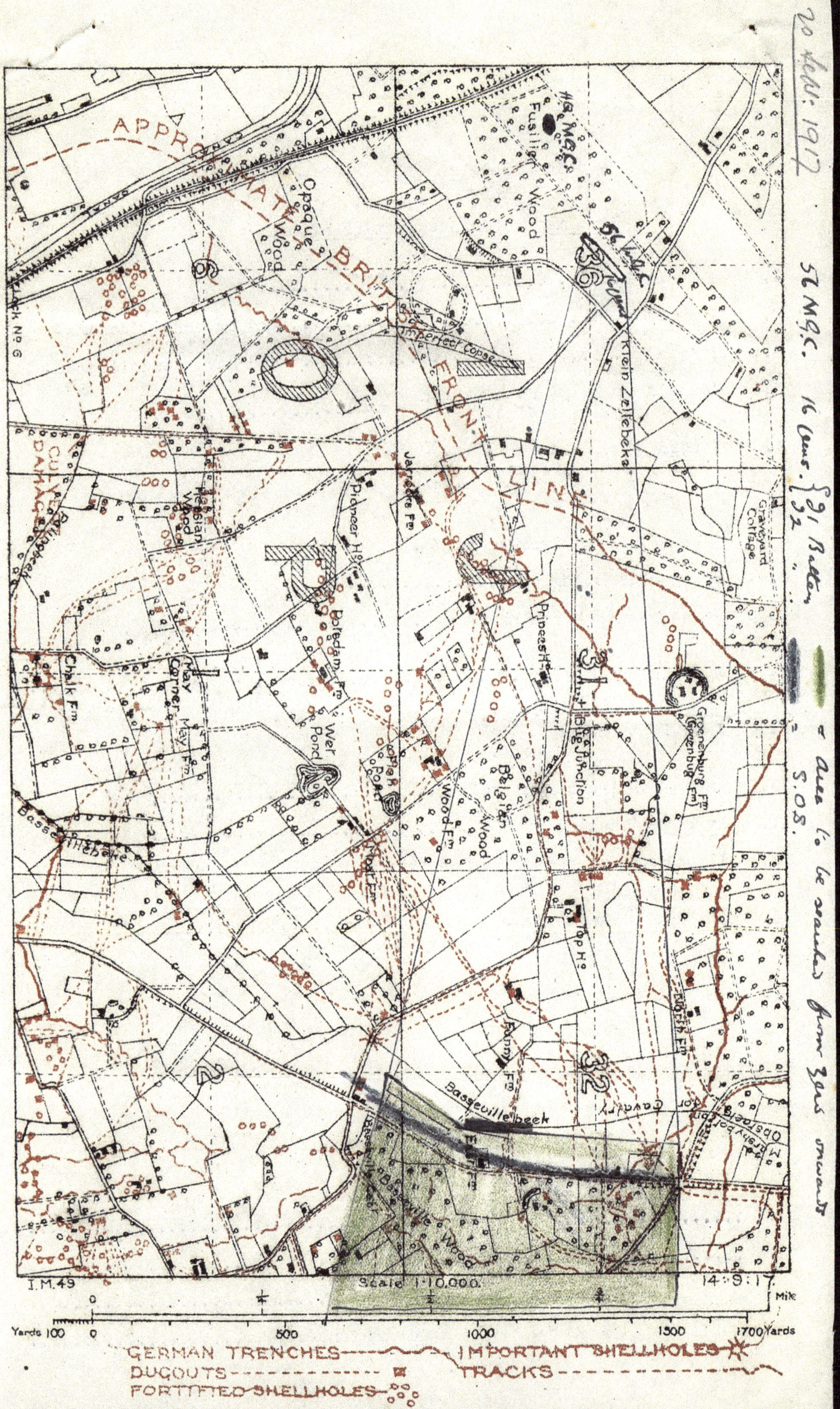
APPROXIMATE BRITISH FRONT LINE
Opaque Wood
Fusilier Wood
Imperfect Copse
Klein Zillebeke
Hessian Wood
Pioneer Ho.
Jarrocks Fm.
Graveyard Cottage
Bodedam Fm.
Pipes Ho.
Chalk Fm.
May Corner
May Fm.
Wer Pond
Belgian Wood
Wood Fm.
Groenenburg Fm.
Basseville beek
Top Ho.
Fanny Fm.
Obsdeerfarm
Bassevillebeek
Basseville Wood
Dammstrasse
Scale 1:10,000.
I.M.49
14·9·17.
Yards 100
0
500
1000
1500
1700 Yards
GERMAN TRENCHES
DUGOUTS
FORTIFIED SHELLHOLES
IMPORTANT SHELLHOLES
TRACKS

- MAKE USE OF PARAGRAPHS AS -
REQUIRED.

Give map reference or mark of map
at back.

1. I am at ....................................

2. I am at .................................. and am consolidating.

3. I am at .................................. and have consolidated.

4. Am held up by ( Machine gun ) at ..................
( Wire. )

5. I need - Ammunition.
Bombs.
Rifle Grenades.
Water.
Very Lights.
Stokes Shells.

6. Enemy collecting at .........................

7. Counter-attack coming from .........................

8. I am in touch with ....................on Right. / Left at .............

9. I am in touch on Right. / Left.

10. Enemy holding strong point ............................

11. Am being shelled from ................................

12. I estimate my present strength at ............. rifles.

13. Hostile (Battery ) active at.................
(Machine Gun. )
(Trench Mortar. )
(Snipers )

14. General information.

Time .............. m.

Date ..................

Name...................................

Platoon................................

Company ...............................

Battalion..............................

SECRET.

COPY No. 14...

OPERATION ORDERS BY:-

CAPTN. F. H. CHAMPION commanding
56th Coy. Machine Gun Corps.

REF. HOLLEBEKE 1:10,000. 18th Sept. 1917.

GENERAL.

The 19th Division will take part in the 2ND ARMY offensive, on a date to be notified later. The attack will be carried out by the 57th & 58th BDES, the 56th BDE being in reserve.

56TH M.G.COY

The 56th M.G.COY is detailed to assist in producing a Machine Gun Barrage and is allotted an area 450x to 600x EAST of BASSEVILLEBEEK from P.2.b.00.85 to J.32.b.30.50.

ORGANISATION AND CONTROL.

The sixteen guns of the company will form part of the NORTHERN GROUP of guns under the D.M.G.O. 19th DIVN. (H.Q. I.35.b.0.8). The guns will be divided into two batteries of eight guns each, designated respectively, I1. BATTERY and I2. BATTERY, both batteries under the command of O.C. Company.

Nos. 1 & 2 Sections will comprise I1 BATTERY under the command of LT. COOPER. Nos. 3 & 4 Sectns. will comprise I2. BATTERY under the command of 2nd LT. BICKERTON.

No. 1 Sectn. will be under the command of 2LT. HODGSON.
2 " " " " " " " LT. COOPER.
3 " " " " " " " 2LT. BICKERTON.
4 " " " " " " " 2LT. GATENBY.

ORGANISATION OF FIRE.

Emplacements have been constructed as follows:-

No. 1. Section — I. 36. c. 8. 9.
No. 2 Section — I. 36. a. 90. 05.
No. 3 Section — I. 36. a. 9. 1.
No. 4 Section — I. 36. b. 65. 15.

The area to be covered by the fire of the sixteen guns of the Company, has been divided amongst the Sections, & again between guns, full details of which appear on BARRAGE CHARTS issued herewith. Both batteries will open fire at ZERO and systematically search the whole area allotted, fire being specially concentrated on the areas and routes marked on maps issued to Officers.

RATE OF FIRE.

FROM – ZERO until ZERO + 2 hrs. 30 mins.
60 rounds per minute per gun.

FROM – ZERO + 2 hrs. 30 mins until ZERO + 4 hrs.
1 Belt in 10 minutes, per gun.

FROM – ZERO + 4 hrs. until ZERO + 5 hrs. 30 mins.
1 Belt in 5 minutes per gun.

From – Zero + 5.30 hrs onwards – 1 belt per gun in 10 mins

S.O.S.

The S.O.S. LINE for both batteries will be the line P.2.b.2.9 through EAST FARM to J.32.b.50.55.

S.O.S. – RATE OF FIRE.

All guns 250 rounds per minute for one minute, 100 rounds per minute for next 10 minutes and 60 rounds per minute until the situation is clear.

ANTI-AIRCRAFT DEFENCE.

One gun per section will be detailed for Anti-Aircraft Defence against low flying hostile patrols.

SYNCHRONISATION OF WATCHES.

Watches must be synchronised three times on Y Day. at COY H.Qrs.

COMPANY HEADQUARTERS.

From 8pm. on Y/Z night. Coy. Hdqrs. will be at I.36.c.30.45.

COMMUNICATION.

O.C. Company will be in communication with the D.M.G.O. by Telephone and Runner. Battery Commanders will be in communication with Coy. Hdqrs. by Telephone & Runner. They will also be in a central position, close to battery, where they can maintain closest communication with Section & Gun Commanders. A Forward Observation Post will be established in conjunction with 246th M.G. COY.

INSTRUCTIONS.

Barrage Charts containing detailed instructions for each section, are issued herewith. Each Section Officer will also be issued with a Map Range Card which will enable him to concentrate the fire of his Section on any point in the battery zone. Section Officers will issue simple Barrage Tables to each Gun Team. Each gun will have assembled at the gun position by ZERO HOUR :- 2 Spare Barrels 20 Filled Belts.

20,000 Rds. SAA. Loose in Boxes. 1 Tin of Oil.

3 Petrol Tins of Water.

The S.A.A. and filled belts are already dumped in the vicinity of the positions.

The First Aid Case will be made up and the Spare Parts Box will not be taken into action

CARE OF GUN STORES.

Section Officers & N.C.O's will be held responsible that no wastage occurs in Gun Stores in the line.

ASSEMBLY.

ZERO DAY will be announced later. Guns of Nos. 1 & 2 Sections will be in their battery positions by 8 pm. on Y. DAY. These guns will take part in the Direct Fire defence of the line on Y NIGHT. A defence scheme for Y NIGHT will be issued later. Guns of Nos. 3 & 4 Sections will not vacate their defensive positions to move forward to their battery positions until midnight on Y/Z NIGHT. Orders regarding this move will be issued separately. The four guns of No. 3 Section will carry out their usual night firing programme on Y/Z NIGHT.

S. O. S. SIGNALS.

In use. Rifle Grenade Signal – Parachute with three colours. – Red over Green over Yellow.

First change } Rifle Grenade Signal. – Parachute – if necessary } White changing to Green.

Second change } 1½" Very Light. – Parachute White if necessary } changing to Red.

As circumstances permit, this last will also be made a Rifle Grenade Signal.

Issued at 12 noon.

ACKNOWLEDGE.

COPIES.

1. O.C. Coy.
2. Lt. COOPER.
3. 2Lt. ECKERSLEY.
4. 2Lt. BICKERTON.
5. 2Lt. HODGSON.
6. 2Lt. GATENBY.
7. 2Lt. VARLEY.
8. 2Lt. BLACK (T.O.)
9. D.M.G.O.
10. 56th INF. BDE.
11. 57th " "
12. 58th " "
13. C.S.M.
14. WAR DIARY.
15. FILE.

Fred H. Champion
Captain.
Commanding. 56 Coy. M.G.CORPS.

H.Q.
56TH INFANTRY BDE.
No. BM 2801
Date 1/11/17

No 56 COY.
MG/B/11
1/11/17
MACHINE GUN CORPS.

To:-
56th Inf Bde

Attached please find Original Copy of War Diary for this Unit for the month of October 1917.

R. [illegible] 2/Lt

for O.C. 56 COY. MACHINE GUN CORPS.

56th M.G. Coy

Instructions regarding War Diaries and Intelligence Summaries are contained in F. S. Regs., Part II. and the Staff Manual respectively. Title pages will be prepared in manuscript.

# WAR DIARY 1.
or
# ~~INTELLIGENCE~~ SUMMARY.
(Erase heading not required.)

~~SEPTEMBER~~ OCTOBER - 1917

Army Form C. 2118.

56 M.G. Coy
Dec 1917 Champion captain
Vol 25

| Place | Date | Hour | Summary of Events and Information | Remarks and references to Appendices |
|---|---|---|---|---|
| KLEIN VIERSTRAAT | 1.10.17 | | LT. COOPER relieves LT. FLAVELL in command of the guns in the line. Indirect fire carried out by barrage guns. | |
| " | 2.10.17 | | LT FLAVELL relieves LT COOPER in command of the guns in the line and takes command over the guns in the right Brigade sector: 8 guns of 56 M.G. Coy and 8 guns of 246 M.G. Coy. Indirect fire carried out as usual by barrage guns. Work commenced on emplacements for barrage guns for coming operations | |
| " | 3.10.17 | | 8 barrage guns placed in position to co-operate with the operations of the Division on the left, see operation orders, attached copy. | App. I. |
| " | 4.10.17 | | 6.3 a.m. fire opened at zero plus 3 mins – 8 guns under 2/LTS VARLEY and CARTER. 2 of our barrage guns relieve 2 guns of 246 Coy. in the Support Line. Dispositions: 4 barrage guns under 2/LT VARLEY at RAVINE I.36.c.2.9; 2 guns under 2/LT CARTER [illegible] at J.31.b.55.25; 2 guns under 2/LT COCKER in the old front line at I.36.d.55.50. | |
| " | 5.10.17 | | Night firing carried on as usual by barrage guns, on selected targets. | |
| " | 6.10.17 | | Night firing carried on by barrage guns. | |
| " | 7.10.17 | | LT. COOPER relieves LT. FLAVELL in command of the guns. Nos 3 + 4 sections relieve Nos. 1 + 2 in the line. Night firing carried on by barrage guns. | |
| " | 8.10.17 | | Night firing carried on. Nos 1 + 2 sections cleaning up. | |
| " | 9.10.17 | | Night firing carried on. Nos 1 + 2 sections training. | |
| " | 10.10.17 | | Night firing carried on. Nos 1 + 2 sections training. | |
| " | 11.10.17 | | Nos. 1 + 2 sections relieve Nos. 3 + 4 in the line. Night firing carried out. | |
| " | 12.10.17 | | Nos. 3 + 4 sections cleaning up. Night firing carried on. | |
| " | 13.10.17 | | Nos. 3 + 4 sections training. Night firing carried on. | |
| " | 14.10.17 | | LT. FLAVELL relieves LT. COOPER in command of the guns. It is announced in D.R.O. that the following N.C.O.s and men have received the Military Medal, viz: 4542 Sgt. C. HILL, 73395 L/Cpl. C. LECKIE, and 31295 Pte. A. TURTON. Night firing carried on. Nos 3 + 4 sections training | |
| " | 15.10.17 | | Nos 3 + 4 sections relieve Nos. 1 + 2 in the line. Night firing carried on. | |
| " | 16.10.17 | | Night firing carried on. Nos 1 + 2 sections cleaning up. | |

D. D. & L., London, E.C.
(A8001) Wt. W1771/M2031 750,000 5/17 Sch. 52 Forms/C2118/14

- 56th M.G. Coy.

Instructions regarding War Diaries and Intelligence Summaries are contained in F. S. Regs., Part II. and the Staff Manual respectively. Title pages will be prepared in manuscript.

# WAR DIARY 2.
or
# INTELLIGENCE SUMMARY.
(Erase heading not required.)

OCTOBER 1917

Army Form C. 2118.

[signature] Captain

| Place | Date | Hour | Summary of Events and Information | Remarks and references to Appendices |
|---|---|---|---|---|
| KLEIN VIERSTRAAT | 17.10.17 | | 2 Lt. CARTER moves his H.Q. from the RAVINE at I.36.c.2.9 to J.31.c.7.3 near JARROCKS Fm. Night firing carried on. Nos 1 & 2 Sections training | |
| " | 18.10.17 | | Night firing carried on. Nos. 1 & 2 Sections training | |
| " | 19.10.17 | | Nos 1 & 2 Sections relieve Nos. 3 & 4 in the line. Night firing carried on. | |
| " | 20.10.17 | | Lt. COOPER relieves Lt. FLAVELL in command of the guns. Nos 3 & 4 Sections cleaning up. Night firing carried on. In a Special Order of the Day by Brig. Genl. F.G. WILLAN D.S.O. 2/Lt. VARLEY is congratulated on having been awarded the Military Cross. | |
| " | 21.10.17 | | Night firing carried on. Nos. 3 & 4 Sections training. | |
| " | 22.10.17 | | Night firing carried on. Nos 3 & 4 Sections training. | |
| " | 23.10.17 | | Construction of barrage positions commenced with a view to co-operation in forthcoming operations. Night firing carried on. Nos 3 & 4 Sections training. | |
| " | 24.10.17 | | Night firing carried on. Nos. 3 & 4 Sections training. | |
| " | 25.10.17 | | Nos. 3 & 4 Sections relieve Nos. 1 & 2 in the line. Night firing carried on. Casualties: Killed: 1 O.R. A gun is knocked out. | |
| " | 26.10.17 | | The Company takes part in a M.G. Barrage carried out under the orders of the D.M.G.O. 19th Divn in order to assist the 7th Divn in an attack on GHELUVELT. For this purpose the 4 barrage guns vacate their positions at dusk on the night 25/26 Oct. 4 guns under 2/Lt. COCKER and 4 guns of 246 Coy. compose "A" Battery, the whole group being commanded by Lt. GASCOIGNE of 246 Coy. The 4 guns of "A" Battery under 2/Lt. COCKER are in position astride the road at I.26.d.85.95 (HOLLEBEKE Map, Sheet 28). The guns are numbered 1-8 from right to left. Targets engaged: Nos. 5 & 6 guns the area J.33.c.25.30 to J.33.c.15.10 to P.3.a.65.80 to J.33.c.8.0. No. 7 gun area, the Railway Triangle Junction at J.33.c.55.35. No. 8 gun, the fork road at J.33.c.13.88. Fire was directed on these targets at | |

D. D. & L., London, E.C.
(A8603) Wt. W1771/M2031 750,000 5/17 Sch. 52 Forms/C2118/14

56th M.G.Coy.

Instructions regarding War Diaries and Intelligence Summaries are contained in F. S. Regs., Part II. and the Staff Manual respectively. Title pages will be prepared in manuscript.

# WAR DIARY 3 or INTELLIGENCE SUMMARY.

(Erase heading not required.)

OCTOBER-1917.

Army Form C. 2118.

Fred H Champion Captain

| Place | Date | Hour | Summary of Events and Information | Remarks and references to Appendices |
|---|---|---|---|---|
| KLEIN VIERSTRAAT | 26.10.17 | (continued) | at Zero + 8 mins (5.48 a.m.) at intense rate until Zero + 90 mins and thence intermittently until Zero + 20 mins. The enemy continuously bombarded with 5.9 shells the old line of trenches approximately 150 yards in rear of the Battery, also the group of dugouts and concrete shelters at I.36.d.95.45 but failed to locate the barrage guns. Casualties: nil. S.O.S. calls: nil. Number of rounds fired 4,000 per gun. Stoppages were numerous owing to the heavy rain which fell during operations. The gun positions were flooded and mud and water penetrated the belt-boxes. See Operation Orders attached. Lt. FLAVELL relieves Lt. COOPER in command of the guns in the line. Nos 1 + 2 Sections cleaning up. | App. II |
| " | 27.10.17 | | 4 barrage guns which co-operated in recent operations moved back to their original emplacements on the night 26/27 Oct. Nos. 1 + 2 Sections training. | |
| " | 28.10.17 | | Night firing carried out. The O.C. Company, Capt. CHAMPION, returns from a month's course of advanced M.G. training at G.H.Q. Small arms School CAMIERS. | |
| " | 29.10.17 | | Night firing carried on. Nos 1 + 2 Sections training. | |
| " | 30.10.17 | | In conjunction with operations further North a M.G. barrage by the 19th Divn. is placed in the left Sub-Sector. 4 guns of 56 M.G. Coy. co-operate by putting down a barrage in front of ALASKA HOUSES (J.33.b.3.6) under the command of 2/Lt. JONES. Approximately 20000 rounds fired. Casualties: Nil. 1 gun blown up (undamaged) 14 Belt Boxes destroyed. Nos 1+2 Sections training. | |
| " | 31.10.17 | | Night firing carried on. Nos 1 + 2 Sections relieve Nos 3 + 4 in the line. Capt. CHAMPION relieves Lt. FLAVELL in command of the guns and takes over command of the guns in the Right Brigade Sector. | |

D. D. & L., London, E.C. (A8001) Wt. W1771/M2031 750,000 5/17 Sch. 52 Forms/C2118/14

Fred H Champion Capt
OC. 56 M.G. Coy

App. I.

Company Operation Orders No. 1.
by Lt. E.W.C. FLAVELL Commanding
56th Machine Gun Company.

1/ In cooperation with the operations by the Division on our left we are placing a Barrage of M.G. Fire on the area.

J. 32 b. 5.4. to
J. 27 c. 4.6 to
J. 33 c. 5.5 to
J. 27 c. 9.8 to
J. 27 c. 4.6.

S.O.S. Line J. 32 b. 5.4. to J. 27 c. 4.6.

2/ This will be carried out by 8 guns. 6 from 56th M.G. Coy & 2 from 246th M.G. Coy under the Command of 2/Lts. VARLEY and COCKER at I 36. b.1.1. These 8 guns will be known as 'A' Battery. Guns being numbered R to L.

3/ Fire will be opened at Zero hour at the following rates.

Zero to Zero + 55 = 200 rds per minute
Zero + 5 to Zero + 30 = 75 " "
Zero + 30 to Zero + 60 = 50 " "
Zero + 60 to Zero + 2 hrs. = 25 " "

after which intermittent bursts of fire throughout the day and night.

4/ S.O.S. On the S.O.S. Signal being sent up all guns will immediately open fire at the rate of 350 rds per gun a minute for 1 minute 100 rds per gun for the next 10 minutes and [illegible] rds per minute until the situation is clear. The guns will remain in position ready to answer S.O.S. signals until Zero plus 8 hours.

5/ After Zero + 2 hrs. 2/Lt COCKER only will remain with the guns & will be relieved by 2/Lt CARTER at dusk. 2/Lt VARLEY will report in person to Coy. H.Q. after Zero + 2 hrs.

6/ The following will be put on the guns

| | | Range | Q.E. | V.I. | Bearing |
|---|---|---|---|---|---|
| No 1 | Gun. | 2200x – 2700x | 4°45'<br>8°41' | 24x<br>26x | 86°–84° |
| " 2 | " | 2250x – 2700x | 4°58'<br>8°35' | 24x<br>28x | 84°–82° |
| " 3 | " | 2200x – 2700x | 4°57'<br>8°3' | 24x<br>28x | 84°–82° |
| " 4 | " | 2400x – 2750x | 6°14'<br>9°17' | 18x<br>18x | 81°–80° |
| " 5 | " | 2500x – 2900x | 7°2'<br>10°47' | 18x<br>18x | 79°–78° |
| " 6 | " | 2500x – 2900x | 9°4'<br>11°17' | 18x<br>18x | 79°–78° |
| " 7 | " | 2600x – 3030x | 9°47' | 18x | 78°–7° |

| | Range | Q.E. | V.I. | Traverse |
|---|---|---|---|---|
| No 8 Gun | 2900 to 3000y | 19° 47' | 18x | 78°–75' |
| | | 9° 47' | 18x | |

For the S.O.S. fire figures will be taken.

7. S.A.A. can be had at Brigade Dump at I 36 c 3.7.
The S.O.S. signal must be known by all ranks and instantly acted upon.

8. 4 men will be detailed as Runners at the Barrage Position. They must be thoroughly acquainted with Coy & Section H.Q. & S.A.A. dumps etc.

9. Zero will be notified later.

10. Acknowledge.

Issued at 2 pm.

J.W.C. Lovell Lieut
O.C. 264th M.G. Coy.

Copies 15
2Lt. VARLEY
O.C. 246 M.G. Coy
2Lt. COCKER
2Lt. CARTER
WAR DIARY
FILE.

31/10/17

App II.

Copy No 3 OPERATION ORDER NO 1 SECRET

By Capt A S WARREN

25 Oct: 17

Machine Gun Barrage for Z Day

1) Control
Guns will be in two groups A1 + A2 Batteries under LT GASCOIGNE + 2LT LOCKER respectively.

2) H.Q. North side of [illegible] BANK

3) Barrage Zones + tasks A1 will keep area marked 4 under fire A2 keep areas marked 2 + 2 under fire
These areas to be searched in depth.

4) S.O.S
All guns will concentrate fire on their allotted targets
S.O.S signal Red over green over yellow.
Rate of fire.

250 rds for 1 minute
100 " 2 "
60 " a minute till all clear.

5. Rates of fire
Until Zero + 2 hrs 30 mins an average rate of fire of 60 rds per minute will be maintained
From Zero + 2 hrs 30 mins onwards burst of fire at a rate of 1 belt per gun per 10 minutes. From Z + 4 hrs to Z + 5 hrs 30 mins double rate of fire 1 belt per 5 mins
From Z + 5.30 fire as situation demands

6. All watches to be synchronized.

7. Each gun position to have
2 Spare barrels
20 filled belts
20,000 Rds S.A.A.
2 tins of water
" Oil

8. Gun No 9 O.F.L 56 M.G. Coy will be mounted for A.A. defence.

9. Guns at Wood Fm will be mounted on attack day to fire at any targets which appear.

10. Acknowledge.

Signed A.S. Warren Capt
O.C. Right Sector

Issued to
No 1a. 2 Lt Cocker
No 2a. O.C. 56 M.G. Coy
No 3a. Lt Cooper
No 4a. File

No 56 COY. MACHINE GUN CORPS.
MG/T/105
11.12.17

To:-

56th Inf Bde.

Enclosed please find Original Copy of War Diary of this Unit for the Month of November 1917.

H.W.C. Howard Lt/O.C.
56 COY. MACHINE GUN CORPS.

Instructions regarding War Diaries and Intelligence Summaries are contained in F. S. Regs., Part II. and the Staff Manual respectively. Title pages will be prepared in manuscript.

# WAR DIARY
or
# ~~INTELLIGENCE~~ SUMMARY.
(*Erase heading not required.*)

Army Form C. 2118.

Sheet I.

Vol 26

No 56 COY. MACHINE GUN CORPS

| Place | Date | Hour | Summary of Events and Information | Remarks and references to Appendices |
|---|---|---|---|---|
| KLEIN VIERSTRAAT. | 1/11/17 | 10pm. | Usual night firing carried out by guns in the line, on Area LOCK IV to KIKI FM to P2. 1.2.8. 10000 rds fired. Raid carried out by 2 Officers. 28 O.Rs on the Brigades left sub-sector. Results 7 Prisoners. Our casualties Nil. Nos 3+4 Sections working on the Camp. | |
| ZILLEBEKE SECTOR in the LINE. | 2/11/17 | 10pm. | 4 Guns carried out Indirect Fire on HOLLEBEKE CHATEAU. 8,000 rds fired. Nos 3+4 Sections Training and working on Camp at KLEIN VIERSTRAAT. Enemy carried out a bombing raid in the evening round the district. | |
| " | 3/11/17 | 12 noon | 2/Lt VARLEY MC relieves 2Lt JONES in the Line. Training carried on by Nos 3+4 Sects. Nos 1+2 in the line. | |
| " | 4/11/17 | 10pm. | Indirect Fire guns carry out usual night firing programme. 2/Lt ECKERSLEY relieves CAPT CHAMPION in command of guns in the line. Nos 3+4 Sections training. | |
| " | 5/11/17 | | Nos 3+4 Sections working on and improving Camp. 2/Lt COCKER relieves 2/Lt SATENBY in command of Barrage Guns. Usual night firing carried out 8000 rds fired. | |
| " | 6/11/17 | 5pm | Nos 3+4 Sections relieve Nos 1+2 Sections in the line. O.C + 2 in C. attends a conference at Adv. Coy HQ to arrange details of relief by 247 M.G. Coy. 10,000 rds fired on selected targets during the night. | |
| " | 7/11/17 | 10pm | Nos 3+4 Sections in the line. 4 guns carry out indirect fire. Nos 1+2 Sections cleaning and resting. | |
| " | 8/11/17 | 9.30pm | Company is relieved in the line by 247 M.G. Coy. Relief complete by 9.30pm. The whole Coy. spends the night at the Camp at KLEIN VIERSTRAAT. Preparations made for the move tomorrow. | |
| KLEIN VIERST. | 9/11/17 | 11am | Company moves by road to FRONTIER CAMP. WESTOUTRE. ROUTE. LA CLYTTE, LOCRE, and WESTOUTRE arriving at 2pm. 2/Lt VARLEY leaves for a Course at IX Corps Infantry School. | APPEX I |
| FRONTIER CAMP WESTOUTRE. | 10/11/17 | 8 am | Company leaves for Rest Area. Marches to BAILLEUL by way of BERTHEN and ST JANS CAPPELL. Entrains at BAILLEUL for EBBLINGHEM. and then marches to REST BILLETS at LE LABOURER near LYNDE arriving at 1pm. The Transport under Lt. FLAVELL and 2/Lt. SLACK proceed to REST BILLETS by road arriving about 3pm. ROUTE. BERTHEN METEREN, STRAZEELE, HAZEBROUCK and WALLON CAPPELL. 2/Lts CARTER and COCKER leaves for Drill Course at IX Corps School BERTHEN | APPEX II<br>APPEX III |

D. D. & L., London, E.C. (A8001) Wt. W1771/M2031 750,000 5/17 Sch. 52 Forms C2118/14

Instructions regarding War Diaries and Intelligence Summaries are contained in F. S. Regs., Part II. and the Staff Manual respectively. Title pages will be prepared in manuscript.

# WAR DIARY
*or*
~~INTELLIGENCE SUMMARY.~~
*(Erase heading not required.)*

Army Form C. 2118.

NO 5? COY MACHINE GUN CORPS O.C.

Sheet. II.

| Place | Date | Hour | Summary of Events and Information | Remarks and references to Appendices |
|---|---|---|---|---|
| LE LABOURER | 11/11/17 | — | Company cleaning and organising at REST BILLETS. LT. COOPER rejoins from leave. | |
| „ „ | 12/11/17 | — | Company Training and improving billets. | |
| „ „ | 13/11/17 | — | Company Training. Inspection by G.O.C. 56th Inf. Bde. who congratulated us on our fine work in the operations of the 20th Sept. | |
| „ „ | 14/11/17 | — | Company Training. Special Courses for N.C.O's under LT. FLAVELL. Signallers, Scouts and Range Takers under LT. COOPER. O.C. Lectures the Officers on Barrage Fire. | |
| „ „ | 15/11/17 | — | Company Training. | |
| „ „ | 16/11/17 | — | Company Training. | |
| „ „ | 17/11/17 | — | Company Training. | |
| „ „ | 18/11/17 | — | Company Inspection by the O.C. and Divine Services. | |
| „ „ | 19/11/17 | — | Company Training. Visited by the G.O.C. 56th Inf. Bde. G.S.O. I and D.M.G.O. who expressed satisfaction with the training being carried out in Range Work and Tactical Scheme. | |
| „ „ | 20/11/17 | — | Company Training. Range Work and Tactical Scheme. | |
| „ „ | 21/11/17 | — | Company Training. | |
| „ „ | 22/11/17 | — | Company Training. | |
| „ „ | 23/11/17 | — | Company Training. 2/Lt. GATENBY rejoins from leave. | |
| „ „ | 24/11/17 | — | Company Training. 2/Lt. CARTER and COCKER rejoin from Drill Course. | |
| „ „ | 25/11/17 | — | Inspection by the O.C. Divine Services. | |

D. D. & L., London, E.C.
(A8001) Wt. W2771/M2031 750,000 5/17 Sch. 52 Forms/C2118/14

Instructions regarding War Diaries and Intelligence Summaries are contained in F. S. Regs., Part II. and the Staff Manual respectively. Title pages will be prepared in manuscript.

# WAR DIARY
*or*
# ~~INTELLIGENCE SUMMARY.~~
*(Erase heading not required.)*

No 56 COY. MACHINE GUN CORPS. O.C.

Army Form C. 2118.

Sheet III.

| Place | Date | Hour | Summary of Events and Information | Remarks and references to Appendices |
|---|---|---|---|---|
| LE LABOURER | 26/11/17 | — | Company Training. Lt COOPER and 2/Lt GATENBY leaves for Drill Course at IX Corps School. | |
| " " | 27/11/17 | — | Company moves from Billets at Le LABOURER to Billets at WALLON CAPPELL by route march. ROUTE: LE LABOURER CERCUS and WALLON CAPPELL. | |
| WALLON CAPPELL | 28/11/17 | — | Company Training. | |
| " " | 29/11/17 | — | Company Training. | |
| " " | 30/11/17 | — | Company Training. 2/Lt SHACK leaves for Transport Course at ABBEVILLE. | |

E.W.B. Havell Lieut for
O.C. 56 COY. MACHINE GUN CORPS.

(A8001) D. D. & L., London, E.C. Wt. W1771/M2031 750,000 5/17 Sch. 52 Forms/C2118/14

APPEX I

11/1/17

# Relief Orders by CAPT. F. H. CHAMPION.

## M.R. 1/10,000 Hollebeke.

1. RELIEF.

The Company will be relieved by the 63rd M.G. Coy. in the line on the night 8/9th November 1917.

2. GUIDES.

The undermentioned guides will be found from the teams at present in the line. Two Guides from the Barrage Guns 11, 12, 13, 14, will be at Dressing Station Spoil Bank at 2.15 pm 8.11.17, with another guide from 246 M.G. Coy Barrage Guns 15, 16; to meet the incoming teams, and guide them direct to Section H.Q. Ravine. O.C. Forward Guns will arrange for 1 guide from each of his teams, 7, 8, 9, 10 to be at Dressing Station Spoil Bank at 3.15 pm, these guides will conduct the 4 incoming teams to the Ravine. At dusk they will proceed independently to their positions. O.C. Forward Guns will send the above 4 guides at daybreak the 8th to Coy H.Q. Spoilbank direct to await the arrival of the incoming teams.

3. Officers

O.C. Barrage Guns will meet the incoming Officers at Sect: H.Q. Ravine. He will detail a guide to conduct the Officer relieving the Forward Guns; to Forward H.Q's. The ~~same~~ Officer who relieves ~~both~~ the 4 Barrage Guns of 56 Coy ~~and~~ ~~will also~~ relieve the 2 of 246 M.G. Coy. ([illegible])

4. Stores etc

10 Belt Boxes per Gun. All S.A.A, T-pieces, Aiming Posts, Special Orders, Range Cards, Indirect Fire and S.O.S. Lines will be handed over and receipts obtained. Sect: Officer will collect these receipts and hand in to Coy H.Q. on relief. (Anti Aircraft Sights will not be handed over)

5. Information

All information concerning the guns will be given by Sect: Officers and Gun Team Commanders to the incoming Coy. A statement to this effect will be added to the receipts obtained for Stores handed over.

The Section Officers will personally examine Belts & Boxes to ensure those in good condition only handed over. O.C. Barrage Guns will see that all belt boxes over the 10 per gun are returned to T. Lines before

Petrol Tins.

Enough petrol tins containing water to last the incoming teams that day will be handed over and receipt obtained. The remainder will be brought out.

Reports On relief, outgoing teams will report complete to their respective Sect H.Q. and will return to T. Lines independently, under Gun Commanders. Sect: Officers will report relief complete to Coy H.Q. at Spoilbank, as soon as possible. 2/Lt. ECKERSLEY will report relief complete to O.C. on his return.

9. Transport. The Transport Officer will arrange to have the following transport at Transport Corner for bringing out the Guns, Tripods, Ammunition etc.

1 Full Limber at 4.15 pm under Cpl: Rosslyn.

1 " " " 6.30 pm " 2/Lt Slack.

2/Lt Slack will be responsible that all Guns etc are loaded, he will not allow the teams to proceed until this is so.

10. Hot Meal. The Q.M.S. will arrange to have a hot meal, if possible, ready for the teams on their relief

11. Accomodation The C.S.M. will arrange to have accomodation for teams on their relief.

12. Acknowledge.

Fred H. Chamberlain Capt.

O.C. 56 COY. MACHINE GUN CORPS.

NO 56 COY. MACHINE GUN CORPS.

[illegible]

[illegible] by CAPT [illegible]

10

[illegible]

[illegible] Company will move to [illegible] CAMP [illegible]

[illegible] ready to move off at 11 am [illegible] Light Marching Order.

[illegible] will detail [illegible] to be at [illegible] CORNER at 8 am to guide lorry to [illegible] Camp.

[illegible] Officers [illegible] Packs & Blankets will be loaded on this lorry. [illegible] Servants will [illegible] this lorry.

[illegible] Mess Cart & Limber containing Cooks & [illegible] Mess Stores will [illegible] the new camp [illegible] to prepare dinner for the Company on arrival.

[illegible]

[illegible]

[illegible] will fall in [illegible] the Company at 10.45 am [illegible]

[illegible]

No 86 COY. MACHINE GUN CORPS.

[illegible] Capt.
[illegible]

8.11.17

APPEX VIII

B Coy. M. G. Corps
[illegible] by Capt. E.H. [illegible]
[illegible] 6.30 am

1. [illegible] lorry [illegible] the Transport will [illegible] at [illegible] for the [illegible].
2. Company will parade at 7.30 am and pass the starting point Rd [illegible] R.11.c.2.7 at 8.30 am. Dress, Light Marching Order. Steel Helmets.
3. All Limbers must be packed by 5.45 am.
4. Officers valises, Mess Packs, Blankets, Officers Mess, Sergeants Mess, Cooks Stores will be loaded on the lorry which will arrive at Camp about 8.30 am. Cooks, Officers Mess and Sergeants Mess Staff will load and travel by the lorry.
5. C.S.M. will detail a reliable guide to be at Brigade H.Q. INKERMAN CAMP at 8.0 am to guide the lorry to this Camp. C.Q.M.S. will be in charge.
6. Rations for the day will be carried by each man. A [illegible] will be ready on arrival in camp.

7. Detailed Orders will be issued separately for the transport.

Copies: 1. Officers
2. C.S.M. and C.Q.M.S.
3. Transport Sergeant
4. File.

[illegible] Lieut

[illegible] COY. MACHINE GUN CORPS

[illegible] MACHINE GUN CORPS

No 56 COY.
MG/I/155.
1.1.18
MACHINE GUN CORPS

To:-

56th Inf Bde.

Attached please find original copy of this Company's War Diary for the month of December 1917.

[illegible]
56 COY. MACHINE GUN CORPS.

December 1917 Sheet I

Instructions regarding War Diaries and Intelligence Summaries are contained in F. S. Regs., Part II. and the Staff Manual respectively. Title pages will be prepared in manuscript.

# WAR DIARY
*or*
# ~~INTELLIGENCE SUMMARY.~~
*(Erase heading not required.)*

Army Form C. 2118.

56 COY. MACHINE GUN CORPS

Vol 27

| Place | Date | Hour | Summary of Events and Information | Remarks and references to Appendices |
|---|---|---|---|---|
| WALLON CAPPEL | 1/12/17 | — | Company Training. Strength. 10. Officers. 169. O.Rs. | [illegible] |
| " " | 2/12/17 | — | Company Training. | [illegible] |
| " " | 3/12/17 | — | Company Training. | [illegible] |
| " " | 4/12/17 | — | Company Training. | [illegible] |
| " " | 5/12/17 | — | Company Training. Aeroplane Demonstration at Brigade Headquarters. | [illegible] |
| " " | 6/12/17 | — | Company preparing for move. 19th Division is transferred to III Corps from IX Corps. 2/Lt. ECKERSLEY leaves for G.H.Q. Small Arms School. 2/Lt. GATENBY rejoins from IX Corps School. Lt. COOPER is admitted to Hospital. 56 Brigade Group starts the move. | [illegible] |
| " " | 7/12/17 | 6.30am | Company leaves for STEENBECQUE by route march for entraining. Entrains at 8.5am for SAULTY (N.E. of DOULLENS). arrives about 4pm route marches to billets at BELLACOURT arriving at 7.30pm. | [illegible] |
| BELLACOURT | 8/12/17 | 12.40pm | Company continues the move, marches to billets at COURCELLES-LE-COMTE via RANSART arriving about 6pm. | [illegible] |
| COURCELLES LE-COMTE | 9/12/17 | 8.33am | Company leaves for ETRICOURT and encamps under canvas just outside the ~~billets~~ village arriving 9.30pm. Lt. COOPER is evacuated to the Base and is struck off the strength of the Company. | [illegible] |
| ETRICOURT | 15/12/17 | — | Company resting at ETRICOURT. Capt. CHAMPION and 2/Lts. JONES E.D. and GATENBY go up to and reconnoitre and arrange the relief of 18 M.G. Coy. 6th Division. | [illegible] |

D. D. & L., London, E.C.
(A8004) Wt. W1771/M2 31 750,000 5/17 Sch. 52 Forms/C2118/14

Instructions regarding War Diaries and Intelligence Summaries are contained in F. S. Regs., Part II. and the Staff Manual respectively. Title pages will be prepared in manuscript.

# WAR DIARY
*or*
# ~~INTELLIGENCE SUMMARY.~~
*(Erase heading not required.)*

Sheet II

December 1917

Army Form C. 2118.

58 COY. MACHINE GUN CORPS.

| Place | Date | Hour | Summary of Events and Information | Remarks and references to Appendices |
|---|---|---|---|---|
| ETRICOURT | 11/12/17 | — | Company resting. No 3 & 4 Sections preparing for the line during the morning, leaving camp at 1.30 pm to relieve 7 guns of 18 M.G. Coy 6 DIVISION. No 3 Section commanded by 2/Lt GATENBY No 4 Section by 2Lt JONES E.D. in the RIBECOURT SECTOR and take over positions on the right flank of 19th DIVISIONAL FRONT opposite COUILLET WOOD between YORK AVENUE and COUILLET TRENCH about 1000x S.E. of RIBECOURT (Reference Sheet 57c/1/40,000) Gun positions:- L32.d.22.55, L32 d 45.78, L32 d 45.80, L32 b 65.50, L32 b 75.55, L32 b 85.78, L32 b 99.98 (reserve positions). COY H.Q. is established at L32.a.5.2. | [illegible] |
| " " | 12/12/17 | — | Nos 1 & 2 Sections resting and cleaning up. Nos 3 & 4 Sections in the line – Quiet day occasional shelling. Our gun at L32 b 75.55, engaged squadron of enemy planes at 11am. Several planes returned over own lines. 1250 rds fired. | [illegible] |
| " | 13/12/17 | — | Transport and Nos 1 & 2 Sections under Lt FLAVELL and 2/Lts CARTER and COCKER leave ETRICOURT at 10.30 am and marches by road to FINS for billets, where HQ DETAILS are established arriving 12 noon. Nothing to report from the line. | [illegible] |
| FINS. | 14/12/17 | — | Nos 1 & 2 Sections training and improving billets at FINS. Quiet day for the Sections in the line. | |
| " " | 15/12/17 | — | The Company relieves 57 M.G. COY. of 8 guns in the line. Nos 1 & 2 Sects under 2/Lts CARTER and COCKER proceed to the line for this relief. New dispositions. Coy H.Q. L36 b 20.30.<br>No. 1 Sect 4 guns. L21 a 25.30, L21 a 12.50, L21 a 00.80, L20 b 65.70.<br>No. 2 " 4 " L20 a 60.50, L20 a 20.30, L20 b 15.50, L19 b 70.25.<br>No. 3 " 2 " L19 a 90.25, L19 a 65.70. 2 Battery guns at L25 a 10.96.<br>No 4 " 4 " Battery at L31 a 84.45. | [illegible]<br>Special Sheet NINE WOOD 1/10,000 |
| " " | 16/12/17 | — | Quiet day in the line. Our Battery guns fire 2000 rds on selected targets. | [illegible] |
| " " | 17/12/17 | — | No change in the situation. Battery guns carried out usual night firing. 3000 fired. | [illegible] |

December 19

Sheet III

Army Form C. 2118.

Instructions regarding War Diaries and Intelligence Summaries are contained in F. S. Regs., Part II. and the Staff Manual respectively. Title pages will be prepared in manuscript.

# WAR DIARY
*or*
# ~~INTELLIGENCE~~ SUMMARY.

(*Erase heading not required.*)

[signature] 59 COY. MACHINE GUN CORPS

| Place | Date | Hour | Summary of Events and Information | Remarks and references to Appendices |
|---|---|---|---|---|
| FINS. | 18/12/17 | — | LT FLAVELL relieves CAPT CHAMPION in command of the Coy who proceeds on leave. Night firing carried out as usual. | [illegible] |
| " " | 19/12/17 | — | 2LT VARLEY rejoins from IV Corps School. No change in dispositions. Night firing on selected positions carried out by Battery Guns. Quiet day. 1 OR wounded by sniper. | [illegible] |
| " " | 20/12/17 | — | 2/LT CARTER admitted to Hospital. 6 Battery guns were moved up to KAISER TRENCH under 2/LT GATENBY for A.A. defence and S.O.S. guns. 2/LT VARLEY takes over from 2/LT CARTER admitted to Hospital. 2/LT JONES returns to the Transport Lines in Command of Details. | [illegible] |
| " " | 21/12/17 | — | A quiet day in the line usual shelling of RIBECOURT. Transport Lines & Q.M. Stores move from FINS to HAVRINCOURT WOOD. | [illegible] |
| HAVRINCOURT WOOD | 22/12/17 | — | 57 M.G. Coy: relieves 2 teams of 2/LT VARLEY at L21a 25.30 and L21a 12.50, these 2 teams are withdrawn to the RAILWAY EMBANKMENT at L25a 10.78. Casualties 1 O.R. killed. | [illegible] |
| " " | 23/12/17 | — | Under the new scheme 57 M.G. COY. take over 2 positions at L21a 00.80 & L20 b 65.70. also 2 in KAISER TRENCH the guns are sent out to the Transport Lines with teams of No 3 Section. New dispositions. 12 guns in the line & 4 in reserve at Transport Lines. L20.a 60.50, L20a 20.30, L19 b 75.25, L19 a 85.25, L20 b 12.50, L19 a 60.70, 4 guns in KAISER SUPPORT at L20d and 2 on RAILWAY EMBANKMENT at L25.a 10.78. All guns in the left sector are now under command of O.C. 57 M.G. Coy. 2/Lt Jones relieves 2/Lt COCKER. 2/Lt COCKER relieves 2/Lt Gatenby who proceeds to Transport as O.C. Details. | [illegible] |
| " " | 24/12/17 | — | Situation normal quiet day in the line, enemy shelled left sub-sector slightly in the afternoon. Weather fine. | [illegible] |
| " " | 25/12/17 | — | Heavy shelling of left sub-sector and KAISER SUPPORT between 2.30pm & 4pm. 2Lt Black rejoins from Training Course at ABBEVILLE. | [illegible] |

D. D. & L., London, E.C.
(A8004) Wt. W1771/M2031 750,000 5/17 Sch. 52 Forms/C2118/14

Instructions regarding War Diaries and Intelligence Summaries are contained in F. S. Regs., Part II. and the Staff Manual respectively. Title pages will be prepared in manuscript.

# WAR DIARY
*or*
# INTELLIGENCE SUMMARY.
*(Erase heading not required.)*

December 1917. Sheet IV

Army Form C. 2118.

[illegible] Lieut.
56 COY. MACHINE GUN CORPS.

| Place | Date | Hour | Summary of Events and Information | Remarks and references to Appendices |
|---|---|---|---|---|
| HAVRINCOURT WOOD | 26/12/17 | — | No. 3 Section relieves No. 4 Section in the line who proceed to Transport Lines. 2/Lt Varley takes over command of No. 3 Section from Lt. LAWSON of 57 M. G. Coy. Quiet day in the line. Snowing. | [illegible] |
| " | 27/12/17 | — | 2Lt. GATENBY relieves 2Lt JONES E.D. in command of No. 2 Section. 2/Lt JONES. E.D. relieved 2/Lt COCKER in command of rear guns, who proceeds to Transport as O.C. Details. | [illegible] |
| " | 28/12/17 | — | 2 men per team are attached from 7. S. Lancs. to the Coy. The following changes in dispositions were carried out during the day. L20a 50.60 to L20b 12.70. L20b 12.50 to L22a 15.30. L19a 65.70 to L19b 45.05. & L20a 30.20 to L19b 25.05. Quiet day very cold snow thick on the ground | [illegible] |
| " | 29/12/17 | — | No change in situation. Quiet day. Emplacements & Shelters improved. | [illegible] |
| " | 30/12/17 | — | Indirect Fire carried out by 2 RAILWAY EMBANKMENT guns. Heavy Artillery activity especially on the right where the enemy attacked the next DIVISION 63rd. No. 4 Section relieved No. 2 Section in the line | [illegible] |
| " | 31/12/17 | — | 2/Lt Cocker relieved 2/Lt Varley in command of the 6 Right Guns. Heavy Artillery Fire on the whole Divisional Front in the early morning 4 am to 7.30 am.<br>Strength of Company. 8 Officers 170 O.R.<br>Reinforcements received during month. O.R 15. | [illegible] |

[illegible] Lieut.
Cmdg. 56 M. G. Coy.

(A8004) Wt. W1771/M2731 750,000 5/17 D. D. & L., London, E.C. Sch. 52 Forms/C2118/14

Instructions regarding War Diaries and Intelligence Summaries are contained in F. S. Regs., Part II. and the Staff Manual respectively. Title pages will be prepared in manuscript.

# WAR DIARY
*or*
# ~~INTELLIGENCE~~ SUMMARY.
(*Erase heading not required.*)

JANUARY - 1918. Sheet I

Army Form C. 2118.

56 M G Coy [signature] Capt

56 COY. MACHINE GUN CORPS.

Vol 28

| Place | Date | Hour | Summary of Events and Information | Remarks and references to Appendices |
|---|---|---|---|---|
| | | | Reference NINE WOOD 1/10000 | |
| HAVRINCOURT WOOD | 1-1-18 | — | Company strength 8 Officers 170 O.R. Weather: clear cold. Slight shelling of the Sector. | [initials] |
| " | 2-1-18 | | Very quiet day. Enemy artillery more active than usual. Guns re organised as follows: Batty of 4 under 2/Lt GATENBY at L.19.d.2.9. Batty of 3 under 2/Lt COCKER at L.20.a.4.2 1 gun at L.20.b.12.70. Under 2/Lt JONES: 2 guns at RAILWAY EMBANKMENT at L.25.a.[illegible] and 2 guns at L.36.d.4.2 | [initials] |
| " | 3-1-18 | | Heavy shelling of Batty at L.19.d.2.9. RIBECOURT heavily shelled with gas shells during the morning | [initials] |
| " | 4-1-18 | | Capt CHAMPION returns from leave. Company is relieved by the Company 47 Division. Relief complete by 5 a.m. All teams return to the Transport Lines for the night | [initials] |
| " | 5-1-18 | | Sections cleaning up and preparing for the line in the morning. No 1, 3 & 4 Sections with 3 teams of 57 Coy. leave Transport Lines at 2 p.m. for the line to relieve 223 Coy 63rd R.N. Divn. Capt CHAMPION and Lt FLAYELL leave to establish Coy. H.Q. at R.3.a.1.9. 15 guns are relieved. Relief complete by 2 a.m. 6-1-18. New positions: 4 Batty guns under 2/Lt VARLEY Res. Sect at R.2.b.00.40; 4 Batty guns (3 of 57 Coy + 1 of Res. Sect) under Lt DUNT, 57 Coy, at L.32.d.85.75; 2 guns at R.[illegible]; 1 gun at L.34.d.00.50, 1 gun at L.34.d.00.60; 1 gun at L.34.c.75.90, 2 guns at R.3.b.8.4 under 2/Lts JONES, GATENBY and COCKER | [initials] |
| " | 6-1-18 | | 6 guns of 57 Coy relieve 6 guns of 189 Coy in the right sector. These guns come under the command of Capt CHAMPION. Weather cold and clear, very quiet day. | [initials] |

D. D. & L., London, E.C.
(A8004) Wt. W1771/M2031 750,000 5/17 Sch. 52 Forms/C2118/14

JANUARY-1918

Sheet II

Instructions regarding War Diaries and Intelligence Summaries are contained in F. S. Regs., Part II. and the Staff Manual respectively. Title pages will be prepared in manuscript.

# WAR DIARY
or
# ~~INTELLIGENCE SUMMARY.~~

(Erase heading not required.)

Army Form C. 2118.

L.R. Jones Capt

56 COY. MACHINE GUN CORPS.

| Place | Date | Hour | Summary of Events and Information | Remarks and references to Appendices |
|---|---|---|---|---|
| HAVRINCOURT WOOD | 7-1-18 | | No change in dispositions. Thaw sets in overnight, trenches in a bad condition. Quiet day with very little shelling. Enemy M.G. fire very heavy during the night. | LRJ |
| " | 8-1-18 | | No change in situation. Keen frost. Enemy shelled CENTRAL AVENUE R.3.a.1.9 and R.3.b.8.4 throughout the day. Considerable enemy movement observed. | LRJ |
| " | 9-1-18 | | Guns are reorganised. 57 Coy send up 3 more guns. Each Coy. has now 12 guns in the line, all under the command of Capt. CHAMPION. New dispositions. Batteries: "D" Batt (4 guns of 56 M.G. Coy) under 2/LT VARLEY, M.C. at R.2.b.00.40; "E" Batt (4 guns of 57 M.G. Coy) under 2/LT POPE at L.32.d.5.3; "F" Batt (2 guns of 56 M.G. Coy and 2 guns of 57 M.G. Coy) under LT DUNT at L.32.d.85.75. In support: 2 guns at R.9.b.1.9 and R.3.d.10.00 under 2/LT RUSSELL (57 Coy). 4 guns (56 Coy) at R.3.b.8.8, R.3.b.8.9, L.33.d.9.5 and L.33.d.9.6 under 2 LT ~~[illegible]~~ JONES. Front guns: 1 at R.10.a.02.95 under 2/LT RUSSELL (57 Coy); 2 at R.4.c.5.9 and R.4.a.05.15 under 2/LT COCKER (56 Coy); 3 at R.4.a.7.5, R.4.a.7.9 and L.34.a.6.1 under 2/LT PARE (57 Coy). Reports received of impending enemy attack, all teams warned to be alert. Enemy heavily shelled CENTRAL AVENUE, vicinity of Coy H.Q. R.2.b.00.50 and support lines at R.3.b. and L.37.d. Much enemy movement seen throughout the day. Casualties 3 O.R. wounded. | LRJ |
| " | 10-1-18 | | Enemy very active. Considerable movement noted in enemy lines. No change in disposition. 2/LT ECKERSLEY relieves 2/LT JONES. 2/LT GATENBY is withdrawn. LT ANDERSON reports from Base Depot | LRJ |
| " | 11-1-18 | | Enemy line barraged at 6.20 a.m. by our Artillery in anticipation of an attack. Our guns opened fire on their S.O.S. lines. Casualties: 1 Signaller wounded remained at duty | LRJ |
| " | 12-1-18 | | LT. A.E.V. COLLINS reports from Base Depot and is taken on the strength. Night firing carried out on selected targets. Heavy enemy M.G. fire round our Battery positions. Enemy shells Coy. H.Q. & vicinity. | LRJ |

D. D. & L., London, E.C. (A8001) Wt. W1771/M2031 750,000 5/17 Sch. 52 Forms/C2118/14

Instructions regarding War Diaries and Intelligence Summaries are contained in F. S. Regs., Part II. and the Staff Manual respectively. Title pages will be prepared in manuscript.

JANUARY - 1918

# WAR DIARY
*or*
# ~~INTELLIGENCE SUMMARY.~~
*(Erase heading not required.)*

Sheet III
Army Form C. 2118.

A. J. Jones Capt.
56 COY. MACHINE GUN CORPS

| Place | Date | Hour | Summary of Events and Information | Remarks and references to Appendices |
|---|---|---|---|---|
| HAVRINCOURT WOOD | 13-1-18 | | Enemy shelled back areas. Night firing carried out by barrage guns on selected targets. | |
| " | 14-1-18 | | Usual night firing carried out on selected targets by barrage guns. Enemy shelled vicinity of Coy. H.Q. | |
| " | 15-1-18 | | Little artillery activity. Usual night firing on selected targets by barrage guns. | |
| " | 16-1-18 | | Weather dull and showery. Trenches in extremely bad condition. Little artillery activity. Coy H.Q shelled. Usual night firing by barrage guns on selected targets - 6000 rounds fired. | |
| " | 17-1-18 | | Weather still wet and dull. Trenches almost impassable. Much movement over the top by both sides. Little artillery activity. The 3 barrage batteries do searching fire from 7.30 p.m. to midnight on squares L.35. and R.5 (S of MARCOING) as an enemy relief is believed to be in progress. 25000 rounds fired. | |
| " | 18-1-18 | | Hostile artillery shells forward areas heavily during the morning. Hostile aircraft active. Usual night firing by barrage guns on selected targets. | |
| " | 19-1-18 | | Hostile artillery intermittently active on both forward and back areas. Lt. HANSON of 57 Coy. relieves Capt CHAMPION in command of Right Group. 2/Lt ECKERSLEY remains as liaison officer | |
| " | 20-1-18 | | Barrage guns keep up a slow rate of fire during the night (19/20) on S.O.S. lines with 1° elevation. Hostile artillery active on forward area. | |
| " | 21-1-18 | | Little artillery activity. Usual night firing by barrage guns. Casualties: 1 O.R. wounded | |
| " | 22-1-18 | | Hostile artillery shells area between our front and support lines from 11 a.m. to 1 p.m. Usual night firing by barrage guns. 2/Lt ECKERSLEY is relieved by 2/Lt JONES as liaison officer. Lt. FLAVELL proceeds on U.K. leave (special). | |
| " | 23-1-18 | | Little artillery activity. Usual night firing by barrage guns. In order to equalise the periods spent in Right and Left sectors of Divl Front (in accordance with 19th Divl Order "G 703") No. 4 Section relieves 4 teams of 246 Coy at "A" Group (Left Sector) (R.3.b.15) & 4 teams of 246 Coy relieve 4 teams of 56 Coy. at "B" and "C" Groups (R.3.b.6.8. R.3.b.89; L.33.d.9.5, L.33...) (Right Sector). This completes the first move in the change over. | |

D. L. & L., London, E.C.
(A8001) Wt. W1771/M2031 750,000 5/17 Sch. 52 Forms/C2118/14

Sheet IV.

Army Form C. 2118.

Instructions regarding War Diaries and Intelligence Summaries are contained in F. S. Regs., Part II. and the Staff Manual respectively. Title pages will be prepared in manuscript.

JANUARY - 1918

# WAR DIARY
or
# INTELLIGENCE SUMMARY.
(Erase heading not required.)

L E Jones Capt

56 COY. MACHINE G[illegible]

| Place | Date | Hour | Summary of Events and Information | Remarks and references to Appendices |
|---|---|---|---|---|
| HAVRINCOURT WOOD | 24-1-18 | | Capt F.H. CHAMPION proceeds to M.G.T.C. GRANTHAM (Authy: A.G/116/26(0) V.A. III. and 19th Div. Order A/14/1) 2/Lt ECKERSLEY is left in command of the Coy. pending the arrival of Capt. L.E. JONES, M.G.C., the new O.C. Hostile Artillery inactive. | [illegible] |
| " | 25-1-18 | | Hostile Artillery and Trench Mortars active on forward areas. Little shelling of back areas. 6 enemy observation balloons up and enemy aircraft active. Usual night firing by barrage guns. Capt L.E. JONES joins from the Base and takes over command of the Coy. | [illegible] |
| " | 26-1-18 | | Heavy shelling during the night (25/26) of back areas by enemy Artillery. Enemy M.Gs very active. Usual night firing by barrage guns on selected targets. | [illegible] |
| " | 27-1-18 | | 4 teams (No 2 section) of 56 Coy proceed from Camp to take over from 2 teams of 246 Coy at "B" guns (Left Group) at R.3.a.9.9 and 2 teams at Nos. 1 + 2 positions (Left Group) at L.33.b.7.8 and L.27.d.25.50 respectively. 4 teams of 246 Coy take over from 2 teams of 56 Coy at Nos 2 + 3 positions (Right Group) at R.4.c.5.9 and R.4.a.05.15 respectively and Nos. 1 + 2 positions of "F" Battery L.32.d.85.75. Enemy Artillery inactive. Usual night firing by barrage guns. Casualties: 1 O.R. wounded | [illegible] |
| " | 28-1-18 | | Heavy shelling of areas R.2.b.+d. and R.3.a.+c. with H.E. (4.2 cm) and mustard gas shells (11pm - 1am night 27/28). Batty at R.3.b.05.50 shelled with H.E. and mustard gas between 2pm and 4pm. Casualties: 15 O.R. wounded (gassed) in No. 3 Section (Battery at R.2.b.00.40) | [illegible] |
| " | 29-1-18 | | Hostile Artillery shells squares R.3.a. and c between 9pm and 11pm (28/29) with H.E. (4.2 c.m) and again between 3pm and 4.30pm. Enemy aircraft very active flying at a good height over our lines. Usual night firing by barrage guns. | [illegible] |
| " | 30-1-18 | | Hostile shelling normal. Enemy aircraft very active. Usual night firing carried out by barrage guns on selected targets. | [illegible] |

D. D. & L., London, E.C. (A8001) Wt. W1771/M2031 750,000 5/17 Sch. 52 Forms/C2118/14

Sheet V

Army Form C. 2118.

# WAR DIARY
*or*
# INTELLIGENCE SUMMARY.
(*Erase heading not required.*)

JANUARY-1918.

Instructions regarding War Diaries and Intelligence Summaries are contained in F. S. Regs., Part II. and the Staff Manual respectively. Title pages will be prepared in manuscript.

W. E. Jones Capt
56 COY. MACHINE GUN CORPS.

| Place | Date | Hour | Summary of Events and Information | Remarks and references to Appendices |
|---|---|---|---|---|
| HAVRINCOURT WOOD | 31-1-18 | | Weather dull and cold. Little artillery activity. 4 teams of 56 Coy take over "C" Battery (Left Group) (L.32.d.1.5) from 246 Coy. 246 Coy takes over "D" Battery (Right Group - R.2.b.00.40) from 56 Coy. | B |

W. E. Jones Capt
O.C. 56 M.G. Coy
31/1/18.

D. D. & L., London, E.C.
(A8001) Wt. W1771/M2031 750,000 5/17 Sch. 52 Forms/C2118/14

Instructions regarding War Diaries and Intelligence Summaries are contained in F. S. Regs., Part II. and the Staff Manual respectively. Title pages will be prepared in manuscript.

# WAR DIARY
*or*
# INTELLIGENCE SUMMARY.
*(Erase heading not required.)*

Feb. 1918 Sheet I. Army Form C. 2118.

Vol 29 56 M. G. Coy.

| Place | Date | Hour | Summary of Events and Information — Ref. NINE WOOD 1/10,000 | Remarks and references to Appendices |
|---|---|---|---|---|
| HAVRINCOURT WOOD | 1.2.18 | | On Feb. 1. 12 guns of this Coy were holding the left sector (see WAR DIARY for Jan.) together with 12 guns of 57 M. G. Coy. | |
| | | | Disposition of these 12 guns: 1 gun at L. 33.60.72, in the front line trench - an open emplacement, conspicuous. Not a good position, a fresh position was about to be made at L. 33. b. 20.62 when Coy was relieved. | |
| | | | 1 gun at L. 27. d. 30.50. | |
| | | | 1 Battery of 4 guns at R. 3. b. 05.45 "A" | |
| | | | 1 do " 2 " R. 3. a. 90.85 "B" | |
| | | | ~~1 " " 2 " L. 33. a. 6.5.~~ | |
| | | | ~~1 " " 4 " L. 27. c. 30.25~~ | |
| | | | 1 " " 4 " L. 32. c. 10.53 "E" | |
| | | | Remaining 4 guns were at HAVRINCOURT WOOD at P. 18. C. central (ref 57C. 1/40,000) | |
| | | | Transport lines were at LECHELLE (P. 25. C.) | |
| | | | 4 guns in line were relieved every 4th day by the 4 guns at HAVRINCOURT WOOD, and front line guns were relieved by Battery guns from time to time. | |
| | 2.2.18 | 6 to 11 pm | Our Batteries fired 5000 rounds during night on selected targets - tracks, posts, sunken roads &c. | |
| | | 9-11 pm | Enemy shelled L.32.a.8.3 with mustard gas, and 77 mm H.E. on L.31.b. | |
| | 3.2.18 | 6 to 10 pm | Batteries fired 10,000 rds. on enemy tracks, posts, & new work. | |
| | 4.2.18. | 6-9 pm | " " 7,500 " | |
| | 5.2.18 | 6-9 pm | " " 8000 | |
| | 6.2.18. | 6-9 pm | " 12000 | |
| | | 6-8.30 am 2-4.30 pm | Enemy fired about 100 H.E. 5.9s in GRAND RAVINE, searching for a "sniping" 18 pr. which moved into that area by night & withdrew by day. | |
| | 7.2.18. | 6-9 pm 5.30-6.30 am | Batteries fired 8000 rds on selected targets. | |
| | | | 12000 " " | |
| | 9.2.18. | 6-11 pm | 14000 " | |
| | 10.2.18. | NIGHT | | |

D. D. & L., London, E.C.
(A8001) Wt. W1771/M2031 750,000 5/17 Sch. 52 Forms C2118/14

Instructions regarding War Diaries and Intelligence Summaries are contained in F. S. Regs., Part II. and the Staff Manual respectively. Title pages will be prepared in manuscript.

# WAR DIARY
*or*
# INTELLIGENCE SUMMARY.

(*Erase heading not required.*)

Feb. 1918 Sheet II Army Form C. 2118.

56 Coy. M. G. Corps.

| Place | Date | Hour | Ref NINE WOOD 1/10,000 — Summary of Events and Information | Remarks and references to Appendices |
|---|---|---|---|---|
| HAVRINCOURT WOOD. P.18.C. central [57c 1/40000] | 11.2.18 | 6-11pm 4-6am | Batteries fired 13000 rds on selected targets. | [initials] |
| | 12.2.18 | 6pm to 11pm 4am-6am | " " 11000 " | [initials] |
| | 13.2.18 | 5-12pm 4-6am | " " 4,450 | [initials] |
| | 15.2.18 | 1.A.M. | Relief of nos 56 & 57 M.G. Coys by 223 & 189 M.G. Coys (63rd Div) complete at 1.a.m 15/2/18. This Coy. entrained on light railway at TRESCAULT at 2 AM, & reached camp at LE TRANSLOY N.24.b.4.4 (Sheet 57c 1/40000) at 8.0 a.m | [initials] |
| | 1.2.18 to 15.2.18 | | During this tour of duty from 1.2.18 to 15.2.18 the Coy. had a quiet time in the line. 10 casualties from gas occurred, due to men removing their masks too soon, before trenches & dug-outs were clear. The feature of the tour was the nightly harassing fire on tracks, posts, roads, new work etc behind enemy lines. Targets were carefully selected from (i) V Corps Intelligence. (ii) 19th Divl Intelligence. (iii) Air photographs. (iv) the targets engaged by Artillery. e.g. if 18 Pdrs took on a new trench one night, M.Gs took on same spot following night when working parties likely to be out repairing. A sniping gun took on one target with direct fire, but unsuccessfully owing to stoppages. ~~The~~ Altogether 106,950 rds were fired by 56 & 57 M.G. Coys (LEFT GROUP) during period 1st-14th Feb. Enemy M.G. fire was fairly active - at its most active fired about 1/4 of our fire. Work was well advanced on a camouflaged shell-hole emplacement, under old Boche wire, at L.26 b 9.5 1.6. The strength of teams averaged 4 men per gun. Very little R.E. or Labour assistance was available - this handicapped progress of work on new emplacements. The constant night-firing & change of targets gave officers, N.C.Os, & men good practice in working out & laying guns on lines at night. | [initials] |
| | 15.2.18 to 28.2.18. | | Coy became part of 19th Divl. M.G. Battn - & a full programme of training carried out. Much stress was laid on DRILL, & smart turn-outs of Guards & Pickets. Firing on Short & Long Ranges, (M.G. Course Pts I & II) daily GAS DRILL, I.A., Mechanism, Aiming Instruction, Ind. and Recog. Elementary Gun Drill and Barrage drill. Lectures by C.R.A, Divl Camouflage officer, & by G.O.C. Divn on Discipline | [initials] |

[signature]
O.C. 56 M.G. Coy

www.ingramcontent.com/pod-product-compliance
Lightning Source LLC
Chambersburg PA
CBHW081400160426
43193CB00013B/2077